Taking It Lying Down

Sexuality and Teenage Motherhood

FRANCES HUDSON

and

BERNARD INEICHEN

MACMILLAN

First published 1991 by
MACMILLAN PRESS LTD
Houndmills, Basingstoke, Hampshire RG21 6XS
and London
Companies and representatives
throughout the world

ISBN 0–333–53177–9 hardcover
ISBN 0–333–53178–7 paperback

A catalogue record for this book is available
from the British Library.

9   8   7   6   5   4   3   2
03 02 01 00 99 98 97 96

Printed in Hong Kong

Contents

Acknowledgements

We would like to thank John Barrett, Ann Burridge, David Burrows, Neville Butler, Hedy Cleaver, Lesley Doyal, David Emmerson, Philip Gammage, Martyn and Joanna Hitchcock, Gordon Piller, and Ann Wilson for their help and encouragement of our work that led to the writing of the book.

Special thanks go to those who have shared their experiences with us. It is they who have provided us with the quotations which are unattributed in the text. All names in the case-histories used in this book are fictitious.

Introduction

Teenage Sexuality and Pregnancy – an Issue for Concern

Why another book on teenage pregnancy? Throughout the 1960s, 70s and 80s writing on the subject has been incessant. In the US it sometimes seems that the epidemic so often feared refers not to pregnant teenagers but to books on the subject. Yet, in spite of research and recommendations, much still remains to be done.

First, existing knowledge needs to be brought together. Very few attempts have been made to consider teenage sexuality, pregnancy and motherhood in depth across international boundaries. International comparative studies (e.g. Clearie *et al.*, 1985; Jones *et al.*, 1986) have largely amassed and compared statistical descriptions of the subject. Few have attempted meaningful comparisons in depth between nations. Discussions of the experience of teenage pregnancy and motherhood, even in Britain and America, have remained largely apart from one another, despite the advantage of a common language. More passengers cross the Atlantic, it seems, than books. And while it is tempting to contrast, for example, the experience of black teenagers in the two countries, both differences and similarities need to be considered.

Other divisions are apparent in the literature besides international ones. Medical investigations are seldom integrated with others. The important work by Russell (1981, 1982), for example, is referred to by few subsequent authors of sociological surveys.

And clearly AIDS adds a whole terrifying new dimension in some parts of the world. For some teenagers, sex is fatal.

Little has been written about historical or policy aspects, although Vinovskis (1988) is a notable exception. There are relatively few long-term enquiries into the subject, although the 17-year-long study in Baltimore (Furstenberg, 1976; Furstenberg *et al.*, 1987) is a major milestone in this respect, challenging a number of widely held views. Longitudinal studies of large samples in Britain are now beginning to provide valuable material over even longer time spans. For example, Kiernan (1980, 1986) has been able recently to demonstrate the consequences of early childbearing and marriage among a sample born in 1946.

In Britain, whose situation we may claim to know best, the literature is scattered and in some respects unsatisfactory. Simms and Smith (1986) have conducted a major study, long on description but short on analysis. Some important research (Skinner, 1986; Birch, 1987) has been printed outside major publishing houses and can be difficult to obtain. Other valuable work (Coyne, n.d.; Sharpe, 1987) has been conducted with very small samples.

Teenage pregnancy in the Third World remains possibly the most important topic of all, yet has so far defied major research initiatives. Sadly, we too will fail to grasp this particular nettle.

Second, much important practical work remains to be done, and we hope that the discussion that follows will, along with those of other writers, point towards some explanation, some understanding and some greater acceptance of the facts. We hope also that it will lead to action on two counts – firstly, early pregnancy prevention, and secondly (where prevention has failed), support for young mothers coping with unplanned children.

Questions of sex education, teenagers' use of contraception, and necessary health and welfare support services need to be looked at carefully. Extended family support must be encouraged. Teenage fathers must not be excluded. But we are still some way from knowing how best changes in these areas can be brought about.

It is widely assumed that early pregnancy and parenthood mean for the parents blighted lives which fail to achieve their full potential, and for the children a disadvantaged start with, as a widely quoted writer has it, '90% of her life script written for her' (Campbell, 1968, p. 238). This is especially cruel at a time of hope, generally true of the last 30 years, that educational, occupational and financial success was becoming increasingly open to all. Research such as the Baltimore study (Furstenberg *et al.*, 1987) has found it less than wholly true, especially when older teenagers and teenagers with a durable partner are considered.

Teenage motherhood remains overwhelmingly a working-class affair. For readers removed from daily contact with adolescent mothers, the pages that follow, describing scenes and attitudes, may suggest another epoch. Yet their persistence remains beyond doubt. The class division they illustrate was brought home to one of the present authors very graphically at one phase of his career. His mornings were spent on research into teenage pregnancy and motherhood, and his afternoons teaching first-year medical students. The contrast between the two groups of teenagers could not have been more extreme. The subjects of the morning's research were interviewed in the hospital antenatal department. Many were pale and anxious, puffing at a cigarette; some into their second or third pregnancies had a toddler crawling around their ankles. Their concerns, beyond their own health and that of their children, and whether or not hospital staff would be punitive in their approach, were centred on topics such as: will this week's giro (welfare payment) arrive safely? is my boy friend really the father of my child? will he ever get a job? will my parents continue to tolerate me in our overcrowded council house when I have the baby? will I have to live in a high-rise flat, far from the area I grew up in, when it arrives? will it involve months of living in a squalid bed and breakfast hotel first?

The female medical students of the afternoon were of identical age, but several inches taller, had healthier complexions and may have been (despite their unpregnant state) a stone or so heavier. Their experience of life had been of growing up in a secure (usually middle-class) household and of succeeding at school in passing a series of exams culminating in achieving entry to medical school. Their current preoccupations concerned coping with the course, achieving social success in their hall of residence and possibly dealing with feelings of homesickness at the initial separation from their parental home. Differences in the long-term prospects of the two groups of young women do not need to be spelt out. Two nations indeed.

'Every child is a wanted child' is an excellent slogan, but – in spite of the efforts of the IPPF (International Planned Parenthood

Federation) – at present it just is not happening. Teenage maternal love is a force-fed emotion. Most adolescent mothers would prefer to have waited. But now they need our help, and we all need to work towards a society where unwanted children are a rare event (some countries have been more successful in achieving this than others) and where those adolescents who do give birth are afforded all the help they need.

SECTION ONE:

What Teenagers Do

Chapter 1

The Changing Shape of Teenage Pregnancy

In this chapter we outline the extent to which teenage sexual experience has become more common in industrialised countries. Rates remain extremely varied from one country to another. There are implications that in very recent years increases are levelling out. Not all sexual activity leads to pregnancy, not all pregnancies lead to births, and not all births occur within marriage. Variations in these processes among countries and over time are discussed.

Teenage sexual experience

Much evidence throughout recent history suggests that young people have become sexually experienced at younger and younger ages. Earlier physical maturity, social pressures and greater availability of contraceptives have all played their part in bringing about these changes.

Human physical maturity has been taking place, for example, at younger ages throughout the countries of the developed world. Accompanying earlier physical maturity has been a decline in the age of menarche. Evidence from Norway shows that, for 100 years up to 1920, the age at which menarche occurred remained fairly constant at about 14 for the upper classes and 16 for the lower classes. It then decreased over the next 30 years to about 13. Other countries show a similar pattern, and the trend is likely to be continuing (Marshall, 1981; Birch, 1987; Hayes, 1987). Recent research (Farrell, 1978; Coyne, 1986; Skinner, 1986; Birch, 1987) suggests menarche among British girls may now be taking place at age 12 or even 11, and about 12 in the US (Vinovskis, 1988) and Australia (Goldman and Goldman, 1988).

Girls who become teenage mothers may be especially early starters. Skinner studied three large samples of teenage girls in South London, over 500 in all. Those who became very young mothers, and those who opted for abortions – both as a result of unplanned pregnancies – began to menstruate earlier than girls who attended family planning clinics. Over a third of the mothers and aborters had started their periods by the age of 11 (1986, p. 31). Some very young teenagers conceive without having started menstruating. Others conceive so soon after their first period that they think they could not possibly be pregnant, that they are simply 'too young'. American research confirms that girls who become teenage mothers start their periods early (Birch, 1987).

Another reason for earlier sexual experience of teenagers has been the growing efficacy, availability and acceptability of contraception. An increasing range of techniques has been created over the past 100 years, although not all have immediately become available to unmarried people, and even when available, a variety of reasons has prevented them coming into immediate use. Much sexual activity among young people takes place without contraception being used or even considered, although the possible consequences of pregnancy and childbirth are not desired. Probably most couples do not even think about such an outcome. This is specifically the case among the under 16 year olds. For many at this age sexual activity has no bearing on the future, since consideration of the future does not impinge on their present daily lives.

The evidence pointing to greater sexual activity among teenagers is substantial, and has been documented in a series of major surveys. Among Schofield's sample of nearly 2000 15–19 year olds interviewed in the early 1960s, only 20 per cent of boys and 12 per cent of girls had had sexual intercourse (Schofield, 1968). Ten years later, over half of a sample of 1500 16–19 year olds reported that they had had sex (Farrell, 1978). Comparing the 15 year olds in the first sample with accounts of what the 16 year olds said in the second, the proportion of those having sex before their sixteenth birthday rose in a decade from 6 to 26 per cent among boys and from 2 to 12 per cent for girls. Dunnell (1979), in a survey of over 6500 women of childbearing age, has shown how sexual habits changed in the third quarter of the century: women became more likely to have premarital sex with their husbands; women marrying in their teens were more likely to have done so, and by the 1970s four out of five had done; the length of time during which couples had premarital sex expanded, and the age for starting sex declined.

Elsewhere these increases have been equally dramatic. In the US the number of female teenagers who had been sexually active rose from 30 per cent in 1971 to about 50 per cent by the end of the 1970s, but signs are that numbers levelled out in the 1980s. Black teenagers became sexually experienced at earlier ages, but this differential has now levelled out somewhat, with 58 per cent of unmarried blacks and 40 per cent of unmarried whites sexually experienced in 1982 (Vinovskis, 1988). Recent Danish evidence (Wielandt and Boldsen, 1989) indicates the median age for first sex is 16.8 years for both men and women. The age for women has declined in recent years, but has remained constant for men.

As long as the teenage culture encourages young people to believe that everyone else is 'doing it', sexual intercourse as an automatic part of a relationship is likely to occur. Prevailing myths such as 'just the once can't hurt' and the notion that extreme youth will prevent conception have an influence on human fertility. Birch (1987), Coyne (n.d.) and Miller (1983) all report conception in very young adolescents as occurring very soon in the relationship, if not the first time of sexual intercourse. The young mothers of Miller's sample were on average just over 13 when they started having sex.

Early sexual experience is reported as not always pleasurable. Only a third of the girls in Schofield's sample and half of the boys said they enjoyed it the first time (1968, p. 67). More recent American research confirms the ambivalence of young people's feelings at this time (Sonenstein, 1986).

Making sex illegal appears to have little impact on young people's behaviour. Statutes prohibiting premarital sexual intercourse in the US are impossible to enforce, and young men are rarely prosecuted in either Britain or the US for having sexual intercourse with a minor. Society's acceptance of youth's sexual activity on both sides of the Atlantic is an indication that the law is way behind in this matter (Rodman *et al.*, 1984).

Physical and sexual maturity among adolescents is not accompanied by an ability to handle their sexuality in a responsible manner. And, as we shall see in later chapters, young people, especially the very young, are faced today with decision-making beyond their experience.

Teenage pregnancy, birth and marriage

Much teenage sexual activity results in pregnancy. In poorer countries this has probably always been the situation, and little notice was paid to it until large populations moved off the land and into the cities, and the traditional tribal structures began to break down. The problem this has created in terms of unsupported young mothers and fatherless infants has scarcely imprinted itself on the world's consciousness: soaring crime rates and mile-long traffic jams are more immediate concerns, which lend themselves more readily to political rhetoric and television documentaries.

Concern over teenage mothers has surfaced much more vividly in the wealthier countries of the 'developed' world. Here a growing concern with democratic rights of access to a share of their enormous material wealth has identified groups who are excluded, and who may be self-perpetuating. Teenage mothers form one such group.

About 100,000 teenagers in Britain become pregnant each year, although not all pregnancies go to term. The peak year for teenage births was 1971, when 82,600 teenage girls (one in twenty in the female adolescent population) had a baby. Numbers later dropped to 54,500 in 1984 but crept up again in the second half of the 1980s. The fertility rate dropped from 50 per 1000 in 1971 to 27 in 1983, and has since risen to 32. The number having two children has been falling steadily: around 14,000 per annum in the mid 1960s to about 3500 in the late 1980s. Of those having three, the number has fallen from about 1300 in the mid 1960s to 300 today.

Teenage sexuality in the US is also active and productive. About a million teenagers become pregnant each year. This figure represents one-tenth of the young women in their teens. Not all of these pregnancies are carried to term: about half give birth, 40 per cent have abortions and 10 per cent miscarry. Between 1955 and 1970 the adolescent share of all births rose from 12 to 18 per cent. Not surprisingly, teenage pregnancy was seen in the US as an 'epidemic' (Alan Guttmacher, 1976; Vinovskis, 1988) and still is. There are, however, signs that the adolescent birth rate (but not the pregnancy rate) has now declined, with the proportion of all births which are to teenage mothers falling back to 13 per cent in 1986.

Teenage pregnancy and birth is perceived as an urban problem. Rural women in America start sex at the same early age as big-city women, though sooner than suburbanites. But they marry younger, which may be why their sexual behaviour is not considered so much of a problem (Heaton *et al.*, 1989).

Teenage fertility has been declining throughout the developed world, generally more sharply than in Britain and America. Between 1976 and 1986 the fall was 50 per cent in several European countries (Werner, 1988). Increases in pregnancy rates among very young teenagers have, however, continued despite the overall decline. Conceptions among 16 year olds in Britain reached 16,512 in 1987. In the US there was a 50 per cent increase in the number of births to younger adolescents (under 16) between 1960 and 1979; the figure rose from 26,380 to 39,076 (Miller, 1983).

Teenage motherhood often means teenage marriage, but this association has become increasingly weak. In 1961, 80 per cent of births to teenagers in Britain were legitimate. Currently the figure is less than a quarter. In 1966, 32.9 per cent of first-time brides were teenagers; in mid 1988 that figure was 10 per cent. In 1986, 40,000 teenage girls married, a third of the 1971 figure. The figure for teenage bridegrooms was a quarter of that for 1971.

This rise in the proportion of illegitimate births among teenagers has been mirrored in the US: out of wedlock teenage births increased from 14 per cent in 1955 to 61 per cent by 1986. Marriage among white US teenagers has dropped dramatically over the last two decades, but marriage among black US teenagers has virtually disappeared. In 1983 four out of ten births to white teenagers were out of wedlock, against nine out of ten to blacks (Vinovskis, 1988,

p. 29). Rising illegitimacy has been reported from many developed countries, although the proportion of births which are illegitimate varies greatly; from 5 per cent in Israel to 83 per cent in Sweden (Clearie *et al.*, 1985).

The declining popularity of teenage marriage is also revealed by the marriage statistics themselves. In 1971, 9 per cent of the grooms and 27 per cent of the brides among those marrying for the first time were teenagers. Current figures are about a third of these. The average age at first marriage has been declining for decades, although very recent figures suggest this trend may have come to an end; marriage has become less and less part of the adolescent birth picture.

To some extent the fall in the number of legitimate births to teenagers has been offset by the rise in figures for cohabitation, and for the joint registration of illegitimate births. However, single parenthood is what many adolescent mothers choose today, a significant indicator of the social acceptance of this state – the stigma of teenage pregnancy and lone parenthood having for the most part disappeared.

Teenage abortion

Discussions of abortion ignore the many spontaneous miscarriages which go unrecorded, and surveys are likely seriously to under-report numbers when past history is asked about (Dunnell, 1979). Even so, in some countries there are more abortions than births to teenagers (Clearie *et al.*, 1985). However, the numbers of teenage pregnancies in Britain which knowingly end in abortion have been rising over the last 20 years, reflecting the greater use of abortion by women of all childbearing years. Numbers have risen steadily from about 21,000 in 1971 to over 41,000 in 1988. In 1984 the age groups 16–19 had a higher abortion rate than any other age group. Today pregnancies among the youngest teenagers are the most likely to end in abortion; one in four of 19 year olds, but three in four of those aged 15 or less (Francome, 1986).

A similar picture is shown in the US. Teenagers accounted for 26 per cent of all US abortions in 1985, twice their proportion of live births (Henshaw and Van Vort, 1989). Bearing in mind that more pregnancies occur in older teenagers, the rate of abortions per 1000 women has been highest in the 18–19 age group. In the whole American female population, the proportion of pregnancies which end in abortion is higher for teenagers than for all older age groups, except women over 40 (Francome, 1986).

If rates of abortions per number of conceptions are considered, the worrying feature is the very young age group, the 16 year olds and under. As sexual activity occurs increasingly among younger adolescents, the number of abortions is likely to increase proportionally. It is significant that the younger girls tend to ignore or reject the use of contraception, risking unwanted pregnancy – sometimes several times over – and choosing termination as a resolution of their predicament.

Chapter 2

Paths to Pregnancy

In this chapter we endeavour to unfold the picture of the vulnerable teenager and the interplay of influences which bring parenthood too soon. Learning our gender roles begins in the cradle, and the messages reinforcing these come crowding in from all sides, in every aspect of society. Learning about sexual functioning involves reliable teaching and guidance, and this is not always available. Even when young people have sufficient knowledge, most appear to be unwilling to put it into practice, or unable to make the connection between knowledge and use.

In spite of considerable advances recently in breaking down some barriers between the stereotypical roles in our society, it appears still to be true that girls are encouraged by our male dominated society to grow up to be emotionally and economically dependent. Many of those who succumb to this role end up by being abandoned by the very men who wanted it in the first place and, it seems, by society which condones it.

The lack of information and discussion of sexual matters for boys is part of the problem. In a world of embarrassment and ignorance, making decisions about sexual behaviour and its consequences is not easy. Many children and even adolescents are more innocent than adults believe them to be in matters of sex and procreation. This chapter focuses on some fears and beliefs of teenagers, and the rationale for their decisions for the future.

Learning the female role

Children's behaviour is inevitably a reflection of adult social life. Adults are direct models for children, and sexual stereotypes are reinforced by the human behaviour that children experience – at home, at school, on television, in books, and so on. Children are inevitably caught up in sexual stereotyping from the moment they are born: neither girls nor boys can help but perpetuate the general view of their female and male roles.

It is generally portrayed and accepted by both sexes that girls expect to become mothers, and thus it is assumed that this is what they wish. Many writers have demonstrated how this is culturally transmitted, based neither on biology nor on what is considered 'natural' (Jackson, 1982). For girls, it is claimed, this is particularly crucial; for them the difficulty of resisting the pressures of gender expectations can have disastrous consequences. Ann Oakley makes the point strongly:

> In Western culture today, motherhood is the chief occupation for which females are reared. It is a major component of the feminine gender role as taught to a female child by her parents, and others with whom she comes into contact. Through this assertion 'all women need to be mothers' comes to be true. (Oakley, 1979a)

We identify three major influences as sources for learning the female role: (i) mother and family; (ii) institutions and the media; and (iii) adolescent sexual discourse.

Mother and family

The influence of the mother as a model for the daughter is crucial. Skinner's (1986) study of 550 girls in South London found two contrasting types of mother whose influence was strong on their daughters; the distant mother who seemed to care little about what her daughter was up to, and the very close mother in whom the daughter confided. The 217 girls who became teenage mothers showed a distinct tendency to cluster around the 'distant' category. These girls were the least likely to have discussed any aspect of sex with their mother or to have had much communication at all with her. They were also the most likely to have been pushed out early and ill-equipped into the world, lonely and seeking affection.

One 14-year-old mother at the Bristol Unit put it more clearly than most girls in her position are able to do: 'What has my mother ever done for me? I ain't learnt bleedin' nothing from her. Look at me now! No wonder I'm like I am!' By contrast the daughter who has a close relationship with her mother identifies and empathises with her to such an extent that the daughter is positively encouraged to become pregnant very young. A symbiotic relationship such as this offers the mother another child by proxy, and the daughter's prospective motherhood is welcomed with enthusiasm. Examples can also be found among mothers of teenage daughters. As another Bristol Unit mother said of her 15-year-old daughter's forthcoming motherhood: 'I've got something to look forward to now. Made my life worth living again.' This about-to-become-a-grandmother was divorced and living with two teenage children. She was 32 years old. A more extreme example of closeness, perhaps, is this 15 year old's mother's comments about her mother:

> I'm never going to leave home. I won't never have to look after myself. My mum'll always be there. No-o, if she dies, I die. No way am I gonna live after she dies. Don't care about my baby . . . My life can't exist without my mum.

Parental influence, particularly between the same sex pairs, does not disappear during adolescence and plays a considerable part in teenage sexual behaviour. Both Skinner (1986), and Fox and Inazu (1980), in an American study of 450 Detroit mothers and their teenage daughters, found that good communication between mothers and daughters meant that daughters were more likely to use effective contraception once they started to have sex.

Another study of teenage girls, this time in Cambridge, England, shows up the ambivalence of their feelings towards motherhood (Prendergast and Prout, 1980). While motherhood was seen as inevitable destiny for women, most of the girls drew on their experiences with their own families to describe motherhood as dominated by sentiments like isolation, boredom and depression.

Actual mothers were frequently described as depressed, but this was considered normal and to be expected.

This comparison of mystical idealism and harsher reality crystallises around the time of childbirth. Women were generally thought by these girls to obtain pleasure in looking after a child. They believed that most women have a mothering and caring instinct, and they had high expectations that it would be the same for them.

From the research a set of beliefs emerges about women which is described as the 'sentimental model'. Embedded in our culture, it causes girls and boys, men and women to view motherhood – not fatherhood or parenthood, but *motherhood* – in a sentimental and possibly a rather unrealistic way. Often it is convenient to explain a way of behaving as a 'need'. The 'sentimental' view of motherhood is explained in this way:

> children need their mothers
> mothers need their children
> all women need to be mothers.

Add to this set of beliefs the commonly held assumptions that:

> biology is destiny for a woman
> to be normal is to be a mother
> to be a mother is to be properly feminine
> (Oakley, 1979b)

and we have the deeply ingrained cultural and social influences which help to create gender identity for girls.

There is evidence that these doubts and contradictions of adolescence frequently take their toll. In a study of postnatal depression evidence was found of a desperate sense of failure among women who felt they had not come up to their own expectations of caring and coping motherhood. Their comments, looking back to their anticipation and expectations during pregnancy, revealed that they had over-romanticised the whole process. The great majority felt their expectations of motherhood had been unrealistic and unduly romantic: the reality was quite different from what they had expected (Oakley, 1979a).

In spite of the evidence – disappointment, depression, isolation, economic and emotional dependence – it appears that the dark side of motherhood holds little sway against social definitions of motherhood as a state which women are bound to want and to enjoy. In other words, personal experience is overridden by the sentimental model – the stereotypical knowledge – in a very dramatic way.

Profound fatalism regarding women's lives and girls' futures is revealed by much of this research: strong among the girls but even more powerful among the boys (Prendergast and Prout, 1980). Motherhood, according to the boys, was something to be endured, there was nothing good about it and there was no escaping it. As one boy said: 'It's the only thing women do, whatever it's like, they have to . . .'. Adolescent boys share their sisters' uncertainties about future dilemmas of sexual life, although their expression takes a different form. One study of working-class boys (Willis, 1977) found they had two quite opposite perceptions of women. First, the sexual object, willing and able to be the receptacle for male pleasure, and as such put down, despised and disposable. Second, but equal with the first, the 'domestic comforter', the faithful and frumpish housewife who is no longer attractive, who services her man and the family while he is free to pursue his pleasures:

> Though there is a great deal of affection for 'mum', she is definitely accorded the inferior role . . . and within the home there is a clear sense that men have a right to be waited on by mother.

Willis provides a graphic example from among his recent school leavers of how rapidly the second role can take over:

> I've got this bird. I've been goin' with her for eighteen months now. Her's as good as gold. She wouldn't look at another chap. She's fucking done well, she's clean. She loves doing fucking housework. Trousers I bought yesterday, I took 'em up last night, and her turned 'em up for me . . . She's good as gold and I want to get married as soon as I can. (1977, pp. 42–3)

Most teenagers push the whole notion of marriage and child rearing to the back of their minds, as not happening ideally until their 20s – when they have lived a bit. However, girls know that both states are their destiny some time in the misty future when they have experienced both fun and romance. It is generally believed by both boys and girls that, for women, fun comes to an end with marriage and raising a family and the drudgery of motherhood is accepted as their sentimental destiny.

Thus it is that boys and girls view motherhood in the same ambiguous way. Not all boys consider marriage; but by those who do, marriage and the female role within it are seen as inevitable. As one boy perceived it, when you marry 'You lose pride in yourself' (Willis, 1977). It seems that, as soon as you have finished striving for your heart's desire and catch your loved one, things fall very flat. But it is the girls who have to carry the load and cope with the practicalities. It is the girls who visibly suffer the physical and emotional effects of this stereotyping and this ambiguity. Reluctant motherhood among young teenage women is more common than is generally supposed. Thanks to the 'sentimental model' – which men and the media do a lot to encourage – this reluctance is not overtly admitted. Thus it is that mothers of all ages, but particularly the young and unprepared, feel guilty and 'unnatural'. They may feel unable to cope, or they may feel negative or resentful about their situation because they think they are failing to live up to the (sentimental) ideal of motherhood. This may herald the start of many problems for both mother and child.

Institutions and the media

It is new to no one that children are impressionable beings – how otherwise would they learn and absorb enough to make them socially acceptable? Adolescents are no less susceptible than younger children when subjected to the endless stream of ideas and images incorporating sexist values (Sharpe, 1976). The screen is an enchanter and we can all of us be beguiled, often without realising the power of the messages. And how we like it! American teenagers watch television 23 hours a week, more time than they spend in any other activity except sleeping. By the time they reach 70 they will have spent seven years watching TV. The stereotypes depicted on the screen are absorbed into adolescents' attitudes and behaviours. Young children who watch a lot of television develop more stereotypical sex role attitudes than those who watch only a little (Strasburger, 1989).

Not surprisingly therefore, the sexual double standards which prevail in Western society ('Be as sexy as you can, but don't "do it" ' or even: 'Take the risk, but don't get caught') are reinforced by the media and imitated by our youngsters. Girls learn quickly and effectively that the world is male dominated and that aspirations towards competing for power and authority in many spheres – from career and earning power to ordinary relationships – are not only futile, but somehow also wrong.

Girls learn to be passive and vulnerable and boys to be disdainful and aggressive. Adolescent attitudes are malleable and television gives teenagers their first real glimpse into the secretive world of adult sex before they can learn from first-hand experience. Masculine sexuality is usually portrayed as assertive, often even violent. Men may come to believe they must dominate and that women like to be dominated. Unknowingly, many girls seal their fate by adapting to the passive and inward-looking roles; romantic love, intimacy, the household, waiting and servicing, sacrifice. Boys are encouraged to look outward, be active, take risks, scorn feelings, and make selfish choices (Jackson, 1982). All these attributes are easily recognisable in the traditional European fairy tales (Bettelheim, 1976), for example: Sleeping Beauty, and Snow-White and the Seven Dwarfs, where the heroine is 'saved' by a man's kiss.

In adapting to this passive role, girls' assertiveness is undermined. So when asked to exercise choice in any sphere they have little experience and even less real encouragement. This is especially so in the sexual and educational choices with which we are concerned here. Teenage television viewers have, by one account, 'the worst of all possible worlds':

> Movies, music, radio and TV tell them that sex is romantic, exciting, titillating; premarital sex and cohabitation are visible ways of life among the adults they see and hear about; their own parents or their parents' friends are divorced or separated but involved in sexual relationships. Yet, at the same time, young people get the message good girls say No. Almost nothing they see or hear informs them about contraception or the importance of preventing pregnancy. (Jones *et al.*, 1985)

Confusion is generated and perpetuated, and communication is stifled by these messages.

Adolescent sexual discourse

Sexual double standards permeate teenage discourse, reinforcing the male sense of his superiority and female knowledge of her inferiority. Speaking for many, one 15-year-old girl was heard to say: 'Whatever we do, it's always wrong!' Sue Lees (1986) has shown how, when teenage girls talk among themselves, there is no admission of the negative aspects of marriage for women: loss of identity in taking on the husband's name, financial dependence, restricted career opportunities, depression, isolation – these sorts of concerns are not part of adolescents' conversations. We have already seen, however, that in a serious, more adult setting adolescents will freely express their feelings on these more negative aspects of family life.

Perhaps most damaging to a girl during adolescence is the madonna/whore syndrome. Surveys of boys' sex talk consistently find that girls and women are held in general contempt at the same time as being objects of lust. Girls notice the changes from one mood to another, depending on whether the boy is with a crowd of mates or on his own. Lees cites a typical example:

> When they're with their mates they're all hard and they call you names. But when they're on their own they talk to you. They say '. . . I like your glasses'. And then, when they're with their mates, it's 'All right, Goggles?' and all the rest of it. That's what makes me sick . . . They're not like it on their own. They only want to act big when they're with someone.

Girls may express their sexuality on the path to marriage by wallowing in romance and falling in love. They may specifically not express a desire for sex. If they do, they are labelled 'slags'. On the other hand, if they do not respond favourably to male sexual pressure they are ostracised – as 'frigid', 'tight' and other such adjectives. 'It's a vicious circle. If you don't like them [boys] then they'll call you a tight bitch. If you go with them they'll call you slag afterwards.' Girls do understand this ambiguity, for in fact it matches their own. But they somehow seem unable to use this knowledge to ride above the boys' insecurity and come out equal, if not winners. Insults abound among the young, and they are used by both girls and boys. They are, however, aimed at girls alone:

'One thing I noticed is that there are not many names you can call a boy. But if you call a girl a name, there's loads of them. You might as well make a dictionary of names you can call a girl (Lees, 1986, p. 32). The following was heard recently in the classroom of a British comprehensive school, spoken by a third-year girl to a boy who was being clumsy: 'You *woman!*' The lack of available terms of derision for a boy in our culture forces this irony on an extremely irritated girl. One wonders if she was aware of what she was saying. The innocence of the comment confirms our point. The insults bear no relation to actual sexual behaviour, and girls on the whole are unwilling or feel unable to stand up for themselves. Neither girls nor boys seriously question – let alone challenge – the double standards they are caught up in.

As Lees makes abundantly clear in her account of girls' attitudes and responses to the double standards, to initiate sex is unfeminine and simply 'not done', and yet girls are held responsible for boys' sexual urges. It is still commonly believed among both men and women, as also among their adolescent sons and daughters, that once a man is aroused and has an erection untold harm will come to him if he does not find relief. As a result of this mistaken belief women are made to feel guilty enough to 'help' the man in his difficulty: 'Since you have caused the erection it is your responsibility and I must have sex with you.' There is much milage in this myth for men. This is poignantly illustrated by the extreme but common example of women being accused of responsibility for their own rape. The fact that arousal and erection for men do not necessarily occur simultaneously is irrelevant here: street knowledge, as we have already shown, seems to have little to do with biological reality or moral responsibility. A woman may be provocative; this does not give the man the right to thrust himself upon her, even if he perceives her as 'asking for it'. The notion of domination and punishment is encapsulated in this little phrase and is unfortunately held by many adolescents (and older people who should know better) to be true.

Such imbalance in relationships means that both men and women lose out, but in different ways. Men expect to dominate and to blame women, and women may allow this to happen. Adolescents express themselves accordingly in their early relationships. A girl's role is inescapably linked first and foremost with her sexual reputation, while boys have a wider field in which to excel, sexual activity being only one of many reputation-enhancers. Girls tread a tightrope, and it is not surprising that many teenage girls topple, or that some of them fall victim and get caught with an unwanted pregnancy. Assuming the role of mother seems the inevitable consequence.

Learning about sex

We learn about sex from the moment we are born. We learn about how our parents feel about our bodies by the way we are handled and by their tones of voice in connection with that handling. We learn to touch and be touched. We learn what and where on our bodies is safe and comfortable for touching. We learn about different types of touch, and what must not be touched, and by whom. Like all taboos, this one operates for our protection, but may also do much damage.

Later we learn to communicate about our bodies through talking. Many children do not get the chance to talk about sex and relationships in a serious way at home.

> Question: 'Do you think you have been indoctrinated with sexual values?'
> Answer: 'Yes, Miss, I have received an indoctrination of silence.' (Carol Lee, 1983)

Alongside this tribute to the adults significant in the lives of inquiring and curious children, Lee quotes the following dialogue between herself and a schoolboy in one of her sex education lessons:

> 'Well, I caught my brother and his girl doing it, you know, fucking, 'cept I didn't know what it was. I was 11, see, and he was much older than me. I asked him afterwards what he was doing and he said it was "fucking" and I said "What's that?" and he told me.'
> 'Told you what?'
> 'What fucking was, Miss.'
> 'Yes, but what exactly did he say?'
> 'He said it's when a man puts his cock in a woman's hole, and I

said to him "What hole, man?" and he said "The one in the
middle and you have to make sure you put it in the right one
because a woman's got two holes".'
'Did he tell you anything else?'
'Yes, he said when I felt something, as if I was going to pee, I
must take my cock out.'
'Did he tell you why?'
'No, Miss.'
'Did you ask him?'
'No.'
'Did you ever learn anything else about sex from your family or
your friends or from school?'
'Yeah, I learnt you mustn't get the girl pregnant.'
'How do you stop that happening?'
'By pulling your cock out, Miss.'

This dialogue had come about because the boy could not relate
touching and cuddling with all he knew about sex, which was
'fucking'. One girl's remark – that they did not know enough
about what sex was about – initiated a very meaningful discussion
and practical exercise during which all the children shut their eyes
and Carol Lee walked round the circle, touching them all on an
arm, a shoulder, etc. They loved it. Such feelings were new to
them all.

A five week old boy had been washed and was being changed.
As he lay a moment naked and free on the changing mat, and his
fifteen year old mother was about to put on the clean nappy, his
still young grandmother exclaimed: 'Now we don't want any of
that naughty business. Take your hand away, you naughty boy!'
She jerked the baby's hand away. The tiny child's hand had
found his penis in a passing uncoordinated gesture and was idly
fiddling. (Hudson, 1985)

This sort of attitude is not uncommon and does nothing to
encourage a good image of sexuality in either the young mother or
her son. They both have their sexual lives before them. Unfortunately the chances are that the young mother is already ashamed
of and covert about her bodily functions and her sexuality, and the
child will grow up in similar damaging ignorance, thinking his body

dirty, and a good deal of his sexual activity will be done secretively and with a sense of guilt.

Yates (1978) discusses 'difficult', 'unacceptable', and 'maladjusted' behaviour in children – i.e. behaviour which embarrasses the adults – and details how such children are likely to grow into adults who have difficulties in their sex lives and in their relating generally. This is not new to us; we know that real, serious sexual awareness is positively discouraged in our society. Whereas being sexy, losing control and giving way to sexual urges – sexual behaviour which in our society is associated with intimate privacy – are continually dealt with in titillating and suggestive ways in the media. Superficial or casual portrayal of intimate sexual relationships does not help adolescents who need answers to serious questions about themselves. Thus it is not a comfortable subject for discussion or activity for many of us. Yates explains how sexual awareness is as important as awareness in other areas of our development – physical, emotional and intellectual. Had we learnt and been allowed as children to recognise and accept ourselves as sexual beings, we would be more confident as adults and behave more responsibly with our bodies, as with those of our children.

A pale light in the sky signals the nearness of dawn as the two bare bodies again stretch upon the bed. He nuzzles her skin, breathes her scent, and quickly rouses. He inhales deeply, presses urgently against her, and unwittingly pinches her nipple in the process. Flinching slightly, she rubs his nose and whispers softly. He fixes his eyes on her, and kneads one breast with his fingers as he relishes the other with his lips. As he forces his hips against hers, an ancient rhythm oscillates and ebbs. Gradually his grip relaxes and he drifts towards a deep, refreshing slumber. She tenderly disentangles her hair from beneath his body. Then she covers him with the blanket and carries him to his cot. (Yates, 1978)

This erotic description of an infant feeding illustrates the essential sexual nature of humankind, how cuddling and touching are vital aspects of a parent/child relationship, and how sexuality is – perhaps surprisingly – present in the tiny infant. 'His whole body is a sexual organ', writes Yates. 'Why is Cupid always portrayed as an infant? To be in love is to re-experience infancy.'

But being in love is not the same as being sexually active. Somewhere along the road to maturity we are taught to forget about the tender side of relationships, we are taught to be embarrassed about our feelings, to hide them. When a group of fourth-year boys and girls were asked what ways there were of showing affection between a boy and a girl/a man and a woman other than inserting the penis into the vagina, they could not answer. When asked to say how parents (but possibly only mothers in many cases) showed affection for their children, the answers came thick and fast. Linking the affectionate behaviour allotted to infants and children with adult sexual relationships was too much for the group of 14 and 15 year olds. They were speechless with giggling embarrassment.

Adolescents are self-conscious about their bodies. Many teen-age girls who indulge in sexual activity (among whom some are mothers) have never seen their partner naked and would not want to. This applies particularly to the younger ones. 'No, did it in the dark. Had me clothes on, anyway, course I did. Wouldn't let him see me nude! Didn't see or touch his thing either' (15-year-old mother). Together with this declaration goes the following, spoken by the same young mother when her son was two years old, and she herself only 17: 'Pull your pants up, Johnny, don't be so disgusting!' He was taking an interest in his body and feeling his penis. Many adults find touching their aptly termed 'private parts' hard to cope with. Negative attitudes such as this encourage youngsters to be furtive in their finding out about themselves, and reluctant to be open about their relationships. If they feel unable to discuss sex, they may find asking questions impossible. Sheer ignorance as well as an instinctive shame are thus partly responsible for unthinking sexual activity and for subsequent unintentional pregnancy.

This taboo on the body's natural functions affects the way soiled nappies are dealt with, with the result that the child soon learns to be ashamed of his daily creations. Breast feeding is also a difficult area, especially for adolescent mothers who are less likely to breast feed their babies than older mothers; they find it 'disgusting' or 'dirty'. Young mothers who have been brought up themselves to be ashamed of their body are unlikely to overcome their aversion to exposure of the breast or to the physical cuddling involved.

'Breast feed? You must be joking! Not having it nibbling at me like a little animal!'

'No-o, it hurts. An' anyway, you can only do it at home, can't you? and you're not always going to be at home when the little bugger wants it, are you?' (an extra rationalisation).

The baby thus loses out on its first real erotic contact. It also starts at this point to inherit its mother's inhibitions and taboos.

Strong sexual taboos can have very damaging consequences. When sexual activity is linked with anger and frustration, sex quickly becomes an aggressive and punishing denial of tenderness. When sexual intercourse takes place without tenderness, it can be confusing, hurtful and damaging. To be sexually responsive is something we have to learn, and this over a period of time. Many adolescent conceptions involve very little tenderness or erotic response. Some may be the direct or indirect result of sexual abuse by the father or stepfather. When such a girl becomes a parent herself, unaware of her own damage, the pattern inevitably repeats with the next generation. As Lee (1983) puts it: 'So many young people . . . suffer from what seems to be rigor mortis of the emotions. They are locked up, and they need an unlocking process which will not endanger them.'

One grandmother who had learnt about sex only from her husband discovered very late in life during her menopause, and thanks to one of her daughters lending her a book on the change of life, that there was a lot more to sex than she had realised, and that her husband had learnt all he knew from talking to other men. She was horrified and said that she thought it was 'completely unnecessary for young people to be kept in the dark' (Lee, 1983).

Girls and boys from puberty onwards find sex and sexual relationships an embarrassing, uncomfortable and exciting topic for discussion and experimentation. It is a 'rude' area of mystery and taboo in spite of specific references to the sexual act and the sexual organs. Physical and emotional maturity do not coincide in the teens, and thus a sense of responsibility and a realistic approach to sexual activity and its connotations are not prevalent in early or late adolescence. It is one of the hardest things to educate adolescents towards sexual responsibility once they are at school. What they already know they have learnt from earliest childhood and it has been reinforced by adult behaviour and representations of adult behaviour all around them. And in the

peer group they are constantly involved in the games of top dog –
status and reputation are at stake.

Sexual experience does not of itself bestow powers of communication. The following is an extract from an interview with a 16-
year-old mother, telling how she explained 'things' (i.e. the facts
of life) to her younger sister who was at risk of becoming pregnant:

> Oh, I told her what to go through – yeah. If she asks me. I told
> her what to go through and what happens. . . . Well, I told her
> [about contraception] – if she ever needs anything, I'll take her
> to the Family Planning with me. She says 'No' – she just laughed
> . . . 'no' that she don't want to go – she'll be too embarrassed –
> be the odd one out. . . . (Hudson, 1985)

Knowledge was not a barrier in this case. She knew what to do,
and so did her mates: 'They all know about it.' What knowledge
do they all have? Where have they learnt it? Whatever it is, this
knowledge is limited and not very clear, judging from the above
explanation, which in our experience is fairly representative.
Perhaps, since sex is something that young (and older) people are
shy about discussing, it is also something they are shy about
thinking about. Hence the difficulty that many young teenagers
have in first of all sifting the facts from the fantasies, and secondly
translating their knowledge of facts into responsible behaviour.

Sex education for this young woman, in whatever well-
intentioned form and by whomever delivered, was clearly not
immediate or relevant or personal enough. If sex education is
unable to cut across the barriers of inhibition and taboo, even an
adolescent's naturally inquiring mind will not win through.

Girls and boys are caught up in cultural pressures. These
pressures either cause restraint and anxious silence about sex –
something which interests and absorbs them passionately – or
they develop into aspirations towards goals of sexual achievement.
The guilt, the ignorance and the general discomfort evinced by
their parents and the other significant adults around them when
young people attempt discussion on sexual matters filters through
with remarkable effect. As for the men, without exception those
Carol Lee spoke with have said they were brought up with the
implicit idea that sex was a 'doing' exercise. They described their
early sexual explorations as learning how to *do* something (mainly

where to put the penis), unrelated to any idea of tenderness, consideration or even happiness. A man of 38 told her:

There was no sharing, practically no conversation, and certainly no consideration. I knew nothing about appreciating women till I'd been having sex for many years. They were things you jabbed your willie into – if you were lucky. And you didn't respect the ones who let you do it to them because everyone said you married the ones who didn't.

While boys and girls believe that male sexuality means actively 'doing it' and 'having it off', and that it brings status and enhances a boy's reputation, and that female sexuality means having things done to you which are expected and not necessarily pleasurable, and which inevitably compromise your reputation, there is little hope for either sex of achieving satisfying, responsible and mutually enjoyable sexual relationships.

Learning about reproduction and contraception

It is a fallacy to suppose that teenage mothers are any more enlightened about their sexuality than any other teenager. Education about the functions of the human body is important, but it is not enough, it seems. And while many adults consider it important to ensure that young people know how to prevent pregnancy, they are often appalled at the prospect that they might enjoy sex.

Sexual behaviour is as much to do with feelings as with physical action. Perhaps failure to take precautions against pregnancy has more to do with an inability to match feelings which are scary, confused and hidden than with what these girls learnt – or at least were taught – at school. Present anxieties can block the absorption of information, so it is the anxieties that have to be dealt with first, not the information. Attitudes, believed misinformation and anxieties about sexual involvement appear to be stronger influences on sexual behaviour than contraceptive knowledge.

Puritan ethics (not to enjoy anything) and Victorian morality (lie back and think of England) are extremely difficult to shake off. Sex education remains something of a problem. Boys receive less sex education than girls, both at home and in school. Girls are closer to their mothers, they identify with them and are more firmly oriented towards relationships than their brothers. They see themselves as care givers and like to know about babies. Boys lose out on initial information when young, partly because mothers are more embarrassed to talk to sons than to daughters, and most specifically because fathers on the whole will not. When we look at the gender role in the context of discussion between parents and children about sex, procreation is considered differently among males and females. Because of monthly periods, girls are made aware of their bodily behaviour – even if the function is understood poorly or not at all – and they look forward one day to being mothers. Boys learn that their penis can behave in strange, exciting and sometimes embarrassing ways, but this is rarely related to the making of babies.

Farrell (1978) made a major study of how young people learned about sex. Three stages in girls' sexual learning help us to understand their sexual behaviour:

(1) reproduction and babies, often from quite an early age;
(2) menstruation, just before or at the time of menarche – usually about 11 years old;
(3) sexual intercourse and what periods mean – usually between ages 11 and 13.

Although most parents and some teenagers thought that the best source of sexual information ('the facts of life') was at school, there was nevertheless considerable ambivalence. Certainly, sex education lessons were considered preferable to learning from friends. Yet a decade later friends continued to be the principal source of sex education (Hill, 1988).

School was felt by over half of Farrell's informants to be the best place to learn about birth control. Parents find it difficult to discuss sexual matters with their children. Only 35 per cent of mothers and 29 per cent of fathers felt parents were the best people to teach their children about sex, but while mothers on the whole practised what they preached, only 15 per cent of fathers did.

More recently, Allen (1987) interviewed 200 families. Evidence of poor communication within families remained strong: 60 per cent of boys had never spoken to their mothers about sex or growing up, and 75 per cent of boys and girls had never spoken about sexual matters with their father. Support for sex education in schools had hardened; some 95 per cent of both teenagers and their parents felt that that was where it should be provided.

Many parents are critical of the sex education they received when young and do not wish their children to grow into equally ignorant adults, or to suffer the distress and anxiety this ignorance caused them. Today, it seems, adults are more willing to face their ignorance and embarrassment, which must in the long run be only a good thing for children, so long as they have the opportunity to learn about sex at school. As a parent said to Allen: 'I don't agree that it should just be the parents' responsibility – nothing worse than passing on your own ignorance.'

Farrell (1978) found parent-child communication on sexual matters weaker in working-class than in middle-class families. Birch (1987) found pregnant schoolgirls in Camberwell, a working-class district of South London, very ignorant about 'the facts of life': 87 per cent learned nothing from their parents, and girls younger than 14 had no sex education at all. Birch notes that where girls have a good relationship with their mother, they are less likely to have early sex, and, as we have noted elsewhere, they are more likely to have more information as well as the good sense to be sexually responsible. The relationship with mother, it seems, is crucial to a girl's view of herself as a sexual being. Where there is no satisfactory sex information forthcoming from parents or from school, the relied sources are friends and hearsay, and an awful lot of rubbish is disseminated as 'information'. Thus 'knowledge' of sexual matters assures teenagers that:

> You don't get pregnant when you do it standing up . . . if you are drunk . . . if you jump up and down afterwards . . . so long as you don't enjoy it . . . if you do it on top. . . .

Such lists are endless and their influence is strong on young people.

Much American research shows that parents provide little in the way of sex education (Birch, 1987).

Boys receive less sex education than girls at school: there is evidence that boys feel they miss a lot. It transpires that many boys do other things like sport or revision when girls have extra sex education lessons. One boy spoke for many a lonely teenager: 'I've no understanding how girls feel, so it may help if we had discussions with girls . . .' (Allen, 1987). Ironically, the fact that girls lose out in the long run may be to a large extent a consequence of the boys losing out on sex education. It is surely essential that both boys and girls understand the functioning and the timing of the menstrual cycle. Yet, when American researchers have asked about the time during the menstrual cycle when women are at the greatest risk of pregnancy, only about one in five has been able to answer correctly. Even among those who had had a sex education course covering the menstrual cycle, only a third got it right (Miller, 1983).

Sex education in schools is unlikely at the present time to relate to pupils' experience because it is not given the time and the space it needs. Whether it is treated as an established school subject or included in other subjects, or even discussed in terms of health, morality or family structure, until there is some overall national education policy, some clarity and vision as to the importance of sex education, it is not surprising that young people remain confused and ignorant. While sex is deliberately excluded from the main curriculum and is part of unplanned, incoherent courses, pupils are unlikely to view sex as anything but a covert matter for discussion and activity.

Unfortunately, in many cases, where teenagers are lucky enough to receive sex education at school, they are generally further instilled with the stereotypes of male activity and female passivity. The programmes tend to have very little to do with the whole concept of sexuality, and are more likely to concentrate on the biological and reproductive facts of sex. Emotions, relationships or the pupils' experiences are not investigated or aired effectively, and pupils in these circumstances remain confused. For example, male orgasm is to do with conception, and male masturbation is believed to be 'natural'. Female orgasm is not discussed, evidently since it has nothing to do with conception. Pleasure is clearly too embarrassing and difficult a subject to air in the classroom. And girls probably do not masturbate.

> The assumption is that sex is important to girls only as it affects their future role as wives and mothers. So they remain ignorant of the means of deriving pleasure from their bodies, given information only on their reproductive, not their erotic, potential. (Jackson, 1982)

An incident from the Bristol Unit provides an illuminating example. In the middle of an English lesson, Janice, a 15-year-old Afro-Caribbean mother, suddenly asked her teacher: 'What's orgasm?' She had apparently asked this question at her comprehensive school and been told that if she asked any more 'rude questions' she would be given a detention. Soon after that she got pregnant. The Unit teacher answered the question by introducing a discussion ranging from male and female sexual parts, male and female orgasm, relationships, touching, etc., etc. to school uniform! The response was exciting: initial squirms of giggling, 40 minutes of intense interest, awakening understanding and enlightening comments such as:

'I didn't have that, did you, Joy?'
'So that's why he huffed and puffed so much.'
'Do you mean we're supposed to enjoy it?'
'But it only took two minutes.'

In the light of evident embarrassment and confusion, it is not surprising that adolescents emerge with poor and incomplete information about their sexual functioning.

The idea that television or other mass media should be used as a channel for teaching about contraception is almost unthinkable in many countries. Even commercial advertising for particular brands of condoms has proved almost impossible. Despite the enormously sexual content of American TV, almost no opportunity is presented for using the medium in an educational fashion. For example, only one mention of a diaphragm was noted in an entire season of US TV, when it required that the user be the Chief of Obstetrics and Gynaecology to accomplish it. Yet a majority of Americans – even among Catholics – favour TV advertising of contraceptives (Strasburger, 1989). The threat of AIDS has produced some small improvements in this situation, and will be discussed in a later section (chapter 6).

Using contraception

Contraception is not popular among many teenagers, particularly those under 16 and those from economically and educationally poorer backgrounds. Confusion, ignorance and embarrassment about sexual matters condemn most sexually active teenagers to possible consequences which will radically change their lives. For in spite of knowing about contraceptive methods, there are psychological factors which affect their ability to use them. Young men are unlikely to consider seriously the consequences of unprotected intercourse; and both obtaining and using condoms require a degree of confidence that many teenage boys lack (Bury, 1984). Boys are generally reluctant to take the responsibility for contraception, considering it the girls' problem. Pressure from partners has been widely reported from American studies as the reason teenagers gave up contraception and became pregnant. This may be especially true of black couples: black teenage men in the US are less likely to use contraception than whites (Sonenstein, 1986). Explicit cases are known to us: 'My boy friend threw my pills on the fire' was one explanation (Ineichen, 1986). Attitudes to single parenthood in the Caribbean have been traced back to times of slavery (Ineichen, 1984/5; Birch, 1987).

Of all the contraception methods *ever heard of*, Farrell (1978) and others recorded the boys' knowledge in this order; the sheath and the pill together, male and female sterilisation, withdrawal, the rhythm/safe period, the cap and the coil together, and lastly chemicals. For girls the order was slightly different: first comes the pill, with the sheath and both sex sterilisation a close second; then withdrawal, the cap, the safe period, and lastly chemicals. Today awareness among teenagers remains in the same order.

The three methods *most commonly used* by young people to prevent pregnancy are the sheath, the pill and withdrawal, although most young people, especially those sexually active, are variously aware of some disadvantages in each method. The unreliability of the sheath, the difficulty in remembering to take the pill regularly, and the timing of withdrawal are obvious examples. Again, it must be stressed, the younger the user, the less reliable the method-use is likely to be. In England and Wales an increasing number of young women today are making use of the 'Depo-provera' three-monthly injection. They may be afraid of their parents finding out about the pill; or they may already have one or two children and know they are not able to remember to take the pill regularly. It is arguable that this is a thin end of a wedge, that it takes away responsibility where it should be encouraged and that the possibly unpleasant side-effects may accompany the woman for three months before the chance to change method comes round again.

Skinner (1986) found that only 27 per cent of her survey group of young mothers had used any form of reliable contraception at first intercourse – 11 per cent the sheath, 16 per cent the pill. Farrell found that out of 433 teenage boys who said they were sexually experienced, 47 per cent had used no contraceptive method at first sexual intercourse, 37 per cent had used the sheath, 9 per cent withdrawal, 4 per cent said their partner was on the pill, 2 the 'safe period' and 1 chemicals. Of 357 girls, 45 per cent had used nothing, 36 per cent the sheath, 10 per cent withdrawal, 8 per cent the pill, 1 per cent 'safe period' and 1 per cent chemicals. The same preference and recklessness seem to apply to both sexes. Much American research confirms this kind of pattern. According to one estimate, only 14 per cent of teenagers use contraception at first intercourse (Foster, 1986). Contraception among girls who become very young teenage mothers is almost non-existent (Miller, 1983; Coyne, n.d).

Simms and Smith (1986) record the classic comments relating to dislike of birth control among teenagers and the reason for not protecting against the risk of pregnancy:

'He couldn't get on with the sheaths and I wasn't on the pill . . .'
'We preferred it without using anything . . .
. . . he wouldn't use French Letters as he didn't like it . . .'

Passing the buck is another excuse to do nothing about it yourself.

'I felt it was up to him . . .'
'She's the one'd might get caught – it's for her to decide . . .'

Many teenagers delay seeking contraceptive help until after they have started a sexual career. Birch (1987), who wrote about young school age mothers in Camberwell, London, points out that girls who turn up at family planning clinics have usually been 'having sex for at least 6 months before they pluck up the courage to come for contraception, many have been taking risks for more than a year'. Skinner (1986) confirms this.

The legal position regarding contraception advice for under 16s and the general confusion as a result of the Gillick case in Britain do not help a teenager to make responsible decisions when embarking on a sexual relationship. In 1981 a local authority refused Mrs Gillick assurance that girls under 16 would not be given contraception or abortion treatment without the parents' consent. Court proceedings against this refusal were dismissed in 1983. However, the following year this dismissal was overruled by the Appeal Court; contraception to children under 16 was deemed henceforth unlawful without parents' consent. This so-called 'Gillick Ruling' met with considerable opposition from a great many organisations and individuals. Currently the position is that a doctor may treat a girl under 16 regarding birth control without parents' knowledge or consent provided that (i) it is in her best interests, (ii) she will understand the advice, (iii) she cannot be persuaded to tell her parents, (iv) without advice or treatment her health would suffer, and (v) she would begin or continue her sexual activity anyway. This compromise is confusing for many: medical practitioners must proceed with caution, adolescents are unclear and parents are unsure.

In the US contraception is available in theory to all teenagers. With the growth in popularity of school-based clinics, where these exist young people have access to reproductive advice, although not necessarily to actual methods. For minors, however, similar ambiguity pertains as in Britain, with doctors advising and prescribing according to their conscience, and also according to individual state legislation regarding the need for parental consent in some circumstances. With the recent changes regarding abortion, it will be interesting to see whether contraception may become more attractive and be made more widely and freely accessible to the young than hitherto. Meanwhile the moral knowledge that sex is 'naughty' and 'wrong' may seem, for many teenagers, a convenient barrier to any action towards birth control. Fear may keep them away from sources of help (Birch, 1987). In Christopher's (1987) words, 'Where sex itself is felt to be bad, the girl may get pregnant to make it good'.

Class is an important influence. Resistance to contraception has traditionally been stronger in the working class. This is especially true among men, whose work role offers relatively little in the way of status and security. If the manual worker's wife goes out to work to help the family finances, that too can be seen as threatening to his pride, his status, his ego. By means of his sexuality he may be sure of dominating in his own home.

Not only are working-class children less likely to discuss sexual matters with their parents, as we have already seen, but females are weaker in the working-class power structure. Working-class girls may be more fatalistic about an accidental pregnancy and give less thought to their long-term future. All the research shows that working-class boys are more sexually active and less likely to use contraception than middle-class boys, middle-class girls and working-class girls.

Scene: Talk, by a teacher working with school age mothers, to a group of fourth year pupils in their own school on 'Sexual responsibility'.

Question to the boys: You want to have sex with your girl friend. You quite rightly say the responsible thing about needing to use a contraceptive, and she says 'Oh – that's all right – I'm already on the pill'. What's your reaction?

Answer:
'She's done it before.'
'She's easy.'
'Spoils the risk – spoils the fun.'
'Wouldn't like it, don't know where she's been.'
'I'd be suspicious . . . you know . . .'
'Well, I might sleep with her, but I wouldn't keep her for my girlfriend.'

Only two out of 18 boys mentioned that this girl was in fact sensibly protected against pregnancy.

Question to the girls: You and your boy friend want to sleep together and he produces a condom from his pocket. What's your reaction?

Answer:
'He gets about.'
'Could be doing it with anybody.'
'He's making assumptions.'
'Looks bad, don' it?'
'Got a lot of confidence, I think.'

But they had to admit also that it showed both consideration and responsibility for his partner.

Premarital relationships

As we saw at the beginning of the chapter, the derogatory and censorious vocabulary used by both boys and girls to describe girls' behaviour or character in a sexual context is a strong influence on the way girls see themselves in their relating with the opposite sex. Terms like 'slag' help to keep a girl in her place. Casual violence often backs up the verbal domination.

> 'Some girls say "Oh he hit me last night" and I say "Did you hit him back?" And they say "No". Then I say "Are you still with him?" and they say "Yes".'

> 'They do it without realising it' [boys hitting their girl friends].

> '. . . he walked out after hitting me . . . he had too much to drink, but we got over it.'

> '. . . he can only hit a girl 'cos he knows the girl won't hit him back.' (Coyne, n.d.)

Why do the girls allow this unequal treatment? Why do they not fight back? Boys' sexual apparatus and performance are visible and thus more open to critical comment than girls' sexual apparatus and performance. And yet, despite this fact, girls seldom seem capable of addressing critical comments to the boys. The reasons for their passivity must be found within a wider oppressive social structure.

When there are difficulties in the relationship it is the girl who is blamed – by herself and by the boy. If he is violent towards her, walks out on her, is abusive, etc., she gets the blame. Many researchers hold strongly to the view that this is the learnt pattern in both fact and fiction. The girls who end up as teenage mothers are among those who have got caught up in this powerful web of sexual oppression and are unable to disentangle themselves. Marriage is seen as a natural progression (Wilson, 1978), justified by notions of romantic love (McRobbie, 1978; Sarsby, 1983), but it will be a marriage which perpetuates the unequal power of the partners. Factory or shop work, if it is achieved, provides little more than a time-filling episode before marriage.

Friends, particularly 'best friends', can be important supports for adolescent girls (McRobbie, 1978). But many girls find that they abandon their friends when they take up with a boy friend, but revert to the old friendships if they drop the boy. In the same situation boys do not give up anything or anybody. They tend to keep their male friends while expecting the girl friend to join in with their usual activities with their mates. While she is with him she often becomes isolated from her friends, since his will and his choices are meekly deferred to. She becomes a hanger-on, an object, a showpiece, a possession and/or a nuisance, depending on the mood of the group.

> Yeah. Like if you're sitting down and there's a whole crowd of boys talking about a girl and you'll be stuck there on your own and you say 'I might as well go home'. (Lees, 1986)

Of course there are exceptions. Some young teenagers pair up in a loving relationship external to the group. If the girl gets pregnant the chances are that if she keeps the baby she will be so much more mature than the boy that the relationship comes to an end. Having a baby makes a girl grow up fast in many ways, as many a teenage mother will testify, and as later examples will show.

Sexual pleasure may not be seen as a shared experience. Certainly, the group of schoolgirl mothers studied by Hudson (1985) gives clear indication that having sex with a male partner was a boring, if not painful event, undertaken by the girl as the inevitable result of passion engendered (by her) in the male. The girl would have stopped the heavy petting or 'larking about' before ejaculation occurred. Even if she too got carried away, actual penetration (and accompanying exercise) would be uncomfortable, short-lived and rarely satisfying or pleasurable for the girl.

The young people under discussion here are playing at it and rightly call it 'having sex'. The finer points have, for the most part, not been glimpsed, let alone achieved. Sexual response is not a subject likely to be much aired during school sex education programmes. Certainly at this stage most young people do not understand and may not have heard about the clitoris: what it is, where it is, how it works and that women have similar – if not greater – potential for climax and pleasure than have men. Such understanding is particularly poor among working-class teenagers.

Choice of partner often reflects a lack of assertiveness and a lack of responsibility among girls. Dowling (1981) and Norwood (1986) in their different contexts expose female acceptance of oppression by male dominance. Where women continue to take a fatalistic and passive view of themselves in terms of their relationships with men, their families and the wider society, there is no call to be in control by taking the pill. In spite of two decades of the Women's Movement, much of what it stands for – working towards greater assertiveness in women, and equal opportunities and treatment for women in all spheres of life – has not touched two significant categories of women: the young and those from low income backgrounds. Far too many girls still expect boys to lay down the law, thus taking many sexual risks, and possibly with a variety of partners. Where they have had poor chances of developing trust, confidence and a sense of identity from their parents, such girls may find relating to boys in an assertive and responsible way extremely difficult.

Many teenagers experience difficulties in managing their relationships in their struggle to find identity and maturity. The double standard, as exemplified by many adults of their acquaintance and as portrayed relentlessly in the media, only helps to reinforce the difficulties for adolescents and subsequently to create another shackled generation.

Justifying pregnancy and parenthood

When pupils in the fourth and fifth years of comprehensive schools were asked at what age they would ideally choose first to have children, that age varied from 20 to 26, by which time they hoped they would have been working a year or so, accumulated some money and have suitable accommodation. They also expected to be married. Those who looked forward in this way held the conventional view of family life with the father as the bread-winner. A few found it difficult to imagine that far ahead, shrugging the matter off with comments expressing a not uncommon fatalistic approach: 'Gotta take what comes, that's how I sees it'. When later in the discussion many admitted to having had unprotected sexual encounters, or even relationships of some duration, the connection between sexual intercourse and parenthood had to be pointed out. For some of them this may have been one of the rare moments when these two ideas came together.

As we saw in the third section of this chapter, one extraordinary aspect of our society is that we expect children to be responsible in their sexual behaviour, and yet education provides no specific training in this very sensitive area. This head-in-the-sand attitude on the part of educators often results in the sort of mental block so often encountered in teenagers, which condones action towards results not intended: having sex is a bit of a risk, but you are unlikely to get pregnant this time. Pregnancy is often not even considered as a possibility. Indirect motives for pregnancy, as seen in this light, can be seen as truly irresponsible, and yet are the direct result of logical responses of the learned role of the submissive female to male dominance. Such responses cannot be attributed to ignorance alone, although that too plays some part.

> 'He said if I wouldn't he'd leave me, so I thought – well, just this once.'
> 'We did it standing up so I thought I'd be all right.'
> 'It was the first time and I didn't think . . .'
> 'He said we loved each other didn't we?'
> 'He was a bit rough so I didn't argue.'
> 'He begged and begged and was all excited and I didn't like to say no.'

It is therefore not surprising that surveys confirm that a majority of teenage pregnancies, even among those that are eventually carried to term, are initially unwanted events. Of Simms and Smith's sample (1986, p. 41) of over 500 teenage girls only one-fifth used birth control around the time they became pregnant; nearly two-fifths had not used any birth control 'because they wanted or didn't mind having a baby'; the remaining two-fifths were using no form of birth control, nor did they want a baby.

Although a small proportion of teenage pregnancies were a mistake due to malfunction or mismanagement of the contraceptive method used at the time, the remaining four-fifths had all been running the risk of becoming pregnant. Half of them were adamant they did not want a baby. Thus more than half these women had not intended to conceive when they did. Nevertheless they kept their babies.

Other research confirms this. Only one in Sharpe's small group of teenage mothers (1987, p. 19) positively wanted to have a baby, and a few did not mind, but the rest had no particular wish to get pregnant: yet four out of five were not using any form of birth control. Research in Bristol also shows a similar pattern. Of 102 pregnant mothers, 29 had planned the pregnancy, 10 were ambivalent, 16 had not planned it but were pleased at the news, and 47 had neither planned it nor were pleased. A majority of each group had had experience of contraception, but many had stopped at the time they became pregnant, not always because they wanted a baby (Ineichen, 1986). Much American research (Furstenberg, 1976; Miller, 1983; Hayes, 1987) confirms widespread fear and unease at this time.

Birch (1987) found that one-fifth of the schoolgirls in her survey did not face up to their pregnancy until a third person (parent, sister, etc) made them do so. She points out that this discovery is a crisis for them and time is needed for them to make one of the most important decisions in their life. Yet time is not on their side. Three-quarters of girls who eventually keep the baby make the decision straight away – as soon as they know. 'My baby didn't ask to come into the world, so I can't get rid of it.'

More direct motives for pregnancy, but still possibly beneath the girls' level of awareness, have been discussed above on the stereotypical female role. Where life at home may be unhappy for the girl for a variety of reasons; where she has not experienced warmth and affection to satisfy her needs; where parents have shown inconsistency and ambivalence in their relating patterns generally; where the parents are separated, divorced, arguing and/ or fighting; where a single mother is too involved in the emotional and physical struggle with her own relationships to cope with her children – any one of these sets of circumstances could motivate pregnancy in the teenage daughter. Far from being put off by the disruption and disharmony in their own family life, some girls set out deliberately to do better for themselves. They hope that, by making a move in this way, they will find happiness with their child, and possibly with their man. Family patterns, however, are not broken easily. Many teenage mothers reproduce a family pattern; for example, a 13-year-old mother whose own mother was 26 and whose grandmother was 46 (Birch, 1987).

Fear of transgressing the social structure which subordinates women, as well as at the same time the feeling of having been cheated by that social structure – both these states maintain the low morale and the sense of powerlessness commonly experienced by many adolescent girls, and indeed by many women also.

Low self-esteem plays a large part in some younger teenage girls becoming pregnant. Such a girl has usually found school and school work uninspiring, has truanted often and emerged from this vicious circle with few or no qualifications. Far too many pupils, both boys and girls, are disaffected in this way. A pattern of purposelessness develops for them and they can become passive receivers of almost anything easy that is offered outside school. Unprotected sex is just one of these.

Looking to the future and possible consequences of any activity enjoyed *now* is a difficult concept for one who has had no joy at or from school, who has received little fulfilment and few rewards in her life so far, and whose employment and financial prospects are low. Today it is an issue of great concern for young people in any industrialised country experiencing economic recession, most particularly for those in ethnic minority groups. Future prospects may appear so bleak that the present moment is everything.

Once their situation is known, young women pregnant for the first time are taken care of by those at home or by the significant adults in their lives, as well as by the health authorities, which attempt to monitor their health needs carefully. Clinic visits, interviews and tests – an anticipatory aura surrounds them. It may seem unlikely, but for many girls their pregnancy gives them the first glimmer of identity and status – as themselves and as women. Not only do nearest and dearest wax lyrical, cosset and worry about them, and supply many of them with more than enough of the material necessities; they are also slotting finally and irrevocably into the pattern of womanhood laid down and expected of them. This, it seems, is their allotted fate, and if it had not been their intention, well – it is now. It feels right.

Pregnancy means also that a girl is regarded differently by boys. If you dislike sex; if you are being harassed by a boy friend who is frequently the worse for drink, or by a group of boys who think you are 'an easy lay'; if you have got in with a crowd who fascinate you but who mistreat you, and you have not got the strength or courage to walk away; if your home life has taught you that affection is bought at a cost . . . getting pregnant may be an answer for you for the time being. A pregnant girl is safely out of reach.

> It was great when I's pregnant – wouldn't let him near me and he respected that – I dunno if he went anywhere else for it. I didn't care anyway. I was glad to have meself to meself. . . . I wouldn't mind getting pregnant again – just to have the peace and quiet.
> (15-year-old mother)

For many girls pregnancy alone enables them to feel confident to say 'No'. For most boys this is a status worthy of some kind of respect, particularly when there may be the question of territorial rights.

Unfortunately, with the passing of time, their sexuality must be confronted once again. Another 16-year-old mother still at school married her baby's father the Easter before she took her exams. Before she left the Bristol Unit she commented:

> Can't wait to get caught again. We're at it all the time – yeah, it's hard work. Once I'm expecting again he'll leave me in peace. I like being pregnant.

This mother went on to have two more children before she was 19, and although she finds life tough and money very hard to make go round, she and her husband enjoy their family life and their children are happy and healthy.

Once an adolescent has become pregnant, the reasons for carrying the baby to term are many. Here are some:

(1) *Genuine ignorance of the pregnancy based on the 'it won't happen to me' syndrome.* Erratic periods may contribute to this feeling. Recognition of pregnancy may be delayed. Venessa, aged 15, managed to conceal her pregnancy from her family, her (constant) boy friend and, it is believed, even from herself. She went into labour at home. A healthy girl weighing 7 lbs was born and her sister's boy friend cut the cord before the ambulance arrived. This girl's periods had continued throughout the pregnancy.

(2) *Rebellion against parents.* To get away from an unsatisfactory home, especially an authoritarian father, and in extreme cases a sexually abusing one.

(3) *To have an object to love*. To have something to call your own. For those who have never had anything, or are forever losing what they have got. To satisfy a need for a loving and dependent relationship. To have someone who demands constant attention and affection. With this baby everything will come right.

(4) *An interest*. Something to do, something that will make you feel important. For those without other ideas, e.g. the severely depressed.

(5) *To keep the father as boy friend*. Or simply to please him.

(6) *To keep a memento of the partner*. If you feel he's about to leave you.

(7) *To achieve adult status*. A cry for recognition and affection on the part of those who lack self-esteem for one reason or another.

(8) *To confirm a self-fulfilling prophesy* in that the adolescent mother is considered a 'bad lot' by her parents.

(9) *Fear of telling anyone, due to absolute views on abortion being 'wicked' (and painful)* and so, if they hang on long enough, it will be too late for adult persuasion in this direction. Putting off the evil moment for fear of being labelled and becoming the target of gossip, comment and criticism.

(10) *The denial system*. Many young teenagers quite simply dare not face the fact themselves, and by not telling anybody they hope the pregnancy will go away. Hence the pregnancy test is put off for months. Josie, aged 14, and her boy friend were so terrified of revealing her pregnancy that she only admitted to it when labour was well under way and her stepfather guessed. Parents also can play this denial game.

(11) *Suspicion of the medical profession*. Many girls fear that doctors will be judgmental to a greater or lesser degree, and indeed examples abound in the literature on adolescent pregnancy of unhelpful biased responses by doctors (see 17 below). The girls in this category probably would not contemplate approaching a doctor for contraception in the first place for fear of their parents finding out.

(12) *There may be strong, unspoken messages coming from the parent/mother* of encouragement to supply the household with another little one.

(13) *Housing problems*. It may be that they want to get away from their family, and see this as a way of jumping the queue for local authority housing. There have been several cases in the authors' experience of a deliberate second pregnancy if the young mother is not happy with her current housing conditions. Because the local authority has a duty to house the homeless/needy/etc., this stratagem has worked in the past and girls have been able to use the system to their advantage by becoming pregnant. Housing problems will be discussed in detail later.

(14) *Disaffection from school*. Some girls who are still at school, hating it and truanting, genuinely believe that they can leave school if they get pregnant. If a fifth year girl plays her cards well, by having a 'difficult' pregnancy, she may put off the authorities who are concerned to see her schooling continued. The various agencies involved with such young people are so hard pressed that this strategy has been successfully employed by a considerable number of adolescent mothers-to-be. Charlotte, a British girl, had succeeded in avoiding school for 18 months before she was referred as pregnant, aged 14. She was allocated a home tutor, whose main role in Charlotte's life became one of surrogate aunt, making sure she kept her antenatal appointments and helping her work through her fear of the birth itself. After the baby's birth Charlotte was rarely available to 'teach' and, when allocated a place in a special centre for school age mothers, refused point blank to attend, requesting again a home tutor, and at the same time finding a job – having lied about her age.

(15) *Negative pressure by family and/or friends to have the child*, whether for reasons of principle or under threat. For instance, it has been known for the parents of a pregnant girl to give an ultimatum: 'Either you have that child adopted or you don't come back to this house after it's born.' If this threat is kept, the girl usually keeps the baby and breaks contact temporarily with her family. Sometimes all is forgiven and the girl brings the baby home – until the next row. A 15 year old at the Bristol Unit claimed: 'I was going to have an abortion, but my friends said that if I did they'd beat me up.'

(16) *Positive pressure* can be just as damaging in the long run. This kind of pressure may come from the baby's father who persuades his girl friend to keep the baby, promising to 'stick by her', etc. Such promises made in these circumstances are for the most part untenable and frequently have disastrous consequences.

(17) *Mistakes and bad advice.* Many examples have been documented. One Bristol schoolgirl went to her GP about her two month pregnancy, wanting an abortion. She was informed the baby was perfectly healthy and she would be unable therefore to obtain an abortion. Not knowing what else to do or whose advice to ask, she felt she had to carry this baby to term. Her plan was to place the baby for adoption, and she eventually received support in this. Others are not so fortunate or so clear in their decisions.

One of Coyne's informants attempted to obtain contraception (the pill) from her family doctor when she was 14, but was told she was too young. 'He said "Well, if you were 15½ I'd risk it". He was talking about risk, and then he said "Oh, no".' This was her only source of advice and help, as she assumed family planning clinics were for married couples. 'It didn't put me off, it gave me the wrong impression . . . I wasn't planning a family!' One of Sharpe's (1987) informants made a similar mistake. She thought that family planning clinics were places where people actually discussed planning their families.

Clinics and doctors who misled young women seeking abortion, among Simms and Smith's (1986, pp. 17–19) sample, put them off with untruthful information, such as enormous costs, they presented too late, it was too dangerous, they'd have to 'go private'.

According to patient claims in the British Pregnancy Advisory Service (1978) survey, 21 per cent of all family doctors consulted made no effort to help schoolgirls obtain abortions.

Of Birch's (1987) Camberwell schoolgirls who went on to have their babies 20 per cent had initially wanted an abortion. Half of these were too late; the other half were not allowed to make their own decision.

Obviously there are some girls who do have a responsible

attitude, once their mistake has been acknowledged. To be thwarted at this crucial stage is an ironical turn of fate for them. Confidence in medical assistance is far from universal among teenage girls. Almost half of Farrell's sample (1978, p. 187) said their doctor did not have time to see them properly for contraceptive advice.

(18) Some girls simply 'get caught' and accept that they will keep the baby because that's life, that's fate – it's inevitable.

Abortion as outcome

The increased availability of abortion to young people in the US since 1973 made this for many a genuine way out of an unwanted pregnancy. Since 1989, however, when responsibility for this availability was reverted to individual state law, those with unwanted pregnancies have been less likely to obtain an abortion. In Britain abortion is available, although there is fairly continuous lobbying designed to restrict the terms under which abortion is legally available.

Many young people feel strongly against abortion, but it is only when faced with the pregnancy and the problem of having to make a decision about its outcome that they are in the position to consider abortion personally. Of those whose sexual activity has resulted in an unwanted pregnancy, a majority seek abortion and for the most part obtain one. Many of the rest, who continue with the unwanted pregnancy, do so because they feel abortion is totally wrong.

Sufficient information around the subject of abortion must be available from various objective sources before a teenager can be expected to make good choices. Unfortunately, most adolescents have limited knowledge of the abortion process. Their formal education says little or nothing about it. Teenagers are guided by street knowledge and old wives' tales, thus remaining in real ignorance while having acquired strong feelings about it.

Feelings among teenagers against abortion run high. One survey revealed that, of the 1540 boys and girls interviewed, only 38 per cent approved of abortion; 49 per cent disapproved (many very strongly) and the remaining 13 per cent had mixed feelings. Girls approve less of abortion than do boys. And working-class girls disapprove of abortion more than middle-class girls (Farrell, 1978) and are less likely to have an abortion if pregnant (Russell, 1982). In other words, those likely to be most sexually active, and without using reliable methods of contraception, are the ones most likely to end up with unplanned and possibly unwanted children.

Many sexual encounters result in unwanted pregnancy, and while abortion of the foetus is one solution to the problem, it is not desirable in very young girls, and as a method of birth control it is hardly satisfactory. When the woman's physical and emotional well-being are involved, it is those at the younger end of the age range who are most at risk and most vulnerable (Russell, 1981, 1982). Abortion may be seen as a quick, easy solution, but the consequences of an abortion may be unsettling and disturbing in the long term unless support and counselling have been offered both before and after the event. The guilt and unhappiness that can accompany the decision to terminate an adolescent pregnancy may result in a second pregnancy shortly afterwards in an attempt to assuage strong feelings of guilt or anger or loss. Women are generally advised – for medical and psychological reasons – not to conceive too soon after the loss of a child, as time for grieving is important to help heal the wound. The younger the woman the less likely she is to recognise her feelings or to impart them to others in seeking help. Help may be offered but can only be given if accepted.

The ability to communicate and make decisions is vital in matters of sexual relationships and pregnancy. Unfortunately sexual maturity does not tie in with intellectual and emotional maturity. Adolescents' attitudes and their decisions regarding abortion can best be understood in stages:

(1) Girls in early adolescence have little awareness of the link between what little they know of contraception, and pregnancy. Pregnancy tends to be denied and responsibility for it disclaimed. If she as a girl accepts abortion for herself, she may not condone it for others. She cannot see herself as a mother or the foetus as a living baby.

(2) In middle adolescence girls have more understanding of conception and contraception and have a more responsible attitude to their behaviour, but even so there is a tendency

to externalise the responsibility for pregnancy, and abortion, if chosen, by blaming boy friends, parents, doctor and others.

(3) Older teenagers know more or less what they are doing and on the whole take responsibility for a pregnancy; as a result they are more likely to feel right about whatever decision they make – including abortion – and not to suffer disturbing after-effects.

Kristin Luker (1975) in her discussion of sexual risk-taking and rationale of the cost/benefit dilemma, puts forward a possible teenage argument from initial sexual activity to its logical outcome:

> If I use ... contraception, certain costs will result, but I probably won't get pregnant, and if I do [get pregnant], certain benefits might emerge; and if they don't, I can always have an abortion.

The costs and benefits are all to do with the different kinds of relationships she encounters – her lover(s), her parent(s), her wider family, her peers, her community – and the values she perceives are placed by each of these groups on (i) controlling her fertility, (ii) young (single) motherhood and (iii) recognising a mistake and choosing to terminate.

It seems that a relatively large number of abortions are sought as a result of sexual risk-taking, that young people would rather risk a pregnancy and use abortion as a last resort than prevent a pregnancy in the first place. If this is so, it is worrying, but it helps us to understand the thought processes and therefore to provide more effective birth control services to the young. Obviously the extent to which abortion is made available to teenagers is a major influence on their decision-making. It is hardly an option if it is not available. As we saw in the last section, it may not be.

Of Simms and Smith's 533 survey teenage mothers, 5 per cent had sought an abortion. Only one admitted to having no intention of carrying this through, but had gone along with the idea to pacify an outraged father. Eight of these young women changed their minds: 'The appointment was made ... I just didn't go ... My sister-in-law had an abortion and ... she was very very depressed

. . . so I didn't want that to happen to me.' Sometimes a boy friend will not only say, 'I'll stick by you', he may also threaten his girl with desertion if she does not comply with his wishes – whether they be for abortion or for keeping the baby.

Of Simms and Smith's total sample, 3 per cent were told by their doctors that they were too late for an abortion. One was first told she was too *early* and later told she was too *late* for an abortion. Sometimes this amounts to deception:

> I wanted an abortion and when I asked my doctor which was more dangerous, having an abortion [at three months] or having the baby, he told me having an abortion. So I believed him and went ahead with the pregnancy. Well, I didn't know, did I? He's the expert, after all . . . (15-year-old mother)

Another, having been told she was too late, 'phoned the hospital, but they 'did not agree with abortion' and she had no further resources. She:

> . . . didn't think it was right, didn't think it was fair. All my mind was upset . . . I'd have one done now if I was pregnant again. I'd try my best to get one now that the baby hasn't even got a father.
> (Simms and Smith, 1986)

Innocence, fear, ignorance and lack of confidence prevent young people from standing up for what they want – if they even know what that is. Sometimes they are given dubious advice.

Skinner (1986) found that numerous women were refused abortions in hospitals, some because of too far advanced pregnancy, others for petty, bureaucratic reasons which bore no relation to the women's circumstances. Skinner states that only a few of all abortions performed 'are by the method and at the time of gestation which could produce a live foetus – a baby so premature that it could not survive independently for more than a few minutes.' She points out that it is this fact that makes the idea of abortion of any kind generally so loathsome. There is in fact much ignorance on the subject of abortion and the different methods. It is not surprising therefore that a young woman in her teens, finding herself unexpectedly pregnant and in an emotional state about it, does not know where to turn, whom to tell or how to tell it. In this sort of state she is unlikely to make thorough enquiries, and is more likely to respond to hearsay. It is at this point that she needs all the factual information and unprejudiced advice she can get, as well as help in working through her feelings towards a decision that is right for her. Yet few had good things to say about those who counselled them at this time: only a third found their GP helpful, for example.

Teenage girls having an abortion tend to have 'late' ones, that is because they make their pregnancy public at a later stage than women intending to be pregnant, or at any rate taking control of their bodies. Only 2 girls out of Skinner's 220 abortion survey girls were offered vacuum aspiration abortion (performed up to 12 weeks). The more dangerous methods, involving catheters, injection or pessaries, are expected to induce abortions between 12 to 18 hours later, and in a third of these cases a general anaesthetic also will be needed.

Pregnant teenagers have little idea of the techniques of abortion and the issues they raise. They are at the mercy of whatever system is available. Most boys disagree with abortion, but as the girls point out, it is not ultimately their decision unless the relationship is perceived by the girl as mature and long lasting. Few teenage boys are mature or well informed enough to discuss abortion with their partners.

Abortion cannot be an option if it has to be paid for by a family with no spare money. It is notionally free in Britain, and for poorer families in the US also, as Medicaid will cover the cost. Quite apart from the realities, though, youthful fantasy on the girl's part also prevents remedial action until it is too late and they go ahead with motherhood with considerable ambivalence. Many young mothers in this position do pick themselves up and manage to make a life for themselves and their child. But many do not.

What of the male half of this difficult decision-making? Unfortunately, little research is available on the potential father's attitude to abortion when it actually affects him. The general picture is that either the boy friend has strong views that his child should not be aborted or he is not involved in the decision at all. However, some of Francke's (1978) informants give us some touching examples of fathers-not-to-be expressing their understanding and their sadness at the decision to abort: 'But you have to accept some things, right? It's not my body. If it was my body, I could make the decision.'

Another reasoned thus, as his teenage girl friend was undergoing an abortion:

> I really love kids. I really wanted to get married but she's still in high school, so I guess it wasn't much fair to her. And I feel really responsible for all this. I knew she wasn't using birth control, but we'd only made love twice . . . She really wanted this abortion. We both cried, I guess. It was real important to me for her not to have the abortion, but I didn't let on, I didn't want her to feel she was hurting me.

When the boy friends are involved in the relationship, whichever way the pregnancy decision goes there are chances for that relationship to strengthen, and a better chance for the well-being of the child if it is born.

There is a deal of confusion among people of all ages regarding sexual behaviour and pregnancy outcome. Values and behaviour of both Americans and Britons have undergone enormous changes in the last three decades. Generally speaking those changes have meant greater acceptance of premarital sexual intercourse and abortion for teenagers. For some this is seen as progress and freedom, for others a lamentable decline of morals and responsibility. This variety in moral approaches is mirrored by variety in both the political and administrative control of access to abortion. While technological advances make abortion more easily available, the vacillating political and legal context in which it is offered means that a great many teenagers seeking it will not find it. The quest will continue to be something of a lottery.

Decisions: teenage pregnancy – a mistake in timing

Unplanned pregnancies form a higher proportion of pregnancies to teenagers than to older women (Cartwright, 1976; Metson, 1988). Yet it is wrong to assume that all teenagers who become pregnant do not want to do so. Those who subsequently marry the father, those who keep the child and remain single, and some of those who have their pregnancy terminated – these young women may have actually wanted a child at some point in the future but not taken sufficient thought to control their fertility.

Although the pregnancy may have been unplanned, unexpected and unwanted, once acknowledged, typical reactions of young teenagers are:

> Didn't want it – but – now it's here – might as well have it.
> I'd planned to have children, yes – but not this young. Might as well start the family now instead. Have 'em all young. Why not?

Older teenage mothers on their second or third pregnancy rationalise it with:

> Get it over and done with young.
> Company for the other(s).

How are decisions made for the future once a teenage girl is pregnant? Who are the people to whom she will turn for help in making those decisions? And will those people ultimately be of any use in her decision-making? Has she already made up her mind? Or will she drift – too scared, unwilling or indifferent – through the pregnancy, taking what comes and making no real choices? Some people she talks to about the pregnancy will be helpful regarding realistic choices, others may not be. Two-thirds of the girls in Coyne's (n.d.) sample had no counselling at all regarding their pregnancy, no one to talk to in any depth about their situation or their choices, despite the fact that a doctor and/or a social worker may have been involved. Of the remaining ten, four talked with their parents and two of these were advised to abort or adopt, while three talked with their doctor and/or a social worker and/or a teacher. Of those who did receive some help in thinking about their situation, only two felt that help had been useful, supportive and unbiased.

Among most of Birch's schoolgirl mothers (1987) most boy friends and two-thirds of parents wanted the baby kept and expected the girl to do the keeping. If, however, opinions vary, then the girl suffers a great deal of stress and conflict. Often girls may be carried along unwittingly on decisions made by others. Considerable stress can be the result of this sort of pressure. The consequences to a girl in this position can be disastrous, as also to her child (see chapter 4). If an abortion has been carried out under duress and without due regard to her feelings, she is likely to become pregnant again. '13% of girls are forced into decisions against their will. In other words, girls lose control of the important issue of pregnancy resolution, just as they have lost control over their bodies in becoming pregnant' (Birch, 1987).

Widespread distress on the initial news of the pregnancy has been reported in several surveys, as already noted. Furstenberg (1976) found many teenagers who were at first concerned about the pregnancy but who grew happier with their position as the pregnancy progressed. The younger the girl, however, the more crucial is the decision-making, for an unwanted pregnancy has a tremendous impact on a woman's life; the younger the girl who is pregnant, the less clear is her vision of her future and the less able she is to appreciate the help, guidance and support of those older than herself.

It seems clear that some teenage girls keep their baby for the simple reason that they were refused help at a critical and crucial time. They were either unaware of their choices and not encouraged to that awareness in any way, or they were explicitly or implicitly discouraged from doing anything about the pregnancy but keep the baby. The immediate practicalities of the problem of unplanned teenage pregnancy can often take over, and the painful emotions and conflicting reactions get jumbled up in a mass of confusion, so that thinking clearly requires considerable effort and support. Among the women Gilligan (1982) interviewed about the question of choices when pregnant, it was found that the gender perspectives (how young people see themselves as specifically girls or boys) were the most influential in a pregnant girl's thinking about her future.

Bearing in mind that in Western culture women are largely perceived as responsible for child care, girls, for instance, are seen and see themselves as close to women in their care-giving role, while boys do not. Gilligan suggests that girls therefore have a clearer basis for empathic feeling. They experience relationships in greater depth than boys and invest them with more significance. It could also be suggested that, by separating too soon from the mother, boys find relationships in their teens quite difficult, while girls invest much in relationships with both sexes and perhaps take a long time to develop away from dependence on mother.

Bettelheim (1976), in his fascinating discussion of the importance of fairy tales, shows how deeply embedded in all of us are the expectations of our culture. Man's identity is with adventure and risk-taking, directing him outward and away from home. Woman's identity is with intimacy and making sacrifices and is decidedly home-based.

Achievement has a bearing here. Considerable research has established that both women and men expect men to be 'successful', first graders, etc. and neither women nor men expect women to reach the same dizzy heights. Girls may actually fear success and have quite a problem with competitiveness, and although they want desperately to achieve, they are acutely aware that their achievement must not surpass that of the boys. If success is a problem for many teenage girls, there is a lot of anxiety around competition and achievement – whether the girl is bright or a slow learner, it makes no difference – either she must not be better than the boys, or she has no chance of being better.

It is on the basis of these perspectives that a girl makes her choices on finding that she is pregnant. Given that she can become socially rejected if she is educationally superior to men, she can, however, achieve success in a sphere which is entirely her own. She can get pregnant and become a mother. By so doing she can achieve various things: she can opt out of the gender competition, and cease to strive for success among her peers; she can make relationships, in this case with her child; she can receive acclaim and social approval.

Girls are brought up with a basic moral stance which has two clear messages that enhance each other. Firstly, inflicting hurt is selfish and immoral – many pregnant teenagers will argue against abortion and adoption as 'selfish'. Secondly, expressing care is a fulfilling moral responsibility – this is the 'sentimental model' discussed at the beginning of this chapter. If a pregnant girl does not think beyond this stage, her needs are not in conflict and she will not question her future. Older adolescent girls are more likely to recognise some of the less positive aspects of motherhood, and as a result will be more likely to experience conflict. Gilligan (1982) quotes a 19 year old disillusioned with her pregnancy: 'The only thing you're ever going to get out of going with a guy is get hurt.' The conflict is between the passivity of dependence and the activity of care, and many women become suspended in a paralysis of initiative in both thought and action. They take the easy way, 'just going along for the ride' and see what happens. Abortion within this mode of thinking can only be justified as an act of sacrifice, a submission to necessity, and may later feel not to have been the right decision.

It is often said that crisis and emotional pain lead to growth. However, this is only likely to be true when an opportunity is both offered, and taken, to confront the impediments to personal growth. For some girls the experience of pregnancy and birth can enhance the quality of personal growth. Sadly, for many others, without the opportunity to work through the difficulties, their lives are not enhanced by motherhood.

Simms and Smith (1986) record that of their group of mothers 15 months after the birth, most admitted they had had the child too soon. One quarter regretted not having enough time to form a good relationship with their partner before having a baby.

> 'I just didn't want a child. I did when I was pregnant, but after I had him I regretted it. After I had the baby I realised what I wanted to do with my life. . . . I don't know what to do about having J. It's hard. I can't see my life being trodden on like this, being shut in the house all the time . . .'

> 'Now that I've got her I wouldn't give her away. If I had my time again it would be nice to have her in a couple of years . . .'

> 'I think I had her at the wrong time although I'm glad I've got her. I was so young . . .' (Simms and Smith, 1986)

The question of timing and decision-making is crucial for a teenager, especially the very young teenager, for she may find herself forsaking her childhood and jumping the adolescent bridge into adulthood too soon (see Maggie's story in chapter 4). She may never catch herself up. And yet she may be unable – simply unable – to see that she has made a mistake and that she could be helped to put it right.

Chapter 3

Becoming a Mother

Although motherhood is as old as the human race, there is no evidence that it is becoming less difficult. The arrival of a baby produces stresses in a marriage which can be devastating, however well the parents have prepared for it. Many people who have planned their future and perhaps delayed parenthood until everything was ready will say that they had not realised quite what an upheaval having a child would entail. The effects of a baby on a teenage couple, themselves not fully mature and without as yet a clear vision of their future, are going to be fairly traumatic. When the mother is a young teenager of 14 or 15, and single, things are going to be far from easy.

Lilian Rubin (1976) describes the world of young white working-class couples in the San Francisco area. The average age of the wives had been 18 at marriage, 44 per cent had been pregnant when they married, and the average period of time between marriage and childbirth for the whole sample was nine months:

> Children born just months after the wedding added emotional as well as economic burdens to the adjustment process. Suddenly two young people, barely more than children themselves, found their lives irrevocably altered. Within a few months – too few to permit the integration of behaviour required by new roles in the new life stages, too few to wear even comfortably one new identity – they moved through a series of roles; from girl and boy, to wife and husband, to mother and father.

They often responded with bewilderment, filled with an

uneasy and incomprehending sense of loss for a past which, however difficult, at least was known; an angry and restless discontent with an uncomfortable present, and an enormous well of fear about an unknown future. . . . They had exchanged one set of constraints for another perhaps more powerful one.

The younger the teenager, the more difficult she will find it to look ahead and see how she wants her life to be. Pregnancy hits hard, motherhood hits harder. But once the decision is made to become a mother, pride takes over and she struggles to cope against all the odds. The economic and emotional burdens, however, take their toll.

The health of teenage mothers during pregnancy

The health of teenage girls is generally good, and pregnancy unlikely to be health-threatening. However, some medical conditions occur more often than in the pregnancies of older women. Anaemia and toxemia are the most commonly noted, but Osofsky *et al.* (1988) add cephopelvic disproportion (which may involve the necessity of Caesarian section), hypertension, abruptio placentae, urinary tract infection, prolonged labour, and difficult or premature delivery. Both Osofsky *et al.* and Russell (1982) point out a raised risk of maternal death, but this is largely restricted to very young mothers.

In developed countries maternal mortality is a rare event. Most investigators have preferred to look at contact with health services rather than health, and this subject will be dealt with later (chapter 8). Many of the health problems encountered by pregnant teenagers are not the result of medical complications *per se*, but spring from inappropriate life styles. Cigarettes, alcohol and drugs are all considered to be particularly health-threatening during pregnancy, and information on their use is available in clinics and surgeries for all women, pregnant or otherwise. Adolescents, ever the risk-takers, often fail to take notice of this kind of information.

Research in the US has come up with similar findings.

Adolescents who are sexually active at an early age are also frequently involved in other behaviours that push towards independence and adulthood, often in conflict with adult norms for them. Among transition behaviours most often associated with early sexual activity are smoking, drinking and drug use. (Hayes, 1987)

The difficulty for parents, teachers and all those in the helping professions is when to treat these behaviours as healthy signs of a passing phase of adolescent rebelliousness, or a learning experience to greater independence; or whether they do indeed represent disturbance of a deviant or delinquent nature. The fact remains that accidents, sexually transmitted diseases, and drug and alcohol abuse among teenagers continue to increase, as does cigarette smoking. There is a particular cause for concern when pregnant adolescents are associated with any of these.

Smoking

Smoking has been growing in popularity among women in Britain at a time when the number of people overall who smoke has been falling. Various surveys have shown worryingly high rates among young mothers. Nearly half of the sample of teenage mothers from a survey in Bristol were smokers at the time of the booking interview (Ineichen, 1986). Wolkind and Kruk (1985) found smoking was more common among teenagers than older mothers in their sample. Another survey, on teenage mothers and their partners (Simms and Smith, 1986) devotes a whole chapter to smoking. Of that sample of 456 teenage women, only 29 per cent had never smoked, 12 per cent had given up, and a majority (59 per cent) were current smokers. One in seven of the whole sample smoked 20 or more each day.

Simms and Smith (1986) also show that smoking in young mothers is associated with problems relating to social disadvantage. Smokers among these teenagers tend to belong to large, lower class families, are less likely to have educational qualifications and are less likely to be married than those who smoke less or not at all. Marriages among smokers are less likely to be perceived as happy. Smokers are more likely to be living alone with their children and to feel trapped by financial problems as well as suffering from depression and nerves. Since a large proportion of these young mothers survive on state benefits, smoking amounts to a substantial outlay each week. One quarter of Simms and Smith's sample were in receipt of supplementary benefit at the time of the follow-up interview. Of those who became pregnant for the second time during the course of the survey, it was disturbing to discover that more than half smoked, one-fifth heavily. Sadly, the majority of these young women live in house-holds or around their extended families where almost everyone smokes, which makes it very difficult for them to give up.

> My grandad said I could have £100 if I gave up smoking during my pregnancy. I used to smoke 20 a day. I stopped just like that. Only when I had Ben – well, I didn't have a very good time – there were complications – I was a bit down, and he wasn't well, and everyone in my house smokes – my mum and step-dad, and the rest of them. I started again. I need to. Calms me down. Ben's been a chesty baby ever since he was born. He's only 4 months old and he's been on antibiotics twice in the last 6 weeks.
>
> (15-year-old mother)

Smoking is described by young teenage mothers as 'the only luxury' in a life which seems dedicated to doing things for others, and getting little in return (Simms and Smith, 1986).

Smoking is said to bring confidence to the smoker, relieve stress, calm nerves, control anger and keep weight down. Clearly this has a good deal to do with conforming to the female role. It may also compensate for what is felt to be a loss of control over their own destiny that typifies the feelings of many young mothers.

Alcohol

In America currently over 77 per cent of adolescent deaths are caused by accidents, suicide and homicide. In spite of continuing concern over drug abuse, alcohol is for the most part separated from the term 'drugs' by adolescents and is consistently consumed by many teenagers, including those under the legal age. This age is 18, except in some districts of the US where it is 21. Alcohol is a factor in 50 per cent of fatal car accidents, many caused by teenagers. A pregnant adolescent behaves in this respect no differently from a non-pregnant one. Alcohol may be drunk fairly widely among teenagers, whether they are pregnant or not. A quarter of the Bristol sample (Ineichen, 1986) were regular drinkers at the time of the booking interview.

Drinking has become the norm for adolescents over the last decade or two. 'Going down the pub' is perceived by many British adolescents as the only available way of spending a social evening with friends. Again, it is those young people with the least resources – in terms of lack of space at home, lack of transport facilities, lack of imagination, motivation and facilities for other activities and low prospects in terms of economic independence – who are at risk of alcohol abuse; again, it is 'something to do'.

The relationship between alcohol and sex is not restricted to teenagers' thinking. Representations of their connections are around us everywhere. 'Alcohol and sex go together, don't they? you can't have sex without a bit of drink inside you, can you?' This 15-year-old mother spoke for many teenagers who hope that alcohol will loosen up their behaviour and drown their inhibitions. In their wish to appear more attractive and more grown up many lose more than their inhibitions:

> I was drunk at the time. I didn't know it was going to happen. It was at this party. Had so much to drink I didn't know what was happening. Can't remember anything about it. Yeah, it was the first time – and the last, I can tell you! Don't want to see him. He was just a mate, nothing special. How could he want to do a thing like that? I mean, look at me! I'm so fat – didn't ever think anybody'd fancy me. But I love my daughter. (15-year-old mother)

Drugs

Illicit use of drugs has become a widespread problem, but the possible consequences are difficult to ascertain. One exception is its involvement with HIV transmission, and this will be dealt with in chapter 6.

Emotional health

Emotional problems among pregnant teenagers are common, although there is little evidence of mental illness at this time. Russell (1982), for example, found that his young teenage sample contained many anxious and difficult-to-manage mothers-to-be, especially those who had been in care or who were of low intelligence. But none, in his opinion, required active psychiatric support at the time of their first pregnancy.

Suicide is something that many teenagers think about, and in recent years there has been an increase in suicide attempts. In the US the suicide rate among adolescents has increased 300 per cent in the last 30 years. Common factors influencing suicide attempts are ill-health, disturbed families, being a child in care, a single parent, a school refuser. Unsuccessful suicides can lead to future attempts as well as to relationship problems.

Teenage pregnancy sometimes appears to be the way a family expresses its conflicts. (This subject is discussed more fully later in the chapter.) In her detailed study of the work of the Chitterton Care Center in Chicago (where pregnant adolescents undergo intensive social and psychological programmes), Bedger (1980) suggests that 'the family already has the pathology' and is programmed for a relationship disaster, while the daughter who becomes pregnant and decides to keep the baby is the carrier. The daughter's behaviour is a symptom of the family disease which had hitherto gone unacknowledged as anything one could do anything about. Both McGuire (1983) and Sharpe (1987) give examples.

It is sometimes difficult to distinguish between what might be seen as a normal adolescent upset on the one hand, and an emotional disturbance, as a direct result of pregnancy, on the other. Given that most teenage girls have problems relating with their parents at some time or other, and given that these conflicts are for the most part around growing up and seeking independence, it is not surprising that discussion about anything related to sex will be perceived as difficult to broach. Parents may often find it hard to allow their children's self-confidence and independence to develop freely, fearful that their (the parents') values might be lost in the process. Adolescents are particularly sensitive to these parental fears and expectations, and if, for whatever reason, the balance is not right, the adolescent years become stormy for both parents and children. Pregnancy does nothing to alleviate the difficulties, although in many cases, as McGuire and Sharpe testify, the mother/daughter relationship may improve for a while, as women's matters can now be discussed in the open. Both authors also point out that the mother/daughter conflict may have helped to bring about the pregnancy in the first place.

Essentially, a young woman in her teens may be far from mature, and if she herself is carrying a child, the changes in her physical and emotional make-up will be difficult to cope with. The fact of her being pregnant in the first place indicates some deviation from the expected path (by adults and also by children themselves) and some degree of antisocial behaviour; her pregnancy does not render her any easier to cope with. 'Normal' negative adolescent behaviour, ranging from stubborn silence and truculence, to the disruptive – if not delinquent – can be difficult enough, but when the adolescent is pregnant it is not unnatural that adult concern be expressed for her health and welfare.

The health of the teenager's unborn child

Like the health of teenage mothers, the health of their unborn children is not easy to study systematically. Pregnant teenagers who move about the country during their pregnancy are particularly difficult to monitor. Miscarriages may not always be recorded.

Russell (1982) notes that low birth weight, congenital abnormalities and perinatal deaths are commoner among children born to teenagers, especially those under 16, than to older mothers. Osofsky *et al*. (1988) add prematurity, neurological difficulties and respiratory difficulties.

Although the general health of teenagers may be good, nevertheless many environmental influences are poorly understood. Studies seeking a connection between diet during pregnancy and hyperactivity, unsociable behaviour, low IQ, low test scoring and poor concentration in the later child are currently being undertaken. Many teenagers who proceed with their pregnancy are in the category of the relatively undernourished. Those young people who have little consideration for their health and who take greater risks with their bodies and their lives are the ones who, having become pregnant, are most likely to want to keep the baby and not attend clinic for routine monitoring. If the mother's health and diet have been poor for many years her baby has a poor chance of being healthy. In our snack-happy society junk food is popular and domestic cooking facilities are sometimes inadequate.

This is especially true of 'bed and breakfast' accommodation, where many British young families are forced to live. These factors greatly hinder sensible eating habits.

Doubt, ambivalence, anger, fear and blame are all part of the story when an unmarried teenager becomes pregnant. The anxiety surrounding the whole circumstance – as well as the decision-making – can cause high blood pressure, palpitations, stress states of many kinds. Poor nourishment is often a consequence as well as contributing to the cause. The unborn child of an adolescent in a state of anxiety may have a fairly traumatic start to its life.

Use of antenatal services by pregnant teenagers

Teenage pregnancy is marked by poor use of medical services. Young pregnant girls often present late to clinics and are, on the whole, poor clinic attenders (Butler *et al.*, 1981; Russell, 1981, 1982; Simms and Smith, 1986; Hayes, 1987). One quarter of the 92 in the Bristol sample had their booking interview in the third trimester (Ineichen, 1986); 36 of the 92 had no discussion with medical or social work staff prior to the booking interview.

In their survey of teenage mothers, Simms and Smith (1986) asked the 27 per cent of their sample who had not consulted a doctor until the second trimester why they had delayed. Nearly half said that it was because they hadn't realised that they were pregnant; 16 per cent mentioned fear or embarrassment; 14 per cent were afraid to confront the possibility of pregnancy; 14 per cent felt they had not been able to tell their parents, and some of this group were afraid the doctor might tell their parents; 13 per cent felt they did not need to go earlier; 4 per cent were afraid of being talked into an abortion. These answers reveal that delayed antenatal care is often a facet of a pregnancy that is not wholly wanted. They also show the need for reassurance about medical confidentiality (Simms and Smith, 1986, pp. 25–7). Some of Sharpe's (1987) sample said simply that they felt out of place among older women.

Other reasons for late presentation include chaotic life styles, language problems, distance from the clinic and fear of physical examination. Some teenagers ignore antenatal care altogether. This may be due to lethargy (rare), ignorance of body signs and functions (not at all rare), fear resulting in pushing it to the back of the mind (common) and lack of trust and perceived lack of support (not uncommon). Alternatively, a few teenagers feel it is not necessary, like Simms and Smith's informant having her third baby, who felt she 'knew it all' (1986, p. 280).

Some slip through the net altogether, not only that of the medical services, but also of the researcher. The boy friend of one of the Bristol sample told this story about his sister:

> She was always fat, so her pregnancy never showed. She told no one. She worked all through it, doing a manual job which included a lot of bending. One day she came home from work early, complaining of back ache, and went upstairs to lie down on her bed. Later she called down to her mother, 'Mummy, the baby's coming!' It was delivered later that day. In the evening her boy friend (not the child's father) came round to take her to the pub. He was told, 'Guess what! She's had a baby!'

In the Bristol Unit there have been several such cases over the years. One girl had always been fat and no one noticed. She came home from school as usual one lunchtime and, realising something was going on, lay down and simply gave birth. Her school friend cut the umbilical cord. Needless to say, she did not return to school that afternoon. It is said the baby was hidden in a drawer until the news was broken to her mother. One visit to the family doctor a few months before 'with peculiar movements in her tummy' led to the diagnosis of the problem as 'flatulence'.

Another 15 year old was extremely thin and in fact had been starving herself to avoid the pregnancy showing. She wore enormous and fashionable sweat shirts to hide her size. She claimed she did not realise what was happening, and later, during her daughter's first six months of life, when she showed signs of eating problems, she explained that she was terrified of getting fat again – 'like before'. Neither her parents, with whom she lived, nor her boy friend (the baby's father) had any idea of the pregnancy, and she told no one. She had no medical attention of any sort during her pregnancy. Her boy friend's sister was with her at home at the time of the baby's birth and delivered a healthy baby, again with no complications.

Yet another 15 year old was, at 9 months, undergoing a routine ear test at hospital. Her parents had noticed nothing and she had told no one. She began labour and had an epileptic fit, and was, in fact, in serious danger. Her baby was delivered safely.

Josie, aged 14, tried to get help when she suspected she was 2–3 months pregnant, but when she rang the clinic and found that the only person she wanted to see was not there, she gave up. She did not try again. She and her boy friend kept it a secret. No one else had any idea, although she lived with her mother and stepfather and went regularly to school. Even when labour finally started she allowed her mother to think it was appendicitis, although Josie herself knew the head was more than engaged. The baby was born 6 weeks premature and needed intensive care for 4 weeks.

Janice concealed her first pregnancy and, already a mother at 15, when asked by her mother, her social worker and staff at the schoolgirl mothers' unit whether she might be pregnant again, she continually denied it. At 5 months she was taken for a pregnancy test. In spite of her age, the instability of her present life and relationships and her grim future outlook, she was determined to be a mother of two before her sixteenth birthday. Their father has so far presented very little support or commitment. Her mother, with whom she lives, has problems of her own and is disinclined to help out in any way. Typically, she 'does not agree with abortion'.

Many adolescent mothers have not got a great deal of confidence in themselves and they have a tendency to project this on to those who offer antenatal services. Indeed, it is a facet of youth to reject care and help sometimes when offered, and during an anxious time such as pregnancy, adolescent defensiveness may dominate, and attitudes may be unnecessarily critical (Skinner, 1986, chs 5 and 8). On the other hand, doctors and clinic personnel are often hard pressed and may not always deal as sensitively as they might with their clients. These may be very young, possibly terrified, possibly feeling guilty, and not clear about their position or very good at expressing themselves. They certainly are not likely to know what questions to ask (Simms and Smith, 1986).

In the US teenagers are less likely than older women to seek antenatal care during the first trimester of pregnancy (54 per cent for adolescents as against 79 per cent for all women). Also they are more likely to receive no prenatal care at all (2.5 per cent of adolescents against 1.3 per cent of all women). Johnson and Ziskin (1988) record that there is negligible difference between white and non-white attitudes towards prenatal care: only half of US pregnant adolescents of all races begin care early in pregnancy.

'I just didn't get around to it.'
'I was afraid my family would find out if I came.'
'. . . waiting till I had a closer relationship with my boy friend.'
'. . . thought it was dangerous to use birth control.'
'. . . afraid to be examined.' (Alan Guttmacher, 1981)

Among other contributing factors, teenage mothers are twice as likely as older women to give birth to low weight babies. Low birthweight (less than 5 lbs, that is 2500 grams or less) is the strongest correlate of infant illness, death and mental retardation, and this is linked to adolescent reluctance to seek appropriate care during pregnancy.

Who and where are the fathers?

Our knowledge of the fathers of the babies of teenage mothers is less than complete. Most teenage mothers are unmarried, and not all give the father's name when registering the child's birth. A very few are unsure themselves as to who the father is. Two features stand out: the fathers are mostly young, and like teenage mothers themselves, mostly working class (Simms and Smith, 1986; Ineichen, 1986; Sharpe, 1987). Qualitative research with the fathers is difficult, as the later stages of teenage pregnancies echo to the sound of slamming doors as fathers make their dash for anonymity and freedom. Many, however, remain trapped by poverty, like their partners.

Simms and Smith (1986) report on one of the few attempts to question large numbers of partners of teenage mothers. They interviewed 553 out of a sample of 623 mothers, and gained permission from them to approach their partners. They managed to find and interview 369 of these men, 59 per cent of the original sample, about 6 months after the birth. Men who were not pleased about becoming a father, who were not involved in baby care, teenage men, unmarried men, and men born in the West Indies were all under-represented in the interviewed sample; 1 per cent could not be interviewed because they were in prison.

Four-fifths of those interviewed reported they had not been using contraception when their baby was conceived; almost half of these said they wanted to have a child. The rest explained the pregnancy in terms of indifference, apathy, ignorance – only one-third had had lessons in contraception at school – or simply contraception failure. Only 5 per cent said they had been definitely upset by the initial news of the pregnancy; they appeared to welcome it more than their partners.

Simms and Smith admit that the distortions caused by the loss of 41 per cent of their sample means that their interviews may present an unduly rosy picture of teenage fatherhood. Certainly their account differs from the highly critical testimony of some of the teenage mothers interviewed elsewhere (McGuire, 1983; Sharpe, 1987).

There are young fathers who do care and want both partner and child, but are thwarted by the partner's decision. Francke's study (1978) on abortion highlights the dilemma for young men when they find themselves in circumstances beyond their control and have difficulty in expressing their feelings – and sometimes no opportunity to do so. It seems a gross irony that while many women, when they become pregnant, feel themselves to be helpless victims of sexual passion (partner stronger than they) or of fate (malfunction of contraceptive), the situation is reversed when, on discovering the unplanned pregnancy, many women leave the fathers out of the decision-making as to the outcome of the pregnancy. It is the man's turn to feel trapped and helpless.

The US Supreme Court in 1973 gave women the absolute right to abortion during the first trimester of pregnancy. The right to abdicate future motherhood is guaranteed – the woman's right to choose. The right to insist on fatherhood is not similarly guaranteed. To the men who do care, this seems very unfair. The case in Cambridge, UK, in 1987, where a pregnant student eventually won her case to have an abortion in the face of strong opposition from the putative father, illustrates this conflict.

The conventional division of roles in the Western developed world means that women are still expected to become the care givers and the child minders, and have a relatively realistic view of what this role entails (see Maggie, chapter 4). Men have little or no experience of this side of child rearing, and tend to live in a world of romance and fantasy, as one of Francke's (1978) examples illustrates. A man who had caused four abortions felt it was 'romantic' to have children, and that it was a man's 'prerogative' to have 40 children if he could.

Francke also points out the importance for many men of having a son, and that many girls want a son for their man. Black men like to 'big' a girl, and this sign of male virility is cause for swagger and a rise in status among their peers. Afro-Caribbean men and women accept the fact that men's status relies to a large extent on the number of children they have created, although they set little store by staying with the mothers.

The sexual development of boys may be seen as having three clear stages, not necessarily relating to age. They compare interestingly with the three stages in girls' sexual learning, described in chapter 2. In early adolescence ignorance and curiosity go hand in hand, and condoms are embarrassing toys; in middle adolescence sex is a considerable preoccupation and even begins to seem possible, but is not associated with pregnancy at all; only in later teenage are boys able to make the connection between sexual activity and the risk of pregnancy. The possibility of parenthood is rarely present. It seems that sex education takes little account of the idea that there are stages in boys' sexual development (Birch, 1987, p. 90).

Boys and men become fathers often for the same reasons that girls and young women become mothers; by default, through an irresponsible attitude towards birth control as well as towards their partner. Teenagers of both sexes may know the facts of conception and contraception, but the gender myths prevail. Whereas it may be easier to use the condom, both partners will say that sex is better without, and anyway 'It's not the same, somehow'. If asked seriously, girls will admit that they could control their own fertility, and since it is they who carry the can for irresponsibility on the part of either party, they should perhaps take the contraceptive initiative. However, it has already been pointed out what a dilemma this is for them. Girls will also say that boys have equal responsibility, and a couple should talk it through together. When it comes to the crunch, however, girls respond to their learnt gender roles: they accept, they love, they relate, they are passive and possibly vulnerable, they may play the cute innocent. Boys, on the other hand, respond to their learnt behaviours: they are often selfish, they take risks, they are active and they dominate. What knowledge they might have acquired through school carries little weight. Neither listens to her/his head but rather goes along with the learnt behaviours.

The young father of a baby by a teenager is often as appalled as his partner. But the macho image may be too demanding for him to dare to express his real feelings, if indeed he is aware of them himself. The girl, equally appalled and possibly frightened, has the physical problem to deal with and may be unsure and confused about a whole range of other feelings she may have.

Some young men father several babies by different girl friends and do not stay with any of them. This may be a consequence of several factors. One, already mentioned, is fear of their responsibilities and desire for escape. Another belongs perhaps to the realms of myth whereby trying to engage an adolescent father's sense of responsibility is either too difficult for everyone, or too traumatic for the mother, or itself deemed an irresponsible idea if it is thought the couple have little or no commitment to each other, due to their age and other factors. Until such time as agencies can address this aspect of teenage pregnancy, and adolescent parents of both sexes accept that help for – and commitment from – the father are as important as that for and from the mother, many young fathers will continue to shirk their parental responsibilities. Young mothers will be lone parents and their children will suffer the known damaging consequences of having no father in their lives.

Adrian, aged 26 and living in a UK city, poorly educated, sometimes a labourer and often unemployed, cohabited with his third teenage girl friend, Chris, when she was pregnant with his third child. Chris had just taken her GCSEs when she gave birth to their daughter. She was aware of his other two children, the first of whom attended the nursery at the same centre that Chris attended. Neither her remarried mother's new home nor that of her father felt like home; Adrian offered something more meaningful perhaps. She thought she would be leaving him. Instead she married him. A few months later he had thrown her out and Chris and the baby were in bed and breakfast accommodation awaiting public housing.

Adrian and others like him find other partners in an attempt yet again to make their nest. Such a father has not been helped in either facing or enjoying his responsibility as a parent. Nor have his various girls friends known how to handle the situation. Work in this area needs to be done in order to harness the good and the positive in the young fathers and to encourage them to own their responsibilities. Just how realistic this is in the long term is certainly a question that must be asked with each couple. Should it be encouraged when these parents are so young and still growing and changing? These are points which we consider further in the third section of chapter 6.

The question of marriage

Patterns of marriage have changed over the last few decades, reflecting the increasing acceptability of both cohabitation and single parenthood. The average age of marriage has risen too; marriage may be delayed but pregnancy and motherhood are not.

The decline in teenage marriages since the early 1970s has been steady and constant on both sides of the Atlantic. Marriage to legitimate the birth of an adolescent pregnancy has become increasingly less popular. Pregnancy in the past led to 'shot-gun' weddings, many of which were doomed to early failure; marriage today is less likely, and often quite simply not contemplated.

Adolescent girls, especially working-class adolescent girls, tend to regard motherhood as almost inevitable, yet look forward to the prospect with mixed feelings (see the opening of chapter 2). Lees (1986) suggests that growing up as a pupil in an urban comprehensive school in the UK can be comparable to being in as closed a society as a Middle Eastern village or an African tribe. Social and geographical aspects of experience are uniformly narrow, and horizons limited. At 15 it is often difficult to realise that your future might be *different* from the present reality around you, and that that difference could be as a consequence of your own actions.

For adolescent girls' attitudes to boy friends and marriage, Sarsby (1983, ch. 7) and Sharpe (1976, ch. 7) provide enlightening discussion. While boy friends are seen as a source of fun, romance, excitement and risk, marriage is seen as important and inevitable, turning every boy into a possible marriage partner (Sharpe, 1976, p. 217). Of Sharpe's sample, 82 per cent wanted to marry; a third of them hoped to marry as teenagers. In her later book (*Falling for*

Love, 1987) the teenage mothers are more disillusioned with the marriage prospect and prefer to wait and remain single for the time being. McGuire (1983) found similar feelings among the teenage mothers in her sample. Very young mothers (16 and under) in Miller's (1983) survey were more optimistic about the prospect of marriage: 58 per cent thought they would eventually marry and a quarter of this group had plans to do so in the near future. The most favoured age for them to marry ranged from under 20 (about a quarter) to between 20 and 30 (under two-thirds). It was not felt that pregnancy or motherhood necessarily influenced a girl's decision to marry; 58 per cent of these very young adolescent mothers felt that the best age for having a first child was under 20.

When mixed groups of 15 year olds (i.e. non-parents) in Bristol, UK, comprehensive schools were asked at what age they would ideally like to have their first child, that age ranged from 18 to the mid 30s, with a few suggesting teens and most the mid 20s. Many of the girls said they would not need to be married, though a good relationship with the child's father was important for both mother and child. Marriage was too much of a tie, while a stable partnership was what they wanted. The boys, on the other hand, generally felt marriage was essential. For both sexes the reasons for delaying parenting were basically a recognition of the need for maturity, for settling down, accumulation of wealth, stability, career and the like.

When teenagers do marry, their marriages are different from older marriages in a number of ways. The proportion who are pregnant on their wedding day is higher (Murstein, 1986, p. 17, for US data), and partners are likely to be chosen from closer to hand (Ineichen, 1979, for UK data). While it is unlikely that many teenagers marry the boy next door, they are much more likely to marry the boy from the next street. Cupid's arrow does not fly far for teenagers, nor is it very robust, for its effects do not last. The chances of survival for a marriage made during the teen years is very small. While the divorce rate overall is four marriages in ten, for those marrying in their teens the rate is currently running at one in two. And the duration of the marriage is often no more than one or two years.

The question of how choice is made is a difficult one, given the pre-empting role of the pregnancy in so many cases. Murstein

(1986, ch. 7) summarises some of the theories of marital choice. Certainly, the younger the mothers, the more unrealistically they view their future, and the more likely they are to leap into marriage if the young father wants it. Miller (1983, p. 94) felt that:

> an accelerated role change into motherhood may mean that some will never explore, as others do in late adolescence, the wide range of possibilities of what they might become as adults. The time for developing a mature sense of identity will have been distorted by adult responsibilities, and the full consequences of this on the young mothers' emotional development are, as yet, unknown.

Most marriages made during the teenage years do not have enough of a firm psychological, emotional or financial base to endure beyond a few years. The likelihood is that neither partner has grown up, and parenthood brings added strains and stresses. Simms and Smith (1986) comment that:

> It is difficult to see why some of these women married in the first place, since their husbands seemed to them so unequal to the role. Part of the explanation may be in the often considerable social and economic pressure exerted on working class women to get and to remain married since marriage is generally seen as their best pathway to support, status and comparative affluence.

Those who have tasted marriage tend to have greater expectations in terms of material comfort, and many might regret marriage breakdown for mainly financial reasons. When marriages break down, the women and children are thrust into poverty and are likely to remain there, while a majority of men are able to make good and become self-sufficient relatively quickly. Of course this happens to older women as well.

However, marriage among teenagers is on the decline, while cohabitation and single motherhood have become more prevalent. For the US the Children's Defence Fund (1987) puts forward several arguments why marriage is viewed unfavourably by young parents today. Research has clearly established the link between male unemployment or low earnings and marriage instability. Adolescent mothers are more likely to marry if their boy friends

are employed full time (Furstenberg, 1987). Marriage postpone-
ment has increased most among poorly educated black women,
women whose partners are likely to have the most limited economic prospects. Absent fathers are classically more likely to have a
history of unemployment than young fathers living with their
children. This is no different from British experience.

Over the last decade the real earnings of young men have
declined dramatically in both Britain and the US, thus the
likelihood has increased that they and their families will live in
poverty. Meaningful support within the home or maintenance
outside the home come to the same thing financially. If a father is
unable to earn sufficient to keep his young family above the
poverty line he may simply give up the struggle. In the US this
decline has affected all races and ethnic groups, but most severely
young black and Hispanic men. Bearing in mind the typical young
(teenage) father: firstly the poorly educated:

> Only four in 10 white male dropouts, fewer than three in 10
> Hispanic dropouts, and a shockingly low one in nine black
> dropouts earned enough in 1984 to support a family of three.
> (CDF, 1987)

Secondly the better educated:

> Three in every four young men with a high school diploma but
> no further education were able to earn enough in 1973 to lift a
> family out of poverty. Only slightly more than half of all
> graduates could do so in 1984. (CDF, 1987)

This state of affairs has had a considerable impact on marriage
rates. The social and economic consequences of fewer marriages
among disadvantaged young people – with few skills, no qualifications and a child either on the way or already born – are of great
concern. The young men who become fathers are the same ones
who have below-poverty earnings:

> Marriage rates have fallen most dramatically among those who
> have suffered the greatest declines in employment opportunities
> and real earnings – young adult males without college educa-
> tion. Losses in real earnings among lower paid young men have

reduced their ability to support a family, diminished their attractiveness as marriage partners, and eroded their motivation and willingness to marry. (CDF, 1987)

Poor employment prospects for the child's father provide the young mother with a reason for not marrying him. The availability of state benefits to single mothers and their families may well undermine the institution of marriage. It is certainly true that many young mothers prefer the reliability of the regular welfare payments from the state to the unreliable irregular maintenance from their child's father.

As Trish, an 18-year-old mother of three, puts it:

What's the point of getting married? No. Too much hassle. I don't know what I want, anyway. Each time it happens – you know – I think this is it, give it time and it'll all work out, then we'll get married. I get caught again, and it's all right for a while, but then he's looking elsewhere and I realise it's not him I want. I'm left with another baby, though.

The impact of pregnancy on the teenager's family

The most significant person in the pregnant adolescent's life is not always the baby's father. It is usually her mother, whatever the overt nature of the mother/daughter relationship, and the younger the girl, the more dependent on her mother she will be. When asked about her initial feelings on hearing the news of the pregnancy, an adolescent will frequently say that she is worried about what her mother will say (Ineichen, 1986; Sharpe, 1987; McGuire, 1983). Generally speaking, after the initial shock, mothers cope well with the news.

As Elizabeth McGee (1982) reports:

Most parents, whatever their race or ethnic background, are disappointed by a pregnancy involving either a son or a daughter. Parents of teen parents who oppose abortion or whose children oppose abortion may be willing to accept and even eventually welcome the birth of an unplanned grandchild, but this reaction is usually an adjustment, not a preference.

Fathers, if they are living at home, are usually less accepting at first and more upset than other family members. The initial anger usually wears off, but there have been cases where a father stopped talking to his pregnant daughter from the moment the pregnancy was announced to long after the baby's birth and, in one or two cases, for years after the daughter and grandchild had left home. One 19 year old in Bristol, whose little girl was 4, had still not had a conversation with her father, and her mother would not intervene.

Absent fathers tend to view their distant daughters' position more favourably, possibly since they feel they have no direct responsibility. When she was pregnant, aged 13, and her relationship with her mother had broken down, Sue's father invited her to live with him for a while, but his tolerance only lasted a fortnight and she was sent home to mother, who justifiably felt abused and angry. This is a common theme.

Simms and Smith (1986) asked their large sample (of whom 45 per cent were living with parents at the time of the pregnancy) about their father's reactions to their pregnancy: 29 per cent were said to be pleased initially; 24 per cent had mixed feelings; 26 per cent of mothers and 30 per cent of fathers were initially upset. Prospective grandparenthood was more attractive among middle-class and Asian parents, and those whose pregnant daughters were married in their late teens or having their second child. On the other hand, some working-class grandmothers are delighted: 'It's lovely to have another little one in the family. Gives me something to do. Makes my life worth while.' (Single mother in her 30s of pregnant 14 year old)

Black girls in Britain may find teenage pregnancy less welcomed by their mothers than do white girls (Skinner, 1986, p. 58). Quite possibly this has to do with the desire of the black girl to 'get on' and have a worthwhile career. While a typical white family reaction may be one of shame – even today – a fairly typical black family reaction may be disappointment. There is a strong tradition among black women both in Britain and the US that they will earn their own living and support themselves – with two jobs if necessary. It is surely significant that proportionally more black than white teenage mothers seek training or employment on leaving school.

Lorraine's mother is a black single parent and has both a day time job and an evening job. Lorraine, aged 15, announced her *second* pregnancy at 21 weeks, and her mother despaired. When this had happened two years previously Lorraine was sent to a foster family and prepared to have her baby adopted. But the child was brought home and grew up as part of the family, sometimes described as cousin, sometimes as brother and some- times as her son. Her mother wanted to know: what made her conceal this second pregnancy, as she had the first, until it was too late for an abortion? For Lorraine wanted an abortion, recognising that bringing another child into the household was neither fair nor sensible. Lorraine did not say much, but she was clear about her answer to this question; she was too frightened to face her mother with another pregnancy, and hoped herself it would simply go away. She claimed she was taking the pill and had forgotten it for a couple of days. The plan once again was to go for adoption. Meanwhile her mother's life felt as though it was falling apart, and indeed aspects of her life important for her were truly destroyed. Lorraine in her teens was perhaps the scapegoat for the family ills; she was certainly blamed for a great deal.

There was guilt, upset and confusion in the family of the 16-year- old boy friend too, another single female headed family. The confusion was about responsibility and the importance of blood ties versus what would no doubt be best for the child. It is important to recognise that, with each unplanned, out-of-wedlock pregnancy in a young adolescent, there may be two families going through varying degrees of anguish and trauma. It is not only the girl's family which is turned upside down.

However, the family background of pregnant teenagers is not invariably problematic. Russell (1981, 1982) found that while social problems were present in over half of his survey families of the 238 pregnant girls of 16 or less, in the families of 274 girls aged 17–19 that figure was just over a quarter. Once again it has to be pointed out that the younger the mother the greater the problems in all aspects of her life.

Typically, many young teenagers about to produce a grandchild for their parents are following in their mothers' footsteps. A 15/16- year-old pregnant girl frequently has a 30+-year-old mother who is now parenting on her own with several children, living on state benefits and with few resources. A new member of the family makes little immediate difference in her eyes for the moment. Especially if, as in some families, teenage sisters are also producing children. Such families are known to the authors; mother is at home with three daughters all in their teens either pregnant or already mothers. Fathers or father figures rarely feature in this type of household. Boy friends come and go but are not always that significant. Producing children – or rather, babies – has become a feature of their lives and it is not questioned. Birch has some interesting and significant examples in her South London sample, e.g. the great-grandmother of 46 mentioned in chapter 2.

In spite of initial upset, today few parents insist on their pregnant daughter leaving home. In Britain it is frequently the daughters who insist on leaving home. With 16 being the age to leave school, many mothers of that age put pressure on the local authority to consider them homeless, and in this way they are allotted bed and breakfast accommodation on their way to their own flat. Those parents who really feel they cannot take any more, and who feel quite unequal to the new situation, may ask the social services to take their pregnant daughter under 16 into care – no easy task for an overstretched agency with very limited foster parents available and a diminishing number of childrens' homes.

Sue, a 13 year old, found that her pregnancy was the final straw for her single mother, who already had an older daughter several months pregnant living at home. Mother was hospitalised for a period due to stress and Sue was put into voluntary care. This child was totally disaffected from school and frequently absconded for days at a time from the children's home where she was placed. While meetings were held over a period of weeks she continued to have no education, and in spite of her mother's absolutely clear statement that she could not return home, Sue retained the hope that her mother would relent. Determined to keep the baby and not part with her boy friend, Sue had nowhere to go: her father volunteered to take her abroad with his new wife and family, but without the child; while her mother would have her home if the boy friend was quite off the scene. Sue was unable to make compromises with such big decisions to make.

Above that age, young mothers on both sides of the Atlantic who are no longer wanted at home are liable to be thrust into the adult world with little preparation and few resources. Many others remain at home very much in the bosom of their family and wanted there. The problem of space is overcome by sisters or brothers sleeping on sofas or doubling up in a single bed. In one Bristol family, Fran (aged 16) and her 3-month-old baby slept in her room, her two younger brothers (aged 8 and 6) slept together in another bedroom, her single mother made room in her double bed for Fran's brother's girl friend (aged 17), whose baby also shared that room. Fran's brother meanwhile slept on the sitting room sofa – he was 13.

Where neither mother nor father are able or willing to offer the pregnant daughter a home, grandmother may step in. Gran's intervention is not always appreciated – depending to a large extent on what has been going on between the different members of the family. On the other hand, Gran may be the one to bring the baby up. Mother and daughter may come to an arrangement whereby the baby either starts life calling its grandmother 'Mom', or is transferred to grandmother's care after a period of months or years. Identity for such children can be a difficult and confusing issue, especially if they find out the truth only in their teens, or when they know the facts from early on but grow up to deceive the world. Families can tie themselves in knots with these sorts of deceits and the damage has ripple effects across the chronologically muddled generations.

There is no doubt that those families who find themselves with an adolescent daughter becoming a mother find one way or another of coping – after the initial shock. Many families cope well with an admittedly unwanted, unplanned teenage pregnancy by dealing with the problem sensitively and rationally; deciding which option suits the girl and the circumstances, and taking it. Unfortunately many other families feel unable to deal with the problem. Pregnancy may drift into motherhood, while the new grandmotherhood is soon tinged with a weary, sacrificial disappointment. This may seem a harsh comment to make, but this is not written to sound condemning. It is written to offer explanations, to offer individual illustrations of a reality of which many people are unaware.

The birth experience

The types of deliveries experienced by teenage mothers in Britain appear no different from those of older mothers (Russell, 1981, p. 187), and their proportion of stillbirths no higher than that of older women. However, their babies are lighter at birth, and more are delivered pre- or post-term. In one British survey of children born in one week in 1970, the average weight of babies born to mothers of 18 or less was 3154 grams (just under 7 lbs) as against 3330 grams (about 7½ lbs) (Butler *et al.*, 1981). Russell also (1981, p. 187) found an excess of low birth weight babies among his sample of young teenage mothers. The proportion of pre- and post-term births was 8.6 and 16.4 per cent for teenagers, against 5.1 and 11.6 per cent for older mothers. For the US Miller (1983) found that in her 1979 sample of under 16-year-old mothers the proportion of premature babies weighing less than 2500 grams (72.4 per cent) was greater than that among all babies born prematurely in the whole of the US (40.6 per cent). There is therefore relatively more concern for adolescent mothers giving birth and for their babies at birth, as well as during the postnatal period. Low birth weight tends to lead to early feeding problems which can persist into infancy and childhood due to lack of patience and understanding on the young mother's part, a situation in itself often due to lack of help and support from the professional and significant adults around the mother during those early vital weeks.

In 1979 the prematurity rate for this age group (16 per cent) was considerably greater than the national rate (8.9 per cent) but comparable to the rate for the US black population for the same year (16.1 per cent). However, the rate for mothers giving birth under age 15 was even higher in the same year: 28.2 per cent for blacks and 18.7 per cent for whites. The need for concern and preventive action is clear (Miller, 1983). Birch (1987) reports similarly low birth weights and premature babies among young teenagers. Young mothers and their children are in danger of getting off to a particularly bad start which can lead to disadvantages for both on many levels as the child grows up.

Most teenagers go through a very anxious time during their pregnancy. The sheer fear of the physical pain can immobilise a young expectant mother, with the result that she may neither express her fears nor attend antenatal classes designed to allay those fears by providing information and techniques. Fear and ignorance in the delivery room can make the pain worse than it need be. Once again, the younger the mother the less likely she is to benefit from any help that may be available for her. Sharpe's (1987) sample report a number of unhappy experiences, due in the main to a lack of understanding of the birth process and sometimes the insensitivity of hospital staff.

If the baby is small and premature it may need to spend some time in intensive care. This happened to Josie's baby, who was initially going to be placed for adoption. Josie changed her mind about that. The baby remained four weeks in the hospital after Josie had returned home and she visited him every evening with the baby's father. It is difficult to make the first bonding when the baby is whisked away into special care without the mother. It is hard for a young mother to be parted from her baby in this way as soon as it is born. Again the younger she is, the less likely it is she will question the way things are handled. Miller (1983) reported a high rate of mother/baby separation (16 per cent) among her very young mothers, whereby the mother went home leaving the baby in hospital. This rate is much higher than for married women of all ages. Other adolescent mothers are able and want to stay with their baby and express breast milk for it as the best they can do in the circumstances.

There is anecdotal evidence (Sharpe, 1987; McGuire, 1983) that young unmarried adolescent mothers are treated differently in hospital from older married mothers. This feeling may also in part arise from the defensive attitude the teenagers themselves may adopt – after all, most of them are aware of their ambivalent position. These young mothers are unsure, inexperienced, sometimes defensive through fear and guilt, and ignorant on many levels. Despite this, they are nevertheless going ahead with motherhood and need all the support they can get. Some are sent home after only a few days, but it has been known for very young mothers to be sent home only a few hours after the baby's birth. It is difficult to see how some hospital staff can justify this course of action. The problem as always is to maintain a balanced view. It may be felt appropriate to send the young mothers home if there are support and home comforts available where they are going. But these are not always present in the homes of teenagers, especially those who are newly independent or those whose family home is already at breaking point.

One aspect of mothering that suffers is breast feeding. Numerous surveys have shown that teenagers are less likely to breast feed than older mothers. Staff may assume greater knowledge and experience than actually exist. This is a difficult area, for there exists a very real danger that genuine help and advice may be taken as patronising. On the other hand, it seems that today young mothers are sent home so early that they have not even had time to get past the colostrom stage of breast feeding. Many do not try feeding their baby this way, and that in itself is a pity, since it helps create the bonding from the start and provides the best nourishment and cherishing a baby can have for its future health and contentment.

Apart from the breast feeding issue, adolescent mothers who are sent home only a few days or even hours after the birth will have had no help or experience in establishing a routine with their baby – the changing, the feeding, recognising the different cries, learning to respond to the baby's different needs, and learning above all to feel confident in handling such a tiny human being without doing any damage and without fear. A midwife's response to a query about sending such mothers home so soon after the birth was accompanied by a shrugging of the shoulders:

What can we do? It's their choice. They claim they're bored. If they want to go home we can't stop them. If the baby's all right, we have nothing to hold them in hospital.

In the US Medicaid will cover a period of four days in hospital, so it is not surprising that over half of Miller's sample stayed four days or less, that is those who had normal births. Obviously those who had a caesarian section remained in hospital a few days longer. Recent experience in Britain, where all services are free, implies that many, many single teenage mothers are allowed home far too soon without sufficient or appropriate support.

With less build up to the birth via clinic attendance, and with less commitment in terms of experience, security, confidence and plans for the future, with youth and immaturity to battle with, bonding with the baby takes longer and is more difficult than for the older mother who has more of these things worked out. Many young mothers are subject to depression (Simms and Smith, 1986). They suffer from exhaustion from broken nights, anxiety and frustration with feeding problems and a new isolation sets in which had not been envisaged. Mothers need a lot of support whatever their age. Young mothers need even more.

It is a myth that maternal instincts come naturally to all women. Many teenage mothers, while pleased and unself-conscious about cuddling their baby, are embarrassed and fearful about physical contact such as keeping the 'privates' clean, and particularly about breast feeding. A good number of service providers do not recognise this fact, making the not unnatural assumption that having a baby implies having had a sexual relationship which means being familiar with your naked body. This is not necessarily so for a young adolescent mother. She may not have seen her own or her partner's naked body, she is unlikely to have experienced a lot of safe cuddling and caressing, and she is likely to carry with her the notion that anything connected with the body is 'bad', 'naughty', 'dirty' (see chapter 2). And until nature takes over and the actual birth begins, many adolescent mothers are also very anxious about the physical exposure involved – as they were about examinations by doctors during pregnancy.

The experience of birth is traumatic for all mothers and babies. For young mothers and their often small babies, the birth repre- sents the real and tangible beginnings of a disadvantaged life. The age of the mother is not considered to be the prime cause of this disadvantage; rather it is considered to be the relatively deprived background from which she has come and the disadvantages that are brought with it. Birch (1987) and others relate the problems of young motherhood in Britain to social conditions, which in many senses are poor and disadvantaged. There is no way that these influences can be totally eliminated, however excellent and sensi- tive the care and support may be, as the next generation arrives. However, unless teenagers are offered support in ways they are able to receive it at the birth, both before and after, we will make little progress with the health and well-being of their children as they grow up.

How education fits into the picture

Teenage pregnancy is clearly associated with school drop out, regardless of which comes first. Girls who become pregnant during their statutory school years and decide to keep the baby are, generally speaking, making one statement about disliking school and another about their own needs in terms of self-value. Parents are not always able to offer appropriate help, and do not know what to do for the best. A significant factor of growing up, which the pregnant or parenting school student is likely to miss out on, is an education which will help her to support herself and her child(ren) in economic, emotional, intellectual and creative terms. Unless enlightened policy-makers provide suitable and congenial facilities for her continuing education as well as for the minding of her child while she does so, early pregnancy very often means a blunted education.

Many pregnant girls still of school age lower their educational targets in preparing for motherhood and assume they will not do as well as they might. This is perhaps so at the time for those who have high aspirations. With opportunity and determination as well as support in their resolve, these may catch up later – sometimes many years later. Furstenberg *et al.* (1987) found in their follow-up Baltimore study that indeed many of them do. Conversely, if those with the drop-out mentality have the good fortune to live in an area with provision for parenting school students, they do a good deal better at school than they expected to – and a good deal better than their teachers expected of them.

There are four eventualities facing a pregnant student and school age mother: remaining at or returning to her original school; transferring to a special centre or small alternative school; receiving tuition at home; or simply avoiding the system and dropping out completely. Factors influencing the course such a girl would take include local policy and provision, alternative child care arrangements, family attitude and set up, andthe cooperation and motivation of each individual girl.

In the US parenting teens are increasingly encouraged to return to school or to continue in an alternative school (where their infants and toddlers are cared for in a creche), for it is deemed more and more vital that school leavers should gain their high school diploma or general education diploma. This is the first passport to true independence. And since this is obtained at age 17/18, the young mothers are obliged to stay on after the end of compulsory schooling. With only one exception, the young mothers interviewed by McGuire (1983) wanted to continue their education.

In Britain the picture is different. A majority of school age mothers do not remain in school, but attend special educational centres to complete their schooling (i.e. to age 16), or have home tuition if such a centre or unit does not exist in their area. Others may return to school if their parents are prepared to look after the baby at home. Others again may have no attention at all. A few certainly slip through the authority's net and manage to avoid schooling altogether – in some cases this simply means that truancy is continuing.

A majority of teenage mothers find it difficult to see the future – that may be one of the causes of pregnancy and the choice of motherhood in the first place – and to girls to whom education has meant very little in terms of interest, relevance, or stimulus, the lure of motherhood is attractive, and is a way of gaining social and family status. However, the continuing education of young mothers cannot take place without adequate child care arrangements with which the mothers are wholly happy. Neither the US nor the UK are anywhere near the forefront, in the so-called 'developed world', of seeing child care provision for any mothers – let alone teenage mothers – as particularly significant in either the nation's economy or the health and well-being of the family.

When earning capacity is limited, when housing is a struggle, when boy friends are not reliable, when women still do not enjoy equal economic opportunities with men, and when child care is impossible – with or without family support – it is not surprising that many young mothers feel they cannot be bothered with education.

/

Chapter 4

Teenage Mothers and their Babies

The majority of teenage mothers, as we have seen, remain single; marriage has not appealed in the current economic and social climate. When having a baby and bringing up the child is accepted as a one person job, many young mothers do not appreciate the nature of that job. Early difficulties range from physical care of and emotional bonding with the new-born to the financial and emotional survival of the mother. This chapter shows how adolescent mothers learn about the routines of parenthood; how they learn to cope with small babies in an environment which is frequently unhealthy and discouraging; and some of the consequences of such an inexperienced beginning. Where adequate diet and health care exist, babies of teenage mothers are as healthy as those of older mothers. The social conditions, however, are not propitious on the whole, and are a major influence on these young mothers and their babies.

Learning to mother

In theory, at least, teenagers have the advantage when it comes to parenting in that their own childhood has happened relatively recently, and their experiences as recipients of parenting skills may be fresh in their minds. In practice, however, it is questionable as to whether they possess sufficient maturity to turn these relatively recent memories to good account when the task of parenting faces them. It would seem appropriate therefore – in the best of all possible worlds – that they draw on the experience of their own parents as guides and confidants at this strange and difficult time, backed by the wisdom of those whose livelihood is derived from offering advice and guidance to new recruits to parenthood. Unfortunately, it is not nearly as simple as that.

A decade ago, Mia Kellmer Pringle (1980) elegantly set out what becoming a parent entails:

> There is one particularly critical period when parents could play a crucial role in offering their own experience; this is just after a couple have become first ever parents. The birth of a new baby is, in most cases, the culmination of joyful expectation shared by relatives and friends. Subsequently, however, learning to live with a newcomer and facing all the consequent changes is all too often a lonely, exhausting and even frightening business.

Changes and pressures which new parents inevitably undergo in their new role have profound personal, social and financial implications. New parenthood can put so much strain on a relationship that great strength is required to keep it together while taking responsibility for a tiny, new, helpless and vulnerable human being.

> At present little help is given to the couple to anticipate the range of likely changes and their impact on their whole way of life. Of course, some preparation is provided in ante-natal groups and parentcraft classes as well as by health visitors during the early weeks of the baby's life. However, the psychological strains and stresses are relatively neglected. And in any case, the most helpful support is the opportunity to have frequent visits and informal talks such as are available to those fortunate enough to have relatives, and especially their own parents, living near enough and with the time to spare.

In the same volume Pugh (1980) notes that approaches of service agencies to preparation for parenthood are piecemeal and uncoordinated, good practice in the area is poorly defined, and that research has shown that younger mothers are less likely than older ones to attend parentcraft classes. It is likely that many teenage girls learn parenting mostly from their mothers. Presumably any parenting skills boys may have were picked up from their fathers' performance.

The above description of first parenthood, although it depicts much that is real and unexpected, does not even consider the circumstances of a single mother, who may only be 16, or even 12, or those of a teenage couple who may not have been together for long. Kellmer Pringle writes of the conventional couple who have planned for and wanted their baby. Even in that situation first parenthood is extremely hard and full of unexpected anxieties and frustrations. For an adolescent mother virtually unsupported the situation is infinitely worse.

Teenage mothers are on the whole totally unprepared for what lies ahead. The support suggested by Kellmer Pringle is seldom available to a young teenager, but even in the event of its availability, it may not feel accessible to the teenager. Parents may not offer the daughter reliable or consistent support; indeed, some are openly hostile and rejecting. Professional services and personnel cannot always make up the shortfall.

Teenage parents are dependent on outside help, but are often unwilling to adhere to professional advice, being of the age when they want to rebel anyway. Further it is important to appreciate that, if they do go for the support that is offered, they frequently do not understand or remember instructions or procedures. Indeed they may not even believe them. After all, many have great difficulty in remembering even to take the pill, sometimes in spite of having had a baby. And finally too often this outside advice contradicts what they have heard from their mothers, especially in the area of feeding and other routines. Many young mothers, for example, are frequently confused by conflicting advice from health and other professionals on the one hand, and how their mothers say they always did things on the other. Their pregnancy may indeed be one symptom of their rebellion.

Very early experience

One of the difficulties for a very young mother-to-be is that she is still at the stage of not fully accepting the pregnancy and the responsibility this places on her. Faced with the reality, her ambivalence remains, in spite of her valiant efforts to care 'properly' for her child. The younger the mother, the more likely she is to be stubborn. She is not likely to be good at accepting criticism or offers of help, as she may still be operating at an emotional level which in times of stress may preclude rational thought. She is likely to see things in black and white terms, unlikely to appreciate the different shades of grey. Naturally, much depends on background here: sadly it is often the case that those least able to articulate, least able to see their future in a positive light, least supported in a long-term realistic way are those who end up parenting their child. The natural mood swings of the immature adolescent can translate into inconsistent behaviour when caring as a mother for her child. When this happens a vicious circle is begun or is continuing, since the child, not knowing how its mother will react next, cannot settle into a routine, which in turn can cause the child to become irritable and demanding. A chain of reactions is set off in the mother and child relationship, and both become miserable and irritable.

Janet, who had bad experiences in every aspect of her life since she was born, and who understandably had not engaged in any way in school life, became pregnant in her third year of secondary school, aged 13. She was loved and wanted by no one. Her parents lived separately, her three siblings were all in trouble of one sort or another. She was shunted from one household to the other and back again. She suffered from asthma and eczema. Her son suffered likewise. Janet was the subject of suspensions from school, child abuse case conferences, and of considerable general concern to all agencies. Her behaviour was typical of a very unhappy, unloved, un-self-loving little girl who was on the one hand crying out for warmth and affection while on the other resisting all that was offered. What was offered was not what she wanted, since it did not come from her family. Her behaviour with her son represented both these sides of her. One moment she was overwhelmingly adoring, smothering him with hugs and kisses, the next she was swearing and shouting at him. The child learnt to take all behaviours with remarkable placidity. And yet Janet showed at times a maturity, an adult appreciation and a clear understanding of her problems. In these circumstances it is not surprising – since she is an intelligent young woman who has great insight into her life – that her physical and emotional care of her child was erratic. There is no doubt at all that she thought the world of him and always meant the best for him.

'Well, what do you expect? Look at me! And don't you tell me to grow up, I'm only 15! Don't tell me to be responsible. I *am* responsible! You expect a fucking miracle.'

Many young mothers have few resources with which to cope. At the same time they will be desperate to prove what good mothers they are. They know that social workers have the power to take the baby away if the mother seems to be coping badly. Naturally the mother is proud of her baby and her new status of motherhood, but sometimes it is difficult to sustain her buoyancy. Even before her baby is born, Donna (McGuire, 1983) expresses this well; a note of adolescent defiance is not absent:

This is what I made, this is something beautiful, this is mine. It's something that I can show off, something that I'm proud of. At first I was nervous about what people would be saying, and then I just figured, well, I don't even care any more. Let them say whatever they want. At least I got something out of it. I got something beautiful.

This desperation can hold back her own and her child's development. The testing, defensive and often contrary behaviour of a teenager is not likely to disappear overnight with the birth of a baby.

So how well do teenage mothers bond with their babies? This is not easy to monitor. From written evidence and from our experience it would appear that they find bonding more difficult than older mothers do. One reason for this may be the natural embarrassment of youth in being demonstrative and openly affectionate. This may be because they find doing the things that create the bonding difficult – breast feeding, for instance. Another cause may stem purely from their inexperience and lack of knowledge of their own and their baby's needs.

Many teenagers have had a rough and traumatic pregnancy (tinged with resentment) especially if undergone in secret denial.

For those who accepted the pregnancy, poor monitoring through missed appointments, inadequate antenatal care, fear of comment, fear of the birth, etc. often meant a difficult labour and a confused first week. Many young mothers are allowed home from hospital too early to have had a chance to establish a confident routine with their baby, and have not been given enough time and encouragement to persevere with breast feeding. Their youth and inexperience act against them during their hospital stay.

Numerous surveys have shown that teenagers are less likely to breast feed than older mothers. There have been cases where a young mother changed from breast to bottle after only a few days' trial because 'it hurt', 'it's too much trouble' and, most significant, 'it's embarrassing'. 'I wasn't making enough milk' is a common rationalisation. Some act out of ignorance:

> I stopped breast feeding Lee at three months. I'm going to breast feed my next baby all the way to weaning. I wish I had with this one, but nobody told me I could have used powder milk to supplement. (mother aged 14)

Teenage mothers may not enjoy the opportunity for rest in hospital after the birth. Many teenagers have poor reserves of tolerance and patience, become bored in hospital and want to go home as soon as possible.

Home circumstances may be far from ideal. Not all teenage mothers return to the bosom of a highly supportive family, though more very young than older teenage mothers may do so. Most teenage mothers in the Bristol sample (Ineichen, 1986) went home to either partner or parent(s) and sometimes to both. Very few returned to a lonely bedsit, but for many a small flat (sometimes in a high-rise block) would be home. Halfway housing with some kind of support services for parenting teens hardly exists in Britain any more, or certainly not to any sufficient extent to make much impact on the need. Prospects are better in the US, and are described in a later chapter.

From the initial euphoria after the birth, many teenage mothers and their infants are thrust into difficulties which they had not foreseen and for which no one could prepare them. It is not their youth alone, but their inexperience and their ignorance due to their youth which act against them. These in themselves represent a disadvantage and only add to circumstances which may already be severely deprived.

Relinquishing the child

The surrendering by a mother of her new-born baby for adoption is becoming a rare event, in both Britain and America. This is true also of teenage mothers. Several surveys (Ineichen, 1986; Skinner, 1986; Simms and Smith, 1986) have found that very few considered adoption, and only a handful carried it through. In New Jersey 94 per cent of teenagers giving birth now keep their babies (Ann Wilson, personal communication, 1989).

It is impossible to say precisely why this reduction has occurred, although the lessening of the social stigma surrounding unmarried motherhood may have played a major part. While not condoning single teenage motherhood, society does not condemn it either. In fact, society as a whole is extremely ambivalent on the matter. Until the 1950s adoption was an answer to an unwanted pregnancy in a world where keeping the baby was out of the question for an unmarried woman. This is not the case today. Among teenagers themselves adoption is the least acceptable option to a pregnancy. While abortion is categorically bad, adoption is seen as unnatural. Many pregnant teenagers regard adoption as 'mean' or 'tight'. Their partners may oppose any course other than keeping the child.

Fran, aged 15, received very clear messages regarding her pregnancy, as she listened to her mother talking to her teacher:

Well, you see, my litt'un, the next one down, he was going for adoption. There was no point in having any more kids. His father had already left me and I had left the decision too late. I was in hospital about to come home and I hadn't seen him. It was all going according to my plans. Then my sister came along and wheeled him in and said I couldn't be so cruel. Well, once I'd seen him, that was that. So I can't have Fran adopting this one. I knows what it's like.

I had an abortion too. That was before this last one I was telling you about. He [husband] beat me about so bad, they told me the baby was damaged. It was late by then, six months, and I

had to go through all the labour. They brought me on, and I had
the whole thing. It was disgusting, I wouldn't wish that on
anyone. Of course she can make up her own mind . . .

Those young mothers who consider adoption may have a clearer
view of the future, and/or a stronger will not to have a baby at that
time. Those who carry out their plan are fortunate in that they have
had appropriate support throughout the pregnancy. Options are
not options unless they are clearly offered and clearly understood.

Where adoption seems too drastic, other options include fostering (voluntary or socially arranged), custodianship, and placement
with extended family members. The latter is especially common in
some cultures: black Americans, for example. Sometimes children
in this position grow up believing that their grandmother is their
mother and their actual mother their sister. It has also been known
for an adolescent's mother to adopt her grandchild officially as
another daughter.

Only one mother in Skinner's sample of 437 girls intended to
have her child fostered initially: again, this may not have been
carried through. Skinner (p. 95) quotes an example of an apparently successful adoption, as the mother came from a background
where it would have been almost impossible to keep her child.
Contrary to all expectations – and this fact too is symptomatic of
the social pressures – this young Irish girl kept to her resolve and
was happy to leave her child with the adoptive parents in England,
whom she had met. In a culture where an illegitimate child is
unacceptable, the trauma of losing the baby in this way is
considerably less than in a more tolerant society.

Elizabeth was 17 and wanted to continue her education
(McGuire, 1983). She was fortunate enough to have a friend to get
her to an adoption agency:

Mrs. W. [social worker/counsellor] made me think about adoption and keeping [the baby]. She really asks you questions, and
you really have to think. You have to think about the pros and
cons of each decision. Up until before I had the baby, I was
going to put her up for adoption. And she was put into a foster
home until I made up my mind. I kept on seeing Mrs. W. during
that time. And I was going back to high school and getting back
involved in things.

In the end she decided to have her baby back and managed to continue school, with much help and support from her family, including her working mother.

> I don't think it's good for every person to keep their baby. I'm not against adoption at all . . . I think giving it up for adoption is the most unselfish thing that anybody can do. Why keep a baby if you can't handle it and just end up giving up the baby for adoption later on? The baby should be in a home right away with parents that will love it and give it attention.

There follow three examples from the Bristol Unit of planned adoption that did not work out for one reason or another.

A 14-year-old girl changed her mind in hospital.

> Josie had concealed her pregnancy and the baby was six weeks premature. The shock to the family was considerable and adoption was the only consideration at first, but it seems there was a misunderstanding between the hospital staff, the adoption agency worker and the family. The result was Josie keeping her son, except that he had to stay in intensive care for 4 weeks. Josie became a mother at 14 with no preparation, no baby to care for straight away and was unable to return to school. That was difficult enough. With almost greater difficulties in adjusting, Josie's mother and step-father became grandparents. She herself took care of her child and started at the schoolgirl mother's unit where she could have him cared for while she studied.

Tracey at 14 was told by her doctor when she had missed two periods that there was nothing to worry about since lots of girls her age miss their periods.

> So when, at six months, the pregnancy was confirmed, she was told she had no choice – 'The family wish to have the child adopted' – the two pairs of prospective grandparents discussed taking the child on, but neither was prepared to. At eight months Tracey admitted she had no feelings for the baby, she wanted the baby adopted, she wanted to get straight back to school. She underwent a complicated and painful birth, the baby weighed ten lbs, and she took him home. Her parents cared for him and Tracey returned to school.

Danielle was herself adopted, along with her adoptive brother. From the age of 4 she was brought up by her adoptive mother alone. Although she was a bright girl, in her teens she truanted from school a good deal and went missing from home.

> When she became pregnant the plan was to have the baby adopted, but Danielle never came to terms with that, and so began a life of turmoil and conflict as Danielle moved away from her mother and back again, set up with a new boy friend, absconded from that relationship – leaving her daughter with him each time, got into debt when she returned as plans were made to start again. At age 19 her daughter was getting on for four and Danielle declared herself settled, and ready now to start a course at the local technical college. Her child was taken care of, part at nursery school, part with a minder. She started her course in September. Plans to marry were set in motion. Then she did another runner. She left her daughter with her fond and forgiving boy friend yet again, and when she finally returned went back to live with her long-suffering mother. The point about this tale is that there are signs here of unresolved issues around her own place and role and also about whether her daughter really should have gone for adoption. The child has been the unwitting cause of much of the conflict, surrounded as she was by unhappy and frustrated people. If Danielle wishes she had taken a different path when her child was born, she is less and less able to say so as the child grows up.

Some teenagers, however, are more sure of what they want, perhaps because they are more confident in themselves. One of McGuire's pregnant teenagers was fairly sure she was not pre-pared for motherhood, as she wanted to remain in college, nor did she want to burden her mother with fostering a grandchild:

> My parents have their life, and it's not fair to them to be dumped with it. I wouldn't want my mother raising my baby. He deserves a life too. . . . When he was born I still felt the same way. I had him for three days in the hospital. He was mine. I felt him. I held him. I had him as much as I could. And I went to see him afterwards. So it was a decision I just knew was right. It wouldn't be fair for him or me. (McGuire, 1983)

She had no second thoughts during the period when the child was in foster care. She was not allowed to sign the adoptive papers straight away. There were no regrets.

Maggie, a British girl of 15 and still at school, found herself accidentally pregnant by her steady boy friend during her fifth year at her comprehensive school, where she planned to take eight GCSEs. After three months of hoping it would go away, she was about to tell her parents when her father suddenly died of a heart attack. She felt she could not add to the turmoil of that time. A social worker from the Fostering and Adoption Department worked with her, as also did a teacher/counsellor from the Bristol Unit in the area. To the latter, Maggie told her own story:

Sometimes I'm really down. I wonder how she is, but it passes. In a way it would have been nice to have kept her, but I'm glad Dad didn't know about it all – feel ashamed. Dad wanted me to go on and do well at school, you see. I'm the only one in this family to be at all academic. I always wanted to stay on and do A Levels. I didn't want to leave school. There'll be time for more babies later. I'm doing this for me.

The whole thing's been quite an experience. The condom broke – such a stupid situation to get into. We split up and he didn't know I was pregnant. I didn't tell anyone. I hoped, if I didn't think about it, it would go away. When I knew for sure, I thought I'd keep the baby. Then I got to thinking . . . no way. It was too late for an abortion, so adoption came to mind. When I told my family, I was back with Stan again, and was fairly sure about the adoption.

I wanted a baby that was unbruised, undented. I had to think of her, but I wasn't going to give up my education.

The whole experience of pregnancy, the anxiety, the decision-making, has made me understand a lot more. I can see more than one side of an argument now – any argument. It was so new and different from anything I'd experienced before. I enjoyed the birth – I can't explain it – and I had no doubts at all that she would be adopted. I felt so happy for the parents.

Stan wasn't happy. He couldn't get used to the idea of adoption for at least a month later. But I never faltered. Stan threatened to leave me – couldn't go out with me after what I'd done – but he didn't. I think he had an unrealistic view of the position we were in. Where and how would we live? He's adopted. My mother couldn't possibly help out. I wanted to go on at school. . . . He felt left out. He wasn't in on my decision. . . . The usual thing, I suppose, he felt guilty and responsible but unable to do anything.

Sometimes my friends make remarks about a pregnant girl – like 'How stupid to get that way' – forgetting about me. I don't usually say anything. I see things in a different light now. And I've learnt to think before doing things or judging anyone. Look before you leap.

If I had the chance to talk to someone who's pregnant at school, I'd do what you did for me, make her work through all the pros and cons of the different options herself. It really helped me to see clearly.

I reckon there are three stages in a person's life: 0–16, 16–20 and 20 onwards. I would've missed out on that very short but vital stage of my life if I'd kept the baby. Those four years are crucial – or I think they are for me. I think it's important not to miss any of the stages.

Three days after her last exam Maggie had her baby. She passed them all and is now in the sixth form studying for A levels, and when last seen was still with Stan. It seems fairly clear from all the evidence that having a positive vision of her future is a strong influence on a girl to consider adoption. Part of this vision is on the education front.

The short case-studies set out above are examples of a minority among teenagers. The younger the girl, the more difficulty she has in expressing her feelings and in having the confidence to stand up for what she wants for herself. Thus it is that the young woman who is least able to sort through the pressures and the confusion more often than not ends up by keeping the baby and convincing herself that on all counts she has done the morally right thing. No one will deny that giving up the baby is hard. It represents loss in the true sense and requires an unspecified period of mourning – but it is the positive, indeed the realistic vision of the future, together with continuous support both from professionals and from the family, that allow the mother to take this generous course of action. And in saying that it is generous, let us also admit that it is selfish too – and there is nothing wrong with that.

Among Sharpe's group of young mothers (1987), Yvonne looks back over the years of conflict, pressure and violence since she first started going out with her child's father, and says:

> If I could turn the clock back, I would, and I would definitely opt for adoption. I'm not saying I don't love her, because I do, but I feel that everything I want to do, she is in the way of. So to those who say they wouldn't swap their babies, let them see how they feel in five years time when their children start school and the real loneliness sets in.
>
> Cheryl still sees her father, a fact that I resent because he now has someone else and I'm left all alone. Once she has gone to bed at 8.30, I chain and bolt the door, and am often in bed at nine o'clock myself. At 24 I feel too young to be among the other mothers, yet too old for people of my own age who are working and getting on with their lives. I also regret that I never finished my education, and that I never joined the army.
>
> I would say to anyone who finds themselves in the situation I did, think very hard, 18 years of your life is a lot to devote to a child, when you're still only a child yourself.

Finally, it should not be forgotten that there is the interim method of caring for a child where a third party has care and control, but where the mother does not completely lose contact with her child. With informal fostering the mother retains parental rights. With custodianship her parental rights are more severely curtailed, as they are with formal care orders. Young mothers of children who are taken into care are those who have not been able to cope well enough. The loss and misery incurred only add to their already desperate circumstances.

The health and morale of the teenage mother and her child

Studies of the health of teenage mothers and their children show they face considerably more risks and problems than older mothers and their children. In both Britain and America children of teenage mothers are more likely to die in their early life. Sudden infant death is more common.

In New Jersey, for example, in spite of the overall decrease in infant mortality over the last decade, babies to adolescent mothers are almost *twice* as likely as babies of older mothers to die during the first year of life (Johnson and Ziskin, 1988). In 1980 the New Jersey infant mortality rate for teen parents was 19 per 1000 live births, while to parents aged 20 and over the rate was 10.7 per 1000. By 1985 these rates were 17 and 9.7 respectively. In Washington, DC, where the infant mortality rate is the highest in the US, the rate soared by 50 per cent in the first six months of 1989 to 32.3 per 1000 live births (*TES*, 13.10.89). This is an extremely high figure and is cause for great concern. Teenage mothers are also more likely to experience miscarriages or still-births (Hayes, 1987).

Teenage mothers are more likely than older mothers to have a baby suffering from congenital malformations (Wynn and Wynn, 1979; Russell, 1982; Grazi *et al.*, 1982) and low birth weight babies (Hayes, 1987). Golding and Butler (1986) report that a wide range of health problems are commoner among children of teenage mothers in their national sample, although social factors, as much as maternal age, are likely to be responsible.

Infants of teenage mothers are more likely than those of older mothers to need frequent medical attention. Accidents and other hospital admissions are more frequent in the first five years than for other children (Taylor *et al.*, 1983). Children of very young teenagers are especially vulnerable. Among Miller's (1983) mothers aged 16 and under the most common problems were to do with colds and chest infections, while bowel-related problems such as diarrhoea and constipation came a close second. Many young mothers are on the one hand overcautious and call the doctor for the slightest thing, while on the other they may unwittingly neglect signs of medical problems. Reasons for not reacting appropriately may well be the consequence of youth, inexperience, inability to take in instructions and lack of support from partner or family. For instance, a simple mistake during the early weeks can cause havoc and misery for the baby and its mother. Many young mothers do not appreciate the accuracy required in measuring the milk for the bottle; making it thicker than instructed is a frequent response by a mother who is eager for her child to develop. Feeding rusks and other solid foods before the baby is ready (which is certainly not before three months) is also common practice. Colicky babies have a lot of pain, cannot take their milk very well and are therefore frequently hungry. Hence they cry a great deal which their mothers find exhausting and depressing.

Environmental factors are often hazardous. If the mother is living with her family, these can include poor housing, cramped conditions, the added aggravation of unsocial working hours by some members of the family, or of unemployed members idle and bored at home all day, little means of escape due to financial hardship, inadequate and irregular meals, and possibly a smoky atmosphere, since many people living in poor conditions smoke. If the mother lives alone with her baby, the stresses are different; these are mainly loneliness, lack of support and boredom through lack of resources. When a teenager's baby is introduced into a household with a combination of some of these factors, that infant has little chance of maintaining good heath. Chest infections and digestive problems are common among young children living in poor conditions. Teenage mothers are especially likely to be smokers (Simms and Smith, 1986) and to have poor eating habits (Hayes, 1987).

Some young mothers find it difficult to attend consistently to their children's health. McGee (1982) comments that in the US sometimes it all seems too complicated:

> To obtain adequate health care for herself and her child, a teen mother may need to consult a pediatrician, a family planning nurse practitioner, a nutritionist, a social worker, a contraception counselor, and/or an internist. She will probably have to arrange several appointments in different places, at different times, during hours that conflict with work or school. The possibilities of getting 'lost in the referral process' ... are endless.

Her child may not be in school yet, she most likely has no work to go to, but it is nevertheless a common feature for an adolescent mother to forget, to miss, or simply to ignore the significance of doctor, clinic or hospital appointments for both herself and her child.

> 'I couldn't face her having an eye operation. I was too scared.'

> 'What's the point of me going back for his hearing test? They'll only tell me the same as before.'

'I know he needs more drops – I forgot. He'll have to wait till after the weekend.'

'I got this card from the hospital. I'm not going. How can I get there? Do they think I'm made of money?'

On the other hand, concern for the baby, trips to the clinic and the nagging knowledge that she can do little to alter her circumstances do much to reduce the teenage mother's initial euphoria of giving birth in the hospital, wearing down her morale and her physical health at the same time. The worst scenario would be a gradual decline of health and morale into apathy and depression and total acceptance of the inevitability of things. Ill-health and poor morale become the norm for teenage mothers in this position. Picture Cynthia:

> She left the Bristol Unit with her little boy, ill-equipped for independence. On-going conflicts with her parents and with her boy friend led her to a council flat at age 16/17 high up in a high rise block. Her second baby, a girl, by the same father who subsequently abandoned his responsibilities, added to Cynthia's problems to such an extent that concerned adults pushed for home help and she was advised to have the Depo-provera contraceptive injection, since she freely admitted to forgetting to take the pill. The children were neglected in every way, but not intentionally. Cynthia had no resources, no strength of any sort. Unable to make any sensible decisions for herself or for her brood, she had been worn down by circumstances and abused by her boy friend.

Her health had never been good, neither had her morale. And yet Cynthia did not come from materially poor conditions; she had been well cared for and well loved. The clue here seems to be a total lack of confidence, partly due perhaps to the family confusion which led to the different levels of unresolved conflict. Stress in one area can lead to stress in others, so that, if it is unchecked, proper functioning gradually deteriorates. She had lived at home with her two natural parents and a good deal of support, although she did not do well at secondary school. It seems that some basic need was not catered for and the downward spiral commenced. When she finally split up with her boy friend she and her children fared a lot better: she lost weight, became more animated, thought about the care of the children and about getting a job. This example of extreme stress and non-coping may not be the norm, but neither is it uncommon. The consequences can lead unmarried and married teenage parents to rates of abuse and neglect far higher than among the general population (Foster, 1986).

Simms and Smith (1986) set out to establish the feelings of their survey teen mothers during a second interview when their children were 16–18 months old. Of the 11 per cent who admitted to being not pleased to be a teenage mother, most were depressed by material shortages, isolation with the baby in poor housing and in unpleasant areas, being unable to work, and the realisation that it would be very difficult to escape from such an environment.

There were many regrets. Missing out on that middle period of their lives between childhood and adulthood was one; there had not been enough time to get to know the baby's father, to consolidate a good relationship or to end a bad one. Another was to do with having missed the opportunity to finish schooling, pass exams and/or train for a skill. With hindsight many of the young mothers felt strongly that they should have delayed having a child, were not ready, were not happy, felt trapped. Those who had had no education in birth control and those who had not intended to become pregnant were more discontented than those who had, as were those whose life was unstable (due to frequent moves and lost jobs). Those who were separated or single were more discontented than those who were married, contrasting their isolation with the lively social life of their childless peers. Large numbers of mothers in both this study and that of Miller (1983) appeared unhappy in their circumstances. Mothers aged 16 and under, if given the opportunity to speak comfortably and unembarrassed among themselves, admit to depression, easy irritability and stress symptoms of various kinds (Hudson, 1985). One 15-year-old mother openly admitted to wishing she did not have her 8-month-old son; she, like her peers in the group, felt trapped by the relationship with the baby's father, and wanted to be free to go out and 'do her own thing'. With these preoccupations weighing heavily, eating and sleeping patterns as well as concentration levels tend to suffer. Children whose existence is regretted even minimally and spasmodically show signs of stress at an early age.

The child's early development

How does the infant of an adolescent mother fare? How do the children of very young mothers develop and grow in comparison with those of older mothers? The youth of mothers is continually emphasised as a disadvantage to both the mother and her child, but how much is maternal age an influential factor in the child's growth?

Both the physical and the mental development of children of adolescent parents appear slower than those of children of older mothers, although factors such as birth order position, poverty and social class appear to play a large part in such differences, making the effect of maternal age alone difficult to establish.

Children tend to suffer disadvantage as a direct consequence of their parents' lack of resources. Children of adolescent parents can be measured against the development 'norms' considered appropriate in our society such as: physical, social and mental health; play; coordination; and an all-round demonstration of thriving. The evidence from percentile charts generally points up the fact that lack of adequate nurturing and cherishing – both physical and emotional – from the earliest weeks can lead to mental delay, poor school performance and distorted psycho-social development in the child in later years. Brierley (1987) points out that significant intellectual and emotional development occurs during the first spurt in brain growth between the sixth month of pregnancy and two years. Clearly it is important to nurture this development.

However, maternal age is of course connected with poverty, by the very fact that a teen mother is unlikely to be fully independent, may not have completed her education, and may not be particularly motivated to attend classes or find work. In the US, of all families with children aged 5 or younger headed by mothers who had given birth as teenagers, 67 per cent were living below the officially designated poverty level (Alan Guttmacher) in 1976. In Britain, six out of ten one parent families were living in or on the margins of poverty, compared with two out of ten two parent families in 1986 (*One Parent Families*, Family Policy Studies Centre, 1986). In the US a Congressional study recently revealed that 45 per cent of all black children and 68.3 per cent of black children in single parent families were living in poverty (*TES*, 13.10.89). It is poor living conditions, poor or hopeless life prospects and a sense of no control over their lives that create and exacerbate the problems for the child.

One of the reasons for poor development in the early years is lack of adequate nutrition. Some general characteristics of very young mothers often include nutritional ignorance and poor diet. Their own upbringing probably provided poor models for sensible eating, and their children are likely to experience similar deficiencies. There is concern on both sides of the Atlantic for the feeding and growth of children of adolescent parents, since such parents are without sufficient knowledge, education and experience to understand fully the nutritional needs of a tiny infant, and tend to eat an inadequate diet themselves.

One young mother, just out of school at 16, decided to wander the streets with her child in the push-chair rather than stay home with mother. Then she went to live with another single sixteen year old mother in a council flat. She herself had always eaten practically nothing but chips and ice-cream and considered this diet adequate for her 16 month old, in spite of all she was 'taught' at the special unit she had attended.

Feeding problems are frequent in babies born to adolescent mothers, and a disproportionate number are admitted to hospital during the first two years of life with gastro-enteritis, blockages, chest infections or other symptoms. Poor management, wrong feeds, neglect and poor hygiene are some of the causes. A disproportionate number of these babies are premature and underweight and therefore difficult to feed at first. The frustration and sense of inadequacy on top of other personal and social problems (such as damp or overcrowded housing) would exacerbate any existing anxieties, one of which would be establishing a regular feeding pattern.

Alison had learnt how to mix her baby's feed and knew about the dangers of making it too rich. Nevertheless, like many a young mother before her, she thought it could do no harm to make it thicker, thinking her baby would be more satisfied. The wakeful and wearying nights that set the pattern for the next few months as a result of prolonged colic due to the over-rich mixture she was giving him tell their own story. The mother herself, though, was hard to convince: 'My mum, she said she always made my bottles richer than it said. I's always all right . . . Nothing wrong with me now, is there?' (Alison, age 16). This lack of assumption of good habits and routines in the first months of a child's life are, it is suggested, the beginnings of poor development in childhood.

A further reason for slow child development is lack of stimulation and play. Like 'maternal instincts', playing with your child does not necessarily come naturally; you need self-confidence and good models. If your mother – or another care-giver – did not play with you and teach you early skills when you were little, then it is most probable that you will not have the skills to help your child learn. Learning about aspects of child-rearing such as nutrition and play in parenting classes or in school does not necessarily seem to be put into practice with the teenagers' own children. This points up a failure on the part of some service providers to impart information clearly and link it effectively with practice. Miller (1983) confirms our own findings that, although teenage expectant mothers wanted more information on child development, interest waned after their baby's birth, and they did not know how to incorporate what they had learned into their daily routines or how to assume habits that would promote the child's learning or healthy development. The ice-cream-and-chips-eating mother mentioned above is not an isolated example.

Simone, age 15 and attending the Bristol Unit, returned from a session on play with her 16-month-old-son, given by the nursery nurse.

> She was astonished and delighted that her baby could play with bricks. When her teacher expressed surprise at her astonishment it transpired that Simone had never played with her son, that he had no toys of this 'educational' or 'learning' nature, that he had never seen bricks anywhere other than the nursery, and that she was not intending to buy him any, nor would she play with them with him if she did.

In her mother's home Simone's son wandered and fiddled as he pleased until he touched something he should not and was scolded. He had little at his own disposal and was not played with at home.

As in other areas of their lives discussed elsewhere in this book, adolescents tend only to believe what they see, and a quiet, seemingly satisfied infant may be enough for its teenage mother.

All too often young mothers do not wish to be told by more experienced adults who see signs of poor feeding, lack of stimulation, or other symptoms. As Deidre, age 16, put it:

> Don't you tell me my baby's ill. He's not stressed. He's not lethargic. He's got eczema, that's all. I love my baby and he loves me. He's all right, my baby. There's nothing wrong with him. I've got this cream, that'll soon clear it up.

The infants of young mothers – who themselves have had little in the way of stimulation and positive attention – are not victims of planned cruelty, but rather of innocent omissions on the part of their parents.

> Janet, whom we have already met, a 15 year old mother and living with her father for a few months, had no money and few resources for herself, let alone for her year old son. She was given a bag of suitable toys for him, but only got them out for him reluctantly when the home tutor turned up and asked where they were. She kept them for tidiness' sake behind the settee, for she could not bear the mess he made with them. In the tutor's absence the child was left to his own devices – and got into constant trouble with his easily irritated mother.

Recent research suggests that Janet's story is typical: teenage mothers spend less time talking to and possibly looking at their babies than older mothers, and use less typically maternal behaviour (Osofsky *et al.*, 1988).

In many children slow development does not show at first, and indeed, in a study quoted by Miller (1983) children of adolescents at 8 months showed a more advanced level of mental and motor abilities than children born to mothers aged 20 to 29. However, by the time they were 4 years old, their IQ scores and motor function were less advanced and they had a higher frequency of deviant behaviour than the children of older mothers. At age 7 these childen had lower IQ scores, were less able in school and showed higher rates of deviant behaviour than their peers with older parents. The effects of environmental deficits in the child's very early life tend not to show up until the preschool years and after; this renders parenting education absolutely vital among adolescent mothers for some time after their baby's birth.

Chapter 5

Very Young Mothers – Sixteen and Under

In both Britain and the US childbearing among girls under age 16 has increased in recent years. Very young mothers face particular difficulties, and are least equipped to cope with the responsibilities of motherhood. Their legal status is anomalous, and continuing their education raises particular difficulties. Taking on the role of motherhood while completing their schooling is by no means a straightforward exercise.

Who are the very young mothers?

In England and Wales nearly 10,000 under 16s become pregnant each year, and in 1985, 4169 went on to have their babies. Around 10,000 births to under 15s took place in the US in 1981. These very young mothers have been the subjects of a number of surveys (Wilson, 1980; Miller, 1983; Coyne, n.d.) and some large surveys of teenage mothers have presented some of their data separately for older and younger teenagers (Zelnik *et al.*, 1981; Butler *et al.*, 1981). Their difficulties resemble those of older teenagers, writ larger.

Wilson (1980) reports on a sample of 44 girls in Aberdeen who became pregnant before they were 16, compared with a group matched by socio-demographic variables. The pregnant girls were underachievers at school, and were more likely to have been in trouble with the police or with the child guidance service. They also appeared more likely to have been illegitimate, to have come from large families and to have been born themselves to a teenage mother.

Miller (1983) interviewed 184 mothers aged 15 or less (67 per cent of those eligible), identified by social work agencies in three American cities, several months after the birth; she reinterviewed 144 of them 18 months later; 85 per cent were black. Only three married in the course of the research. Like Wilson's sample, most were themselves children of young mothers, who at the time of interview were single parents. Not surprisingly they were poor: the babies' fathers were on average under 18, and the amount of financial support they provided was small. Most relied on welfare payments, and this sort of income appeared to be of growing importance as the baby grew older and other sources of financial help decreased. What seems especially worrying is that the real circumstances of very young mothers and their children in America may be even bleaker than Miller suggests, in the light of the large initial losses from her sample. Like Simms and Smith's (1986) enquiry, those who talked may have been doing better than those who did not. Reliance on welfare will be discussed further, later in this chapter.

Coyne (n.d.) interviewed a sample of 30, several of whom, like Wilson's, had been in trouble with the law. Not surprisingly, their feelings around motherhood betrayed immaturity; when expressing concern for their child's welfare, they did so only in relation to themselves; 'Having my baby has given me a purpose in life'.

The younger the persons concerned, the less likely they are to use any form of contraception. While older teenagers take more responsibility and control over their lives in general and their fertility in particular, the younger ones take enormous risks without realistically anticipating the consequences. It was this attitude which led Paula McGuire to write her book *It Won't Happen To Me* (1983). If a girl were to go for contraception advice it would mean she was making a conscious decision about her sexuality. Sexual activity is equated with immorality, and with illegality for an under 16 year old, bearing in mind the age of consent. Unplanned and unprotected sex, since it has not been contemplated, is therefore more moral than immoral and can be easily excused by herself and society. As one of Christopher's

(1987) informants said of her baby's conception: 'I wasn't really there'!

Girls who seek contraceptive advice are not always praised or condoned by society, their family or their peer group. The younger they are the more difficult it is for them to be responsible. Their partners also are likely to be young teenagers. The sexual relationship may be kept secret and they will be aware of the 'naughtiness' of it. Thus, when the girl gets round to taking some responsibility for herself, going for contraceptive advice frequently means she is already pregnant (Christopher, 1987). Family planning clinics are finding that they have less and less time for the essential counselling in these circumstances, since their work emphasis has changed radically from helping a young woman control her fertility to dealing with the consequences of lack of planning.

Birch (1987) found among her very young mothers that sexually active under 16s are poor contraceptive users, and that premeditated, planned sex is inexcusable (see also chapter 1). Therefore to be on the pill, or to expect your partner to use or even to have a condom, is tantamount to being a prostitute.

> I know it's a risk but what can you do? You can't say 'It's OK I'm on the pill' or 'just a minute while I put my cap in' or 'would you like a sheath, it just so happens I've got one here'. Right away he'd think 'fucking slut who's she got them for, then?'
> (Cathy, 18-year-old mother of 3-year-old boy: Birch, 1987)

The potential shame of being responsible for the rest of your life from this moment of truth (unprotected sexual intercourse) holds an irony which is hard to get across to a young adolescent. It is also hard in many cases to get it across to parents of adolescents. On the one hand, there is a mixture of pride and shame in discussing your sexual life with your peers. On the other hand, discussing your sexual life with your parents is difficult – or felt to be difficult – by teenagers. In either case little is achieved. 'My mum would kill me if she found out I was on the pill, she'd think I was easy, that I'd go with anyone' (Birch, 1987).

Girls, those who become pregnant, and typically those who keep their baby, tend to find difficulty in making and sustaining good relationships, and yet a good relationship is what they most need. Few are promiscuous; many have more than likely 'got caught' first or second time, and their relationships with their sexual partners are seldom deep. They are also very likely to have decisions made for them 'in her best interests' (see Coyne, n.d.; Sharpe, 1987; McGuire, 1983; and others).

By contrast, pregnant schoolgirls who decide themselves on a termination or who do not keep the baby once born – these girls are most likely to appreciate their schooling and to want to realise their potential in terms of education and a career (see particularly McGuire, 1983), and to have full parental support in this view. In such cases the girls have families who are truly supportive and are not so needy themselves as to deprive their daughter of her own vision of her future. Sensible and sensitive decisions can be made, bearing in mind all that is at stake and putting the adolescent and her need first. The adolescent who is fortunate enough to have the opportunity to admit her mistake within a supportive setting does not need to bear the scars of loss and guilt into her adulthood.

Those who are able and allowed to make thoughtful decisions about the future have obtained a level of confidence which enables them to have a clear idea of what they want – and of what they do not want in this case – and it goes beyond the christening party and the congratulatory relatives. Realistically they do not see a baby as part of the life they have planned. Carlotta, aged 17, who had her first abortion at 14, her second at 17, describes the school age pregnancy scene in the US as she saw it:

Everybody's doing it. Some of the girls in my high school have 2 or 3 kids. I don't know who takes care of them. Welfare, I guess. My mother's on it, and I have two sisters and three brothers already. My mother didn't want another baby.

On the first day of the month, my high school is empty. All the girls is home waiting for their checks. Maybe 40 of them in the school have got babies. There are little girls walking around pregnant, around 13 or 14 years old. I'm disgusted. They don't take care of themselves at all. They don't even wear maternity clothes but just stuff their stomachs into their jeans. I don't know what's wrong with them. We have sex education in school, but it just goes in one ear and out the other. I want to go to college. I don't want to be on welfare. (Francke, 1978)

15 year old Maggie [who tells her own story in chapter 4] suspected she was pregnant by her steady boy friend but did not

have the courage to tell her parents. When she was 4 months pregnant her father died suddenly of a heart attack, and so, just when she had geared herself up to admitting the pregnancy and going for an abortion, the family was thrown into such an emotional trauma that she felt unable to burden her mother with another problem. A month later the pregnancy showed and she told her mother. She felt it was too late for an abortion and decided to go ahead with the pregnancy and give the baby for adoption. Her mother discussed it with her and, upset as she was, left the decision to Maggie. Maggie and her less sure boy friend were given support and time by teachers, social worker and clinic personnel, and she stuck to her decision. She sat eight GCSEs just before the baby was due, had an uncomplicated birth and completed the adoption procedure. After a good summer holiday, she returned to school into the sixth form, sure that her decision was right for her.

Other plans for adoption do not fare so well, as was discussed in chapter 4. It is clear from the experience of those who work with school age mothers and their families, and from sound research (Francke, 1978; Luker, 1975; Petchesky, 1984; McGuire, 1983), that if the girl has not been able to work through her own feelings – with the support of her family – about what to do about her pregnancy, and make up her own mind in her own time, the course of action taken may be regretted, often with severely and emotionally damaging results. If the baby goes to be fostered with a view to adoption without the committed resolve of the mother and her parents' backing, she is likely to want to take it back at any time – and she may do so – possibly still with unresolved feelings. Whatever educational and other provisions have been made, the situation requires reassessment at every stage in the young mother's decision-making, since she is still a dependent in every sense. This process takes up considerable time and energy on the part of the various services involved. The confusion of mother and child may continue for many years as a result of this, to the sad disadvantage of both.

The schoolgirl who becomes a mother tends to follow a certain pattern of family background and attitudes. Many girls who, on becoming pregnant, decide to go through with the pregnancy and keep the child, themselves come from homes where decisions are often made as a result of limited judgment, and where deprivation on material, nutritional and emotional levels is prevalent, and where the father figure is either weak or absent (Birch, 1987; Miller, 1983). Thus, paradoxically, and according to our society's double standard, masculine dominance is expected and yearned for by many of these ill-equipped young women, who tend to reflect their own mothers' attitudes. And thus, too, abuse by their menfolk is often their expectation of normal behaviour: to be abused and left is what many have become used to, and it feels right. To be treated this way themselves feels comfortable because they have never known any different.

Inevitably the younger the girl the less experience she has of decision-making, the less knowledge she has, and the more she has experienced external (family) control. As has already been discussed (in chapter 2), a girl in her early teens will tend initially to deny the pregnancy and subsequently to absolve herself from all responsibility. Contradictory as it may seem, if both these factors are accompanied by conspirational parents (whether consciously or unconsciously), the girl is very likely to insist on becoming a mother.

A school age adolescent who keeps her baby has only had her own experience to go on. She has looked at the pros and cons of motherhood for herself, and tipped the balance to the side of keeping the baby. She has seen her mother (possibly herself a lone mother) doing 'all right'. She may have a poor sense of achievement so far, she may feel alienated from or unable to compete in her peer group, she may feel a lack of stability and affection in her world. Having and keeping a baby brings her a status beyond any previous experience. The fact that the status is short-lived is of little consequence to one who has had little practice at planning for the future and who looks no further than her immediate family for financial, physical and emotional support.

Fourteen year old Lesley in an English city lived happily and cosily with her divorced mother. They did everything together, from going out to clubs to having baths. Until, that is, another man came into her mother's life, and Lesley was suddenly excluded. The rejection can be imagined. Lesley became pregnant 6 weeks after her mother did. Estranged from her mother, once the baby was born, she went to live with the mother and step-father of her boy friend in their one bedroom council flat (her boy friend lived elsewhere with his father and step-mother). Lesley slept on the settee while her baby slept in the pram. This arrangement could not last long and tensions all round led to Lesley moving into bed & breakfast accommodation, at the authority's expense, while waiting for a council flat – she was still under school leaving age at this time and was entered for several public exams at the local Unit. She was badly treated by her [alcoholic] boy friend, there was no communication from her mother, and any relationship there had been with the boy friend's parents had long since broken down. The council eventually found her a flat on the outskirts of the city where her emotional state and her living conditions went from bad to worse.

The care of her child was of great concern to the Unit staff and the rota of social workers and health visitors involved, but, as in many similar cases, neglect of the child was not quite sufficient for her six month old daughter to be considered officially 'at risk'. Lesley was an intelligent girl who had had high standards and of whom high expectations had been entertained at her school. It was generally felt she would eventually emerge from this wild phase. Had something been done sooner, her child might not have had such a long period of relative neglect. On the other hand, everything that could be done at the time was done, bearing in mind poorly resourced services and the individual circumstances.

Lesley's exam results were disappointing, and for over a year after she left the Unit she was flitting with her infant from one squat to another. The latest news was that she and her child had settled with her new boy friend and they were trying for another baby, but that her child's father had beaten her up so badly and her insides were in such a mess that it was unlikely she would conceive. . . , so Lesley said.

Very young mothers often come from a family background where early childbearing is an established feature. Miller (1983) and Birch (1987) found that many young adolescent mothers belong to families where mothers were young and sisters also were pregnant or had babies. Two-thirds of South London pregnant schoolgirls had a close family member who had also been a pregnant teenager and 35 per cent of their mothers had been through the same experience. This finding is borne out by the authors' experience. Many 15 year olds and younger at the Bristol Unit had sisters who were also either pregnant or already a mother. In one single mother's family of four girls, three had babies, two of whom attended the Unit over two consecutive years. With careful planning, the youngest daughter may be saved from motherhood so young. In another mother-headed family of three daughters, two were already mothers and the youngest at age 15 was pregnant.

It also means that very young mothers often do not stop at one child. One in five of Miller's sample had had a second pregnancy by the time of their follow-up interview. A midwife, working in a newly established Young People's Club at a hospital in the north of England, found that in the first six months of 1987 the maternity department saw four 16 year olds who were in their second or third pregnancy (Jowett, 1988).

Health risks to very young mothers

Russell (1981, 1982) has carried out an extremely thorough survey into the health of very young mothers. Russell was involved in the care of 267 pregnant schoolgirls in Newcastle-on-Tyne between 1960 and 1974, as well as 317 pregnant unmarried older teenagers. He kept in touch with many of them over a number of years, including the great majority of those who stayed in the Newcastle area.

The younger pregnant teenagers were twice as likely as older ones to have their first antenatal consultation *after* the twelfth week of pregnancy. Other research (Simms and Smith, 1986; Birch, 1987) confirms this picture of late consultations. As a result, more of Russell's samples who had therapeutic abortions did so by prostaglandin, and many more suffered immediate complications (Russell, 1982). Among those who went on to have their babies, more of the younger teenagers gave birth to low birthweight babies, often following premature onset of labour. Such a situation is likely to increase the necessity to involve care in special baby units.

American research confirms this bleak picture of health among young teenage mothers, who have higher rates of pregnancy complications including toxemia, anaemia, prolonged labour and premature labour; maternal death; and giving birth to low birthweight babies. Poor and black teenagers suffer from these disadvantages more than middle-class and white teenagers. Younger teenagers still do worse than older ones when the effects of race and income are discounted (Hayes, 1987, pp. 124–5). Frequent health checks and recurrent illnesses marked the early life of infants of Miller's (1983) sample.

Some specific medical problems are more likely to affect very young mothers. One is pre-eclamptic toxemia, which has been reported worldwide (Russell, 1982). Another is anaemia, iron deficiency. The diet of many pregnant girls of school age is poor (Birch, 1987). During the teenage years children have a growth spurt for which they require a nourishing and balanced diet. Diet affects every aspect of the teenager's life, including her attitudes and behaviour, as well as her physical development. Calcium is another important mineral in pregnancy, for its deficiency in the diet means that, while the foetus takes all it needs, the mother may well not be getting enough. This deficiency will affect her later.

A 12–16 year old who becomes pregnant, and then a mother, undergoes a rapid, confusing and frightening period of hormonal changes while still expected to continue her schooling, and – perhaps more importantly – feeling in many ways like a child still. Her physical development may not be complete. The physiological and emotional manifestations of the pregnancy in an already confused, rebellious and volatile teenager – or possibly a passive, sullen, unresponsive one – require respect, and firm, careful handling.

Many girls in their early teens take pregnancy in their stride, undergo a normal birth and assume motherhood in a fairly calm if slightly bewildered manner. Many others, however, do not. Both sorts of mother need help in different ways. The calmness of the first often belies the ignorance and inexpertise of their coping, while the childish, demanding behaviour of the second tells us how young they are and how desperate the situation is.

Sue, a British girl aged 13, pregnant and in the care of local authority, had decided to keep the baby by her 18 year old boy friend. Yet she seemed to have no sense of her baby's needs, nor any responsibility for herself. She was hardly ever in the children's home, she went missing for days, returning starving, wet, bedraggled and exhausted. Next day she was off again. The only commitment she would make was to keep the specialist's appointments once or twice. There was naturally great concern for this child's health and for the health of her baby. When last heard of Sue had been missing from the home for four days, having left one morning early with packed suitcases.

This may sound like an extreme case. But such a situation is not uncommon. A young adolescent like Sue, out of control of her divorced mother, playing mother and remarried father one off against the other, breaking the law in many little ways, determined not to go to school and deliberately trying to get pregnant since the age of 12, clearly has a lot to be angry about. Pregnancy seems the answer when everything has gone wrong. Sue certainly thought that when her baby was born her mother would have her back at home. That her mother was adamant this time that this would not happen had absolutely no effect on Sue at all. She needed to know that, in spite of all the dreadful things she had done, her mother would forgive her at last.

Meanwhile Sue lived in a fantasy world, taking no care of herself at all, and having very little idea of what her pregnancy entailed, let alone motherhood. Many very young pregnant teenagers live in similar limbo, inarticulately frightened at the prospect of the birth but unwilling to seek help or to think positively. It is often extremely difficult to help girls in this situation to minimise the health risks of their pregnancy and birth, and to support them in their untimely motherhood.

Legal and financial confusion

The legal situation of the school age mother is a very grey area: the law relating to the age of consent; the legal battles over contraception and parents' consent in Britain and the US; the confused issue of whether or not to prosecute a prospective father for having had unlawful sexual intercourse with a girl under 16; the girl's right to choose the outcome of her pregnancy; the social and/or family pressure to keep the baby; and the not uncommon second pregnancy after being pressurised against her will for the termination of her first. All these facts, and more, are confusing for young people as well as for their parents, and indeed for lawyers. The confusion continues into the life of the young mother and her child.

The school age mother is a contradiction in terms. She considers herself essentially a child still – she is, for the most part, aged 15 or under – and yet she is expected to be responsible for, and expects herself to be responsible for, a baby. She is unlikely to think of her commitment in terms of a future 'child'. Our society's expectations of these two conflicting states are quite opposite, and yet, in the case of the school age mother, they must exist together. School age mothers put themselves into an anomalous category from almost every societal point of view. Legally too young to have sexual intercourse, they are nevertheless allowed the freedom to choose the fate of the foetus created.

Legally, economically and for the most part emotionally dependent on parents, in Britain teenage mothers under 16 are eligible now to claim free milk tokens and free dental care only, and child benefit when the baby is born, regardless of the economic status of their own parents, whether they are on Income Support or Family Credit; only on their 16th birthday may they claim income support in their own right, even though they may still be living at home. From July 1982 the maternity grant was made available to mothers of all ages – previously it was only available to 16 year olds and over – but from April 1987 this grant was again not available until their 16th birthday and then only if their parents were themselves on benefit. In 1990 the grant become £100, with no extra payments to be made. Loans from social services are available, but are of little use to a new mother who has no means of her own and no opportunity or experience of saving.

In the US, standards differ from state to state about when a teenager can start receiving public assistance, but, as in Britain, their eligibility depends on the economic situation of their parents. In New York state, for example, provided her parents are on welfare, a teenage mother can start claiming AFDC (Aid to Families with Dependent Children), food stamps and Medicaid (free medical attention) during her fourth month of pregnancy – whatever her age. She is eligible for public housing in her own right at age 16 (McGee, 1982; Levitan, 1985).

Very young mothers often find home life overcrowded and intolerably conflict-ridden, a situation they have unwittingly worsened by their pregnancy. There is no alternative home for them unless other family members have room for them. This is unlikely, given the characteristics of a 'typical' pregnant under 16 year old. Voluntary care proceedings may offer an alternative home, but this is a drastic step and only taken in a time of crisis.

Although legally still obliged to attend school, or at least to receive education until school-leaving age, not all are able to benefit in this way. As awareness of the problem grows, there is currently considerable expansion of special educational provision for pregnant schoolgirls and schoolgirl mothers in Britain. There is no law requiring that schools retain pregnant or parenting pupils, unless, that is, the parents of such pupils wish it. Such a wish is rare. The numbers and proportions are greater in the US, and although the law requires no discrimination against pregnant and parenting pupils continuing to attend the local school, alternative courses and sites are often made available for this particular category of student.

The financial situation of school age mothers varies according to the status of their families, their age and the birth of the child in relation to the mother's age. Of Miller's young mothers of 15 and under (1983):

> 60% were receiving financial support from the government, predominantly AFDC, within several months of giving birth to their first babies. The proportion had risen to 85% a little more than a year later [when the mothers' mean age was 15.1 years]. About half of these respondents had relied on their parents' income at both times. These young mothers were more likely than older mothers ... to be receiving public assistance at 18 months postpartum.

It remains questionable whether reliance on the state so young may be called self-sufficiency. Mothers under 16 in Britain were only recently eligible for the single parent benefit and child benefit, since the changes in maternity and other benefits in April 1987. For the second year running (1989), the government saw fit to 'freeze' the amount of child benefit, so that its value became completely out of step with recent escalating inflation. Adolescent mothers still at school are therefore more dependent than ever on their parents for financial help. This illustrates the 'Child with a Child' paradox. Some families can and do support; others do not.

The double standard continues. Legally the under-16 mother is a child. Actually, whatever else she is, she is a parent, in receipt of child benefit in her own right while her mother continues to receive child benefit for her. Although she has given birth to her child, she is not entitled to the maternity grant – at a time when cash is crucial – until her 16th birthday. If she gives birth at age 12 or 13 she will never receive this 'maternity' payment. Her parents may claim for her, but only if they themselves are claiming benefit, either Income Support or Family Credit.

Some may argue that, since she is still a child, the parents of the under-16-year-old parent are and should show themselves to be responsible for her, are in part responsible for her behaviour and the outcomes of that behaviour. Some parents do respond in this way and manage to absorb the daughter's pregnancy and mother-hood into the life of the family with little agency involvement. However, the chances are that the family is in need of help and support on several fronts, and last straws like a daughter's pregnancy are just another difficulty to be taken on. As Birch (1987) points out with great clarity, the young adolescent who gets pregnant very often has sisters in the same position, a mother who was also pregnant very young, poor home conditions and low economic status. Families headed by a mother with all this against her are already in a poor position to monitor behaviour and to cope adequately with a daughter's pregnancy.

For a variety of reasons, living at home can prove problematic for young mothers and their children. In Britain an increasing proportion of pregnant schoolgirls are taken into care each year due to intolerable family circumstances. Girls under 16 are not eligible to apply for local authority accommodation; they may, however, find themselves in bed and breakfast accommodation at public expense if home life has proved impossible for whatever reason; when the baby is due they may have the opportunity to stay in a Mother and Baby Home for a short period, though this sort of accommodation is less and less available in Britain and the US, as the social stigma of unmarried pregnancy and motherhood wanes. Just-16-year-old mothers may find themselves in severely inadequate bed and breakfast accommodation with their babies, lonely and isolated, on their way to substandard housing in a run-down area often on the edge of town with all the related problems that invariably ensue from such a move. For a young single mother on welfare benefits the prospect is bleak indeed (see Lesley above).

It has been argued that school age mothers should have proper legal and therefore social status, with more financial assistance as single mothers. The counter argument is the fact that they are blatantly too young to take on the responsibility of motherhood, since they are both emotionally and physically immature. They may themselves be aware of the grotesqueness of their situation. As one put it to the authors: 'Well, it's children having children, ennit?'

The education of very young mothers

That the education of a pregnant or parenting teenager of school age has to continue may seem obvious. But it is problematical. At the basic level there are side-issues like morning sickness and clinic attendance. Then there is the whole question of tiredness during the third trimester of pregnancy. And then there is child care after the birth. Beyond this there is the moral issue: should we be separating this category, thereby giving them 'special' treatment, or should we insist that they continue their education with their childless peers?

In 1979 the Miles report on pregnant and parenting schoolgirls in England and Wales recommended that these very young women should be encouraged to remain in school as long as possible, and to return to school after the birth. Despite this recommendation made over ten years ago, it is still not general policy. Each education authority handles the problem differently; indeed, a few appear not to address the problem at all. However, all children up to or a little beyond their sixteenth birthday are obliged to receive education. Thus provision must be made for all categories who are unable, for whatever reason, to attend school for any period of time. When they leave at 16, all children should have had the chance to obtain some meaningful qualifications.

In the US the picture is similar. However, although legally a girl may leave school during the year of her 16th birthday, she would do so with no qualifications. There is now considerable pressure put on pregnant schoolgirls and school age mothers to remain in or return to high school in order to get their diploma at 17/18. Without it they have very few chances of employment. The financial hardship and all the aspects of poverty that this brings with it has brought the problem of teen motherhood in the US to the forefront of social policy in many states most recently. Schemes are being set up in many states to support these adolescent mothers in a desperate attempt to improve the educational attainment of the mother and the future chances of the child. These will be further discussed, in chapter 8.

Along with other categories of disaffected school children, many school age mothers and mothers-to-be manage to avoid their last months and sometimes years of schooling, due to many factors. These include difficulties in parental control and the overloaded education welfare teams.

There is evidence that girls who become young teenage mothers have long-standing difficulties with education. Wilson (1980) found in Aberdeen that they were academic underachievers, performing less well in arithmetic and English at age 11 than their measured intelligence would suggest. In her sample in Camberwell, London, Birch (1987) found that a considerable proportion of mothers aged 16 and under were considered by their teachers to be below average ability, felt themselves to be failures and had truanted regularly from school. Half of them had been visited by Education Welfare. More significantly, one-third had already been to child guidance, 12 per cent were attending special schools and 45 per cent were illiterate. Having a baby felt like the only thing they could do right. Their mothers had probably behaved similarly. Their children were likely to fare just as poorly. Society and the education authorities have been slow in accepting that teenage pregnancy is a problem for educators, but with the growth of new education schemes now well under way there is greater hope for young mothers completing their education. In the US as in Britain policy and provision vary from state to state and from authority to authority, for the problem of school age motherhood is not yet sufficiently recognised for there to be a consistent overall campaign for provision or prevention. In the US, where the legal requirement is the same as in Britain, no discrimination is allowed against pregnant and parenting school students. And while support and advice centres are beginning to be set up for teenage parents of both sexes across the US, in Britain concentration is still on the younger teenage mother, and here the emphasis is almost wholly on those aged 16 and under. This is undoubtedly due to the examination system whereby children can leave at 16 with GCSEs and go on to training. There are, however, a few enterprising exceptions, where education provision for the under 16 mothers extends to A level opportunities up to age 18 (see the final section of chapter 3 and chapter 8).

Home tuition seems to be the form of education most favoured by education authorities in Britain, although in some urban areas special centres have been set up to cater for schoolgirl mothers, and a number of these have creche facilities. While education authorities are legally obliged to provide education for all under school leaving age, schoolgirl mothers represent such a comparatively small number (on average, one girl in 50) that authorities are understandably reluctant to spend public money on a category of girls who, after all, according to many, should not exist in the first place.

Educational provision for these girls variously offers basic curriculum subjects to exam level, life skills, parenting skills and sensitively structured education in relationships of all kinds, including sex and birth control. It has been commented that, as they are mothers already, it is too late for sex education. But in fact their knowledge is extremely limited, and with education and support they may make the choice not to go on to have more babies until their circumstances are more stable.

Whatever education is offered to school age mothers in Britain, it is in many areas insufficient in quantity and limited in quality. This paucity of provision has to cater for students with generally a poor self-image and a fairly fatalistic attitude towards themselves and their futures. But, however poorly resourced the service offered, it is agreed that those who have the good fortune to attend one of the special centres or to receive home tuition from specialist teachers may leave education not only with a few qualifications and their baby, but also with social and personal skills beyond their expectations. However, they leave, aged 16, to embark on the adult world, where all the social, financial and housing problems discussed earlier become a greater reality, now that the support of whatever full-time education they received has been removed.

At this stage for most British 16 year olds the prospects and choices are many. Government training schemes are in theory available to all school leavers at 16, for none is eligible for income support for two years. For the young mother, however, almost all channels are blocked. If she wants to continue to study or take a job or opt for training under a government scheme – compulsory now for all school leavers without children, but deferable in special cases – she needs a child minder. She cannot pay for one, since her financial position is, with benefits, precarious. Sponsored child minding is available only for those considered most in need, for children considered most severely at risk, and like every other publicly-funded service, budgets are being cut annually as the need increases. Young adolescent mothers are not at the top of the priority list.

In the US, since the mid 1970s, mandatory equal rights for pregnant and parenting students have meant a growing provision of special school programmes, most of which are state funded and in local school settings. Some are funded and housed by social services. Many of these programmes provide general as well as specialist education. Some provide child-oriented programmes only. As in the UK there is discussion as to whether a pregnant or parenting teenager should remain in her regular school or attend a separate and specialised centre. While such deliberations continue, without a nationwide policy or a source of funds, these young people are insufficiently catered for in the nation as a whole. However, as Miller points out, where these programmes do exist, their design 'depends largely on the views of the prime mover in the community for such activities, and the school superintendent'.

More than half of her sample of mothers under 16 had attended special school programmes for pregnant adolescents and young mothers both before and after their baby's birth – another indication of no overall policy. The mean number of months before delivery was 4; after delivery was 1.2. It appears that many young mothers returned to their regular school and that alternative child care arrangements were made. It was not clear how these were funded, a crucial factor. Miller's sample included mothers from three sites: Chicago, where 96 per cent of the respondents attended special programmes, Cleveland, where 83 per cent attended and Minneapolis/St Paul, where only 43 per cent benefited from this provision.

Miller (1983) sums up the general feeling about special educational provision for young parenting teens:

> The positive program attributes cited by those using them were the chance to make up educational credits, being with others who were also pregnant or rearing young children, and the convenience of obtaining a variety of services at the same location. There were few complaints except for not being with regular classmates.

Dawson (1987) found similar responses to special provision at centres in England and Wales. Where such a centre includes care for the babies, the impact on the infants of these mothers is great and can only be beneficial. She found that the mothers experienced similar disadvantages, similar social and financial hardship, and that the emotional poverty which discretely and inextricably impinges on the mothers also affects their children. The cycle continues if it is not given a chance to break – even a tiny bit. Thus care for mothers and babies during the mothers' final year(s) of education is seen to be worthwhile. Children who attend special centres for parenting school age adolescents develop well and benefit from the care of professionals as well as a good sleeping and feeding routine.

Without further training and child minding schemes, very young mothers may decide that having more babies is an easy enough answer to their immediate needs. In the main these are those students who were switched off school anyway and did not have high aspirations for their lives. Others who are more motivated may be encouraged and cajoled into work experience and training and possibly college courses. Current government thinking suggests the idea that the best place for these young mothers is at home with their tiny and vulnerable offspring, or that, if they must seek employment or further education, then the responsibility for child care rests entirely with the family. What is not understood is that firstly, good alternative child care for a very young mother can only be beneficial to both child and mother; secondly, the parents and other relations of 16-year-old mothers may be unable or unwilling to offer child care that is both consistent and reliable.

The benefits of child care by someone other than the young mother for at least part of every day will be discussed in chapter 6.

Specifically for these very young mothers, Miller found that 86 per cent of her sample had their child cared for for some part of each day. It must be taken into account that her sample emerged as 67 per cent of those invited to take part in her study, and it is likely that those who did not want to be part of her study were less inclined to seek out resources generally. The majority of her respondents' babies were cared for for 5 to 8 hours daily, and in many cases by their maternal grandmothers. This figure is much higher than found in other studies, but is no doubt attributable to their younger age, their dependence on their parents and the requirement to attend school.

Given that the US education system means a diploma at 18, the pressure to remain in some kind of schooling or to return to high school to complete the courses is high. Students in special programmes are well motivated (McGuire, 1983), but they cannot always find work when they need to, on qualifying (McGee, 1982).

The problem is the same in Britain. Weighing up the pros and cons of working for a minimal wage which is the same as their income support, or staying at home – without the effort of getting to work every day plus the child care arrangements – one can understand why a young mother of 16 might be reluctant to bother. In spite of this, many centres designed for young parents go out of their way to provide career guidance, work experience and as much support as the students will accept. Very often it is the world of work which puts these young people off, for the system as a whole is not yet fully formed, and training schemes are not perceived as satisfying their needs. Staff working on teen-parent programmes noticed how motivation increased among young parents with increased self-confidence (McGee, 1982). Such programmes would provide both educational goals and vocational assistance, as well as personal support to mothers and (in some cases) fathers. But with all the training, preparation and enthusiasm possible, there is no future for them in the world of work unless they are first of all able to leave their child reliably and regularly. And secondly, granted that the best place to learn about work is the workplace, that workplace must offer them something more than a humdrum filler for minimum wages. These young potential workers should not be discouraged by their first experience.

Chapter 6

The World of the Teenage Mother and her Child

As the children of teenage mothers pass through infancy and into early childhood, they and their parents are exposed in a new way to forces and influences from which they were hitherto protected. The relative disadvantages during teenage motherhood produce an over-representation of social problems in the lives of young mothers and their children, which are discussed in this chapter. AIDS is a new and particularly dangerous threat. However, despite this gloomy picture, many young mothers create happy and loving family lives.

Family support

It is important to remember that teenage mothers are daughters too, and many of them are likely to be still living in their parental home. They may be surrounded by one or two nephews and nieces as well as brothers and sisters, with single mother/grandmother at the head of the family. The home can become a cocoon, a warm and safe haven where all share in the care of the babies. Young mothers receiving all-embracing support of this nature may find it difficult to establish their independence when they need to leave the overcrowded nest. Another variant is the adolescent daughter and her baby in a family headed by the grandparents. As a young mother herself, she will have altered the focus of attention in the family as a whole.

Furstenberg (1980) discusses the impact on families when a teenage daughter becomes pregnant and some of the changes that occur in the family as a daughter becomes a mother. The baby's arrival may be seen as a unifying force, or as the replacement of a lost family member. Unplanned pregnancies are not uncommon following a funeral, for example, nor are they uncommon in situations where father has left and not been replaced; or even, over a period of time, when a stepfather has taken his place. The status of the young mother-to-be often rises within the family, in some cases changing from scapegoat to favoured child. When this occurs the youngest sibling may lose his/her favoured place and sooner or later become a problem in his/her own right. Meanwhile the baby receives all the fuss and attention, and although the teenage daughter may feel put in the shade, she has pride in her new status and is respected for this within the family. This support is very important for her.

In some cases the extended family assumes a paramount role in enabling young mothers to cope successfully with early parenthood. Grandmothers (usually the maternal ones) are often a source of alternative care, advice and support. Birch (1987) and McGuire (1983) both found evidence of this among their teenage mothers. In her study of US mothers aged under 16 Miller (1983) found that two infants in three were cared for by someone other than their mother for five or more hours each day during their first 18 months. This figure is slightly higher than is found in other studies of adolescent mothers, but is explained partly by their extreme youth, their need for continued education, as well as dependence on their parents, with whom they were for the most part living.

At a regional public hearing of The Task Force on Adolescent Pregnancy in Trenton, New Jersey, in October 1987, many of the young mothers attending spoke realistically and movingly of the conflicts faced by a teenage mother today. One of the more fortunate young mothers described her daily life: 'I go to school, go home, take care of my son and go to bed. That's it' (Johnson and Ziskin, 1988). This young woman had a support system to help her manage her dual role. She lived at home, had access to reliable child care, she was able to continue at school, and in spite of the constraints, she had encouragement to glimpse the future and to plan for it. Positive support by her relatives means that the teenage mother can continue her education, improve her job prospects and get better care for her child.

Unfortunately, not all teenage mothers receive support from their family. Many have a very difficult time. For a number of reasons they may be excluded from home. Those who end up in hotel accommodation at the state's expense while awaiting public housing – especially if they are still under school leaving age – are particularly vulnerable.

> Fiona, aged 17, had no family who would recognise her, let alone care for her. She had no home. Her new born baby had no father who would recognise him. They were classified as 'homeless' and, although theoretically Fiona was 'in care', her social worker was helpless against the ruling bureaucracy. They lived in bed and breakfast where Fiona was unable to boil a kettle to make the baby's bottle without it being made abundantly clear that she was a nuisance. She had nothing to do all day. She could not handle her meagre income support benefit economically.

There are many Fionas in Britain and the United States. This particular Fiona eventually got her own independent accommodation in the form of a flat on the edge of town.

Janet, aged 14, whose family could not cope with her volatile nature, was shunted from one divorced parent to the other according to the tolerance threshold of each.

> I don't know what to do – where to go – who to live with. They don't neither of them want me. I knows that. But my baby won't know where home is. He won't know whether he's coming or going.

Neglect and lack of any affection helped neither her nor her child to adapt to changing circumstances. Feeling unloved prevented her from giving lovingly to her child. Since she herself was treated inconsistently, she found it impossible to be consistent with her child. Within this vicious circle of unhappiness she was unlikely to function well in any capacity.

Many adolescents are headstrong, and parents may be forgiven if they find it hard to support a pregnant or parenting daughter. On the other hand, there is no doubt that support is vital for a mother still in her teens, and if it comes from her own family it is worth a great deal more than from elsewhere. McGuire (1983) gives examples of two kinds of family support: the extended family and the mother who asserts her independence.

Inez's support were her aunt and uncle. Her mother had tricked her about the unavailability of further pills because she wanted Inez to get pregnant as she herself had done, with Inez, at age 13. Inez was very resentful when she found out her mother's deliberate lie, and went to live with her aunt and uncle to have and keep her baby.

Billie's mother's responsibilities were over; she made that quite clear. Billie could have the baby but there was absolutely no way her mother would help her in any way. She had her own life to lead. She had done all the child rearing she intended to do.

This may sound unsupportive, but it was clear and it was strong. Many parents are less able to be clear and strong enough about what they will and will not accept. Lack of clarity is not helpful to teenagers who have got themselves in a mess. But it is often those teenagers whose parents are themselves confused. When this is the case, help and support must be sought from a different source; if the extended family cannot provide this, an outside resource agency such as social services must be approached.

Adolescent women who decide to bear and raise a child risk never growing up properly. This was discussed in chapter 2. But with support, such parents may find the motivation and the means to organise and stabilise their lives, and to finish the practical and emotional business of growing up, while at the same time taking on and carrying out responsibly the parenting role. These young parents are lucky if such support derives from their own families.

A majority of families with young parenting teenage daughters are themselves in receipt of welfare benefits. In such families, economically speaking, another mouth to feed and body to keep clean and healthy may be a considerable added burden on family resources.

How involved are the fathers?

Not all fathers to babies of teenage girls are themselves teenagers, but many are. In Britain in 1980 one-fifth of all legitimate births to teenage women had teenage fathers, and three-fifths had fathers aged between 20 and 24. Much less is known about the fathers of illegitimate babies, and we have to rely on information from individual surveys. Many are themselves young (Sharpe, 1987; Christopher, 1987) and a large proportion play little part in their child's life. Their own families play even less. Miller (1983) found among very young teenage mothers that, when asked who, if anyone, looked after the baby apart from the mother, only 2 per cent said they used the baby's father or his family for this purpose.

Miller also found that, even though the baby's father had probably known the mother for up to a year before the birth, his attentions became less and less after the event. He provided the odd necessity, such as nappies and money, but infrequently and inconsistently. Most significantly, the extent of support he did provide came nowhere near the expectations of the mother.

As might be expected, fathers' involvement increases with their age and maturity. Nevertheless, whatever the father's age and whatever the likelihood of the couple staying together, the evidence from research, and from programmes designed to support partners of pregnant and parenting adolescent women, suggests that involvement at the time of pregnancy and birth – and into the infant's early months and years – is vitally important. The father's involvement over this period strongly influences the emotional stability of both mother and child (Elster and Penzarine, 1979).

In the Bristol sample (Ineichen, 1986), of the 35 fathers who were neither married nor cohabiting at the time of the hospital booking interview, 16 had gone from their pregnant partner's life by the time she gave birth. Many fathers were not ready for parenthood when it arrived, still less were they ready for a full-time relationship. The younger the father, the less ready he was, especially when the pregnancy was not planned, and if the relationship had not focused seriously on 'settling down'. The different gender perspectives on relationships have been discussed earlier, in chapter 2; the teenage girl may be more ready and willing than the boy to embark on and to keep the relationship, yet it is likely that neither is able to engage in dialogue to make 'informed choices' together.

The general feeling amongst the girls in McGuire's study (1983) was that boys run away from responsibility. Susan, who at the age of 19 felt 'stupid' to have got pregnant, spoke for the majority of girls in her position: she was devastated when the father turned out to be unsupportive; he kept putting off making decisions; 'Boys are unrealistic', 'ignorant' and 'make assumptions'; President Reagan was changing the laws for the worse in that financial help was negligible; Medicaid was only available to those earning less than 100 dollars a week.

But how do people expect teenage fathers to behave? What would Susan have liked? Did she know? Did she ask him? There is very little support for a father such as Susan's partner. He may not be able to express his feelings, he may panic about his responsibilities, he may not be able to offer any financial assistance, even if he has been bound by the court to pay minimal maintenance. Often he is rejected by the girl and her family. He may be unable to acknowledge his responsibility in the pregnancy and subsequent son or daughter; and sadly he may not be able to express his pride either. If these feelings are not recognised by someone with whom he can express them in a useful and relevant way, his sense of rejection and loss may encourage him to prove his manhood again – elsewhere. This is the same logical sequence as for the girl who is forced into decisions against her will – an abortion, for instance – and who gets pregnant again.

Some fathers are initially delighted at the prospect of a baby, but totally unprepared for the reality, and unable to cope with the responsibility. Such young men have not matured and are still at the self-centred age when they expect to come and go as they please. They are not so much rejected by their girl friends, rather they are perhaps scared off by the strength of their love, their need, their dependence. Young couples in this sad situation need much support and counselling; yet they are not likely to obtain it. Young fathers may have had only a passing emotional involvement in the relationship. Whatever the nature of the emotional commitment between girl and boy, the fact of pregnancy alters the balance of the relationship. Adolescent mothers have invested considerably more in the relationship (see chapter 2) than have the fathers. Thus, with sadness and, for some, bitterness, they may accept their lot and sacrifice their youth, while teenage fathers are not ready to give up their 'freedom'. As one such young man put it, he was not prepared to forego all the girl friends he might go out with (Sharpe, 1987).

A teenage boy is seldom used to recognising his feelings, let alone sharing them with others, and although he may feel genuine affection for his girl, it is likely that he finds discussing the situation both embarrassing and emasculating. If she is under 16, he may even deny paternity out of panic and fear at legal consequences. He may fear financial responsibilities. The 'indifferent' stance – or the bravado – he may be demonstrating publicly may very well belie his private sadness and loss in a situation which has suddenly become too complicated for him to cope with. Whatever age he is, he may be viewed with hostility by the girl's parents, especially if he is not working and has no real means of paying maintenance in any amount worth claiming. Maintenance in this context equals punishment, and anyone in his position would want to avoid punishment. In any event, the likelihood is that he will find himself in a dilemma and with little means of dealing with it.

Julie, aged 15, concealed her pregnancy until it was spotted at 9 months during a hospital appointment for ear treatment. She was rushed to Maternity, where she had two fits. She and her baby son survived, against most expectations, and so did her parents after the shock. No one had noticed her pregnancy. She had split up with Tony, but when he knew about the baby they got back together again. The relationship had its ups and downs until she sent him packing as he was, she said, 'sleeping around' and 'that wasn't right'. He and his family began to make a fuss about visiting rights, and probation officers were involved. Times and venues of visits were arranged, some of the aggravation vanished, and, as she was rather bored, she accepted his advances again. Yet neither of them are at all sure of what they want in the long run. Julie was then afraid she had caught VD. Tony seemed to be out for what he could get. Neither of them had really talked things through.

Support agencies often leave youthful fathers out of the picture. Julie needed continued support to remember that she could control her own life. Tony was so lost in his peer-boosted, macho gender role, he seemed incapable of caring for or considering anyone else. Both Julie and Tony were in a state of irresolution, and the baby was between them. Julie was given support from the moment her pregnancy was discovered until she left the Bristol

Unit with her 9-month-old son. Tony, on the other hand, having just left school at 16, was denied three important things. Firstly, getting any help himself; secondly, sharing in the decisions about his son; and thirdly, the chance himself to give support and affection to his girl friend and their child. He may not have wanted to provide support, but, had he been given the chance, it seems likely that the relationship (or non-relationship) might have been clearer and caused less suffering for everyone concerned.

Men, as well as women, feel trapped by circumstances. Christopher (1987) reminds us that, although the young man is often considered the villain when a girl gets pregnant, it may well be that he was deliberately made use of by the girl to this end. It is not difficult to see how responsibility can be passed back and forth in such a situation, with little chance of resolution. Boys, like girls, can also fear failure. One way of being a peer success for a girl is to have a baby; and for a boy, to have 'had it off' with as many girls as he can boast of, and, for some, to father a child. Tony, mentioned above, was reported to have said to Julie: 'I bet my mates I'll be a father by the summer.' Julie claims in solemn retrospect that he wouldn't have minded who had his baby: 'even my mum'.

The horror of the consequences of their lack of responsibility is not realised by either sex. The girl has been irretrievably trapped into making decisions. The boy can escape and often does. In this case mother, child and father miss out on much needed affection and support.

Louise, a 16-year-old mother of a 10 month old, unsure about her relationship with the baby's father, having fluctuated between great plans for settling down with him and dismissing him entirely in favour of other young men, decided at last to spend a week with him and their child in a caravan by the sea. On her return she commented:

> I never let him have the baby. He wouldn't know what to do. He never knew the half of it – changing, washing, sleepless nights, the crying – you know, all them things you takes for granted. . . . Till we went down Sandbeach together. Then he realised how hard it is with a baby. Till then he never knew. To think I been through all this. An' it's his baby too!

Despite this, the couple married 15 months later.

In Virginia, recently moved after a 5-year wait to a public housing estate on the edge of Washington DC, a 42-year-old, hard-working and devoted black grandmother of five talked of her circumstances. Three of Evelyn's six sons fathered children in their teens. Only one of them, the eldest, was still with the mother of his two at the time Evelyn told her story. The other two teenage fathers stood proudly by their girl friends until the child began to walk, and then they simply got tired of it. Neither was able to sustain any sort of commitment.

Delroy's girl friend, Lilly, took another boy friend after he'd left her, which gave Delroy the excuse not to go back. Since he got picked up on a drugs charge, went to jail and then on to a community programme, Lilly has moved from one unsuitable home to another. Twice when made homeless she dumped the children (the second child by the second man, who also left her) on Evelyn for periods of weeks, expecting her to feed and clothe them – which she did. 'What else could I do?'

Andrew's girl friend, Rosie, was more responsible and remained with her parents. She openly grieved for the lost relationship and talked things over with Evelyn. She used Evelyn as a comforter but not as a dumping ground. Evelyn said of her sons:

> They're so selfish. But that's men for you. I don't know why they all grow up that way. They just don't seem to think about other people or about the future. My home now – I waited so-o-o long for this home, I got it with three bedrooms, one for me and one for each of my two youngest sons. But they all come in – in and out – all six of them – whenever they please. It's not really my home, after all, however much I looked forward to my real own place. And when Lilly asks to leave the children with me – well, what would you do? I lo-ove children. Once they're in this world, you just gotta look after them. How can I say no? . . . Sometime I get mad – really ma-ad – and I think they all get scared then. But I love them all. And I sure done my best.

Evelyn had indeed not shirked anything. Abandoned by her first husband after three sons, she formed one relationship after another, ending up a single mother with six much loved boys who wanted for nothing, within her means. Evelyn had never been without employment, sometimes doing two or three jobs in order to make ends meet – and getting into trouble when she was on benefits as well, so she had to work harder to pay off the 2000 dollars fine. She had had more than her fair share of illness, too, in and out of hospital, with complex financial problems as a result and a continuing morbid interest in ill-health.

Yeah, Delroy and Andrew, they're irresponsible, they should have stuck by their girls and babies. I dunno what it is, they're all the same nowadays – my husband was the same, too – none of them use their brains no more.

I think they learnt their lesson now. I don't think they will get a girl caught again. I told them. I talked to them. I tried to make them see reason. I told them to be careful. . . . What do I tell them exactly? Sure, I told them not to put it there no more! But who knows if they listen to their mother?

Evelyn was caught in the female gender trap: sacrifice. Caring was her role, always had been, always would be, in spite of her attempts at rationalisation and justifiable selfishness. She would admit that she always seemed to allow men to abuse her generosity and, one suspects, had not been able to provide clear models for her sons regarding responsible parenthood for themselves. Nor did she know an effective way of teaching them about birth control. She was specifically asked how she thought, by talking to them, they could be brought to change their ways and become sexually responsible. Her answer was: by telling them 'not to put it there no more'. Since her sons always knew that she would not let her grandchildren suffer, they and her badly coping 'daughter-in-law' would not be able to learn independence until she herself learnt to 'let go'. So long as she continued to pick up the pieces and forgive everyone (after a spell of shouting), the family processes were unlikely to change, and her sons would learn neither to accept responsibility for their own actions and mistakes, nor to recognise female independence and freedom of choice.

When the baby of an adolescent mother is fathered by a boy younger than herself – a not uncommon occurrence – there is little chance of support or involvement on his part. When John, aged 13, got his 17-year-old girl friend pregnant, the two families (with absent fathers) raised their hands in horror, and accepted it. When the baby was born, premature and underweight but healthy, John joked about it being dead. How should one expect a boy of 13, still at school, to respond to his baby? Fatherly commitment may not reasonably be expected at such a young age.

Craig and Dora, both aged 12 and at the same comprehensive school in a small town in England, started a pregnancy, and since the parents were willing, Dora continued with the pregnancy. Not surprisingly the by then 13-year-old father could not handle the situation and drifted from Dora's life. She, forced into a premature adulthood, learnt to adapt to motherhood (shared with the care offered by her parents) while continuing her education at school, after a brief period with home tuition. Much of her confusion was dealt with through all the support she got from tutor, teachers, parents and social workers. Craig got nothing. It was not surprising, therefore, that about a year after the birth of their child, he demonstrated some very disruptive behaviour which threatened Dora and her family. His problems, seething beneath the surface for lack of recognition, were beginning to emerge. Who knows? – if he were able and willing to receive help, he might have wanted to return to Dora and his child to offer support. Meanwhile, Dora was growing up and away from her first love, and the child would no longer know its father. This father was not involved from the start, but who knows whether he would have been welcomed back if he chose? Admittedly this father was very young. However, this boy's difficulty illustrates the all too frequent dilemma faced by many young fathers left out of the equation.

Some adolescent mothers experience conflict between the need to recover from the birth and establish a routine with the new baby, and the need to get back to their partner for fear of losing his affections. He may put pressure on her to resume sexual relations far sooner than she wants to, but she may feel a need to do this to restate her claim on him. His involvement with his baby may be marginal. Such a couple is likely to part and the father's contact to cease.

Fatherhood may be a dream of many a young man in or just out of his teens, but economically for most, when it occurs, unplanned fatherhood is not just bad news, it is a disaster. In the United States the problem has been specifically highlighted by a report on young men's earnings and their effects on family formation. Due to the rapidly falling real earnings among young workers in the US, apart from their lack of skills as a result of dropping out of school, hope for financial independence diminishes and poverty becomes a reality. In 1973 nearly 60 per cent of all males aged 20–24 were able to earn enough to lift a family of three out of poverty. By 1984 this figure was 42 per cent. This means, as the decline steadily continues, that more than 60 per cent of young families are below the 'three person poverty line' (Children's Defence Fund, 1987). The problem is worst among the young black and Hispanic males. The CDF report goes on to say that these young, poorly educated and unskilled men are unable to support any family, and yet they are more likely to father children when young than are those better educated.

Other relationships and subsequent pregnancies

Pregnancy is often a far from isolated event for teenagers. Many young mothers get pregnant for a second time while still a teenager and unmarried. In 1983 more than 27 per cent of children born to 18–19 year olds were second or more births in the US. For black 18–19 year olds, 37 per cent of the births were not first children. Even among younger teenagers nearly 13 per cent were second or third births (Foster, 1986).

Follow-up studies in the first year or two after the baby's birth (Simms and Smith, 1986; Furstenberg, 1976) suggest that the subsequent rate of family building would be relatively fast among teenage mothers, and outstrip their desired intention to limit their families. However, the long-term follow-up of Furstenberg *et al.*'s Baltimore study (1987) found that family size did not grow as large as had first appeared likely: most had fewer children than they originally intended, due principally to sterilisation and an increasing resort to abortion. It must be considered a hopeful sign that those young mothers found alternative interests and goals in their lives which motivated them away from having more children than they felt they could cope with.

Having more children to follow the first at an early age is perhaps a natural consequence of seeking and maintaining status in a world which offers very little in the way of fulfilment. If a teenage girl gets locked into motherhood with no other aspirations, whatever her material circumstances, she is likely to continue to bear children, and in many cases by different fathers. Such a girl will be unlikely to make good lasting relationships and will attract towards her similarly impoverished young men. The poor economic and emotional tenor of her life renders her vulnerable and susceptible to unsuitable relationships which cannot endure. It seems that, in seeking the ideal, she has little notion of reality. Many children of single young mothers experience a series of uncle figures and stepfathers. Although it is good for a child to have a father figure in its life, such a relationship has little value for mother or child if it has no stability, no genuine long-term commitment. Too often, sadly it has not.

In her study of very young mothers, Miller (1983) found that those mothers of under 16, who had no one else to help care for their child, were more likely to have become pregnant again by the 18 month follow-up interview. She comments that:

> It may be that these mothers are more committed to the one role of being a parent and therefore want to continue having children right away. Lacking child care, they may also be isolated from services and other contacts that might allow them options for roles other than being a full-time mother. (Miller, 1983)

There is some evidence to show that teenagers may be heavily influenced by their peers in continuing pregnancy. Although friendship among very young mothers is by no means automatic, for they are not necessarily confident in this area and may not seek out friendships with other women in their position, it is generally found that those teenagers with babies had friends who were also young mothers. For example, 76 out of 87 in Ryan and Sweeney's sample (1980) from Memphis, US, had friends with babies; 80 per cent of Birch's sample (1987) had friends who were pregnant – yet only 12 per cent had friends who had used contraception.

US studies from the 1970s raise wider issues. Teenagers influenced by their friends rather than by their parents have higher levels of premarital pregnancies (Shah and Zelnik, 1981). The majority of both black and white subjects felt that 'society' and their neighbourhood condemned unmarried mothers, but a larger minority of blacks rather than whites felt they did not. Stigma was reducing in the early 1970s (Zelnik *et al.*, 1981, p. 48) and subsequently has reduced even further.

Janice, age 15, became pregnant for the second time, her first child being 4 months old. The circumstances of Janice's life are not unfamiliar to those who work closely with teenage mothers. She lived with her divorced mother in an unstable, unhappy situation, and was still seeing her boy friend who had been on the scene for some time, and who was the father of both pregnancies. Janice freely admitted that Mike's presence irritated her if they were together too long. At first Janice refused to believe she was pregnant again and would not even face the possibility. When she finally accepted the harsh truth of the pregnancy test, in spite of her less than propitious circumstances, there was no question but that she would keep this baby too.

> Mike said 'We ought to see if I'm pregnant so's we can go for an abortion. He just assumed – it made me very upset. I don't believe in abortion. Got to have it [the baby]. My mum doesn't believe in getting rid of it either. Didn't with the last one . . . I can cope all right . . . Marie's no problem . . . Two babies and my exams? Well, I never was much good at school work . . .
>
> I already got two cots – I been trying to sell the other one. Won't have to now . . . Mike – now he says he'll stand by me and be more of a help with the second than he is with Marie. Only my mum won't let me see him now . . .
>
> I was on the mini pill. I copped out with Marie on that – not strong enough, that's what the doctor said. My mum did too . . . Yeah, he put me on the mini pill again after Marie was born. I was going to go for the stronger pill, but, well, I hadn't got round to it.

Janice was lucky to have a place at a Unit where she would get daily support during the school year as a mother of two and a GCSE student. Outside school hours consistent support would in all probability be hard to find.

Janice is an example of a young woman who saw little chance of roles for herself other than motherhood. She seemed to accept her second child as inevitable. Although the relationship with the children's father was continuing, even she would admit that it did not amount to much, and she did not have much hope of his support. Although her (divorced) mother would not allow an abortion, she also declared herself unprepared to help with the care of her grandchildren, as she had her own life to lead. Other 15 year olds who attended the same Unit were able to make the decision to terminate a second unplanned pregnancy, for they had at that time a clearer idea of themselves in relation to their circumstances and their future. However, Janice is not alone in her lack of control over her own life, in her sense of fate, and in recognising that she is isolating herself even more. For having children in early and mid teens is an isolating process; there is little time to make or keep friends, and there is certainly very little confidence to do so. Like so many others in her position, she left her unhappy home as soon as she could, relying heavily on all state services available and accessible to her. Her suspected third pregnancy will lead to further difficulties.

Young mothers like Janice will find it very hard to manage their life with two small children, poor housing and very limited financial resources. Other resources will also be few and limited. Loneliness may be one of the major problems for them, and the need for company may well lead them along the wrong road. Needy people are very vulnerable, and a prey to exploitation.

Poverty and deprivation

The isolation of many teenage mothers is due to a number of factors, not least among them being their need for relationships, their need for support. When they find that life is not what they hoped and imagined it would be, in an already disadvantaged position with one child, they may bring even greater disadvantage upon themselves and their family by having yet more children. Their hunger for affection can begin a devastating downward spiral of poverty on many levels. The contribution of poverty to the relatively poor outcome for young mothers and their children has already been suggested. Poverty can be seen as both cause and result of the multiple problems faced by adolescents, who in seeking fulfilment too early become trapped in a way of life which depresses and limits their options in a number of different ways.

The issue of poverty is significant in any discussion of teenage parenthood because it affects both parents and children so closely. It affects their families in general and the communities in which they live as well as the services provided there. For as the number of children in a household increases, their corporate and individual needs increase too, and destitution is a probability. A large number of studies in both Britain and the US have shown that lone mothers and their children are the most deprived members of our society. In Britain women who give birth out of wedlock are predominantly from the lower socio-economic groups (Christopher, 1987). A majority of these mothers are teenagers, and a majority of these are on income support and living in run-down areas with few amenities.

In the US the situation is probably worse. In 1981 six out of ten women dependent on grants from Aid to Families with Dependent Children (AFDC) gave birth while they were teenagers. Reliance on federal and state support programmes is very important for teenage mothers in the US. One in ten is likely to be in receipt of maintenance payments from the child's father, compared with one in four of older mothers (Alan Guttmacher, 1981). America may boast of being the richest nation in the world, but it also has to admit to an enormously high proportion of the poorest people. In a recent Congressional study, it was revealed that 45 per cent of all black children in the US and 63.8 per cent of those in single parent families are now living in poverty (*TES*, 13.10.89).

The US also has by far the highest rate of teenage pregnancy, and teenage mothers in America do not get a good financial deal. Poverty as it is known in the US is virtually unheard of in Europe; American state welfare payments are not so generously allocated. The Netherlands and Sweden have succeeded in reaching reasonably egalitarian societies, and even in Britain and France the gap between rich and poor is not nearly so great as it is in the US. Adolescents who have been emotionally as well as economically deprived, and who look for fulfilment in a child of their own, have an unrealistic view of their future and make up the major proportion of those in need of welfare support (Jones *et al.*, 1985, 1986).

Evidence from the US shows a definite link between teenage birth rates and poverty; 60 per cent of teenage mothers receive welfare at some time, more than 60 per cent of women under 30 on AFDC grants are teenagers. More than half the annual AFDC expenditure in the US is to families where the mother was a teenage mother. Poverty rates are still rising while benefits are being curtailed in efforts to control state costs. This is the case both in Britain and the US. As Foster (1986) says:

For many families, these benefits programs provide the difference between total and partial destitution. The structure of our programs to aid the poor maintains some groups below the poverty level, provides disincentives to independent status, and ignores large categories of the poor and needy. As a result, many teenagers find themselves in a vicious cycle wherein the problems of poverty compound the chances of teenage pregnancy and teenage pregnancy compounds the problems of poverty.

In many states in the US one in five children start life with a teenage mother, and this has a significant impact on health care, education, child welfare and other public systems such as housing. From deprivations engendered by reliance on state services for basic requirements there arise social, economic and psychological problems which are almost impossible to eradicate, since they begin at the cradle and are absorbed as a way of life. It does not take much imagination to see that families with these sorts of multiple difficulties and needs are a burden on state systems like health and housing. While realising this and attempting to control and economise, the respective governments fail to see that such action amounts basically to shutting the door after the horse has bolted.

McGee (1982), a social work administrator, feels that teenage mothers are satisfied neither with the appropriateness of the help provided, nor that help is provided where, when or for as long as it is needed. 'We see young mothers who expect to get, not give. When they don't get, they are disappointed – again – and angry about their continuing deprivation. Some become resigned and passive towards their future.' Public assistance is generally inevitable for a teenager who has her first baby before she is economically independent. In the US standards differ from state to state about when a pregnant teenager can be in receipt of financial assistance, including food stamps, Medicaid and WIC (Women, Infants and Children food program), and about when she can establish her own household. New York City, for example, allocates AFDC to any young woman during her fourth month of pregnancy regardless of age, and she is eligible for her own household after age 16. In Britain a pregnant teenager is not eligible for Income Support until her 29th week of pregnancy, and she may only receive that if

she is over 16 or has left school (whichever is the sooner). Until
that time she is considered – reasonably, many would argue –
dependent upon her parents for everything. Whatever her age,
once a mother, she claims single parent benefit. The official age for
setting up an independent household in Britain is 18. However,
today more and more young mothers in their early teens are being
housed by the local authority, since their family circumstances
have caused them to be homeless.

Williams *et al.* (1987) interviewed 911 women in Glasgow having
their first baby in 1984/5, including 283 teenagers; 71 per cent of
the teenagers were wholly reliant on state benefit, compared with
42 per cent of the older women. Only 32 per cent of the teenagers
receiving state benefit said it was adequate. Blondel *et al.* (1987)
conducted two national surveys of several thousand women in
France in 1972 and 1981. Teenagers were significantly under-
privileged compared with older women at both dates, and their
social circumstances deteriorated between the two dates. Longitudinal studies in Britain and the US suggest that the pattern of
relative poverty persists both during the child's early years
(Osborn *et al.*, 1984) and for considerably longer (Furstenburg *et
al.*, 1987). Without good employment prospects there is no route
out of poverty.

In her book about poverty and politics in Britain in the 1980s
Beatrix Campbell (1984) describes the life of young single mothers
in the North of England, where enormous debts are commonplace.
With inadequate resources on all levels, the poor are often blamed
for their own poverty. Good budgeting means having a budget in
the first place as well as the wit and motivation to organise it. But
when all other facets of a young mother's life are well below her
and society's expectations, spending money is one of the few
pleasures available to her and getting into debt is perceived as a
relatively minor difficulty.

To take but one example: in the era of fast food, subsistence
incomes do not make for a culinary culture. Creativity in the
kitchen for these young mothers is unknown, and junk food
provides relatively few nutrients.

The mass production and marketing of family food expresses the
dissolution of domesticity as a way of life . . . For the poor, food
is always functional: 'It just fills a hole, doesn't it?' said one

single mother, 'I can't stand watching television because it depresses me, there's always food on.' It's never the endless toast and tea, beans, bread and chips which are the staples of poor people's diets. 'Toast, I look like a piece of toast.'

Many families nowadays do not eat their meals together, and a common dining area is for some a thing of the past. A regime of TV snacks is likely to take its toll: without proper nourishment both mothers and children will suffer.

Weekly budgeting is meaningless in a world where poverty, loneliness and boredom are commonplace. Cooking on a very tight budget requires nutritional planning skills, storage space, equipment and cheap local shops – resources which poor young mothers seldom have at their disposal (Levitan, 1985).

Social problems: the effects on life style

Most teenagers are single as they start out on motherhood. Many have a series of partners in unsatisfactory relationships. Most are caught in the poverty trap. Employment prospects are few. Most young fathers maintain an ambivalent attitude to parenthood, since they also are caught in the poverty trap. While the difficulty of unscrambling the relative importance of all these factors remains, their combination is undoubtedly potent: a 'vortex of disadvantage' even among the married (Ineichen, 1977).

Many will have been doing poorly at school, and the pregnancy will interrupt and possibly curtail schooling. Reliance on state benefits is virtually universal for those who lack an employed partner (Ineichen, 1986). Very few will have a job to go back to after the baby is born. Constantly applying for subsistence living is neither easy nor enjoyable, but can become a way of life. The indignities involved reduce morale, hope, motivation, and both mental and physical resources.

Housing

Teenage parents are at a grave disadvantage when it comes to housing. 'Maternity homes' for wayward young women whose pregnancy was a matter of shame are definitely a thing of the past.

Since unmarried motherhood, even in teen years, bears no stigma today, young mothers openly demand and expect to be independently housed. However, with no resources, starting from scratch, in urgent need of a place for two, and little, if any choice in the matter, reliance on the state for a home is an additional burden to their already considerable problems. The situation may be summed up by a US report compiled by the New Jersey Network on Adolescent Pregnancy (1986):

> ... many pregnant and parenting teens are told they cannot remain at home, others have no homes, while still others must initiate a move for a variety of compelling social-psychological-financial reasons. Their needs cover the spectrum from short-term, emergency forms of shelter to long-term housing for up to two years after the baby's birth. The settings themselves can be varied: from a parents' home to a group home, from an independent living arrangement to a maternity home to a foster care placement.

The survey this report was based on was undertaken in 1985, subsequent to a similar one in 1982. There was little evidence of change. Two-thirds of the respondents, from voluntary organisations and individuals focusing on the issue of teenage pregnancy, felt that, of four major unmet needs of teenage mothers, housing was number one; 66 per cent felt that, whatever the present circumstances (federal, local state, private, voluntary), it was not feasible to meet the housing needs of teenage mothers and their children. Since then foundation-funded innovations have been put into operation in New Jersey; these include a teen mother residence to house temporarily those very needy young women with literally nowhere else to go.

In Britain, recent legislation to curtail the building of new state housing and to encourage private housing development has reduced the chances of the adolescent mother finding a place of her own when she needs it. Encouragement from the government for all adolescents to remain at home until age 25 has resulted in a chaotic situation regarding emergency housing and homelessness among young people. Young mothers fare marginally better in that they are quickly found bed and breakfast hotel accommodation as a halfway measure. It is true that a young mother with a baby usually takes priority when it comes to housing. With two babies, it is a certainty; as one young mother said:

> I wanted to leave home, my mum and I weren't getting on, there was no room for the baby. They told me at the Housing Department that if I had another baby, they'd give me a flat, no problems. So I got pregnant again.

Leisure activities

One of the most frequently heard adolescent responses to pregnancy is the grim resignation in recognising that they will have to stay in now, and may not be able to enjoy themselves with their friends, relying heavily on television for their entertainment instead. Even if they could afford to go out and leave the child with someone, child minding is an extra expense and therefore unthinkable. Many teenage mothers find it all too much effort to get together; this is not surprising, since public transport is expensive and money is scarce. On the rare occasions when they are able to get out, leaving the baby overnight with mother seems the most popular form of child care. Babies have been left alone at night; with a young sibling; even on occasion in a children's home without informing the staff. Some very young mothers are disturbed and damaged enough not to realise the full implications to their child in the pursuance of certain selfish activities. They still need to behave like the children they are. Coming to terms with the responsibility of motherhood is extremely difficult for them.

Young mothers who are needy both on the material and the emotional level are particularly vulnerable to false flatterers and short-term morale boosters. Their need to be valued is paramount. Financial and emotional needs are strong motivators to seek out relationships. The poverty and loneliness which young women in this position experience render them prey to exploitation by men who see sexual relationships as having no commitment. Apart from the emotional damage that such relationships perpetuate, the risks of further pregnancies are very great, since, if sex is not taking place on a regular basis, contraception once again is considered pointless.

Sheila, aged 17, had no family who would recognise her, no boy friend, but she had a baby. From various bed and breakfasts she moved to a flat provided by the local authority and was so lonely she advertised for a man and some fun. She received many replies. . . .

Prostitution

It is generally recognised that teenage prostitution is linked with poor relationships at home, absent fathers, violent or criminal families, divorce and child abuse. Young mothers who are drawn into prostitution have a particularly hard time. Many live in run-down areas where prostitution is already part of the scene. Some girls are already on the edge of it before they become pregnant, and some become involved unwittingly once they have a child. Once this life style is established, it is difficult to relinquish it. Firstly the pimps exert pressure and the young women feel powerless against it. Secondly, if it raises their standard of living even a little, it may feel worth while. The prevalence of child and teenage prostitution in Britain has not been adequately documented, but Birch (1987) found that 9 per cent of pregnant schoolgirls (16 and under) in her sample were involved in prostitution. Many girls suffer sexual abuse and prostitution in silence while society continues to keep the facts well and truly under the carpet.

Clara and Leila were both aged 16 with a baby. Clara's boy friend, her baby's father, turned out to be a pimp. Both young women were exploited by him and his gang. Leila and her baby were robbed, her flat was broken into and her equipment smashed, and she and her son were severely beaten up. This was in order to intimidate her into submission to go on the streets.

One British 14-year-old girl was abducted by her boy friend, who was also a pimp, to another city where she 'worked' for a few weeks, before escaping and returning home and back to school. During her later pregnancy she attempted to keep out of harm's way, but was drawn back into prostitution, leaving her child with its maternal grandmother. Another – lonely, unhappy and in need of affection, although living at home with her mother – was attracted to prostitution after her baby's birth at age 16. Yet another at age 16 was drawn back into this way of life as her only perceivable means of survival after her baby was born. She had been living out of plastic bags at different addresses for many months. With her baby's arrival she made a desperate attempt to escape her pimp. It appears that once this way of life has been glimpsed, the immediate attractions are too much to lose and compare favourably with loneliness and poverty. As with pregnancy, their sight is short and they are not inclined to look ahead and see the dangers; nor have they had the good models or the practice in their upbringing. The possible link between youthful motherhood and prostitution is an area where good research would be extremely valuable.

Family violence

Nearly one-third of Birch's (1987) sample of pregnant schoolgirls came from violent backgrounds. Several of Lees' informants described the boy they would like to marry as 'someone who doesn't beat me up' (1986, p. 89). Searching for an ideal family life and seeking affection, impoverished young parents are thrust into adulthood deprived of the maturity to make and sustain good relationships. It is not surprising that they may fight each other as a familiar means of expressing their frustration with life, each other and themselves, since this is one of the main ways they have seen relationships function in their own families. Some of Sharpe's (1987) teenage mothers tell of violent experiences with boy friends. Many a mother has arrived in school with bruises inflicted by boy friends. They take it in their stride with a shrug of the shoulder (see chapter 2). Love bites may perhaps be considered in the same category. There are even more of those in evidence, worn with distinct pride. Poverty and lack of employment or valued occupation are strong motivators to violence. Add youth, inexperience in relationships and rapidly evolved responsibility, and the recipe is complete for confrontation. The implications for the children of parents in these circumstances are obvious. Their experience of family life may lead to disturbed behaviour.

Divorce

Teenage mothers in Britain are more likely than older mothers to have their first marriage end in divorce. This is especially true of lower occupational class couples. Youthful spouses, low social class and premarital pregnancy have been described as a 'powerful cocktail' leading to marital instability (Thornes and Collard, 1979). In the US the experience has been similar, extending also to their second marriage (McCarthy and Menken, 1979). This should surprise no one. Teenagers from unhappy or deprived backgrounds are unlikely to have had good models for relationships. Without some knowledge of themselves and each other and some experience in this, it seems marriage has little chance of survival.

Child abuse

Considerable research has been conducted into child abuse in both Britain (Corby, 1987) and the US (Bolton *et al.*, 1980; Kinard and Klerman, 1980) which suggests a higher likelihood of abuse among youthful parents than among older parents. Of course, not all young parents batter or abuse their children or each other; however, the frustrations of their circumstances may well lead to destructive behaviour of this kind. Battering parents may be defined as inadequate, self-defeating, immature, isolated, wanting immediate gratification for impulses, having a poor sense of identity and very little self-esteem. Much of this list describes many of the young mothers we have been discussing, who with their youth and inexperience are ill equipped to cope with the stresses of life. And battering parents marry young perhaps for similar reasons that they have children young: wanting to leave much that was unhappy and unresolved behind them, searching for an ideal and unable to wait for adulthood.

Some adolescents who become pregnant have been sexually abused by their father or – more likely – their stepfather or uncle. This is not to say that their babies are necessarily the result of this incest. Early secret sexual activity with a father figure can lead to sexual promiscuity and early accidental pregnancy that way, or it can lead the girl to seek security in her own chosen relationship, with a baby to seal it. Girls between the ages of 10 and 15 are the most common victims of sexual abuse (65 per cent of known cases), and in almost three-quarters of these cases the perpetrator is the father. But it is estimated that 90 per cent of cases go undetected (Christopher, 1987).

The most important factors associated with sexual abuse within a family are to do with poor or faulty family relationships. Where incest is the result, but not the cause, of a disturbed situation, this too can be associated with sexual abuse. It is a complex and sensitive issue to deal with, as the controversy surrounding the detection and management of child sexual abuse in Cleveland, England, in 1988 showed. Identifying genuine cases of child sexual abuse remains difficult, and perpetrators seldom own up. Since many of our young and very young mothers were themselves victims of abuse, help is needed for them and their children in order to minimise the chances of continuing the patterns. As we have already seen, many damaged and unhappy people choose partners with similar unhappiness or difficulties in their own lives.

AIDS and other sexually transmitted diseases

About 30 known diseases can be transmitted sexually (Christopher, 1987). The poor record of teenagers as contraceptors means they are at particular risk. Broverman and Strasburger (1989) list some of the consequences for Americans in 1986:

> Some 224,000 cases of teenage gonorrhea (including over 8000 among under 15s);
> Over 3000 cases of teenage syphilis (including 155 among under 15s).

Other social problems are often associated with these conditions. Reports from several countries (Britain, Denmark, US) show that young people with sexually transmitted infection tend to be involved in prostitution, alcoholism and crime, and to lead unstable lives in many respects (Birch, 1987).

One in eight sexually active American teenage girls have pelvic inflammatory disease, which can lead to infertility, ectopic pregnancy and other problems (Broverman and Strasburger, 1989). Cancer is a major threat. The cervix of young teenagers is vulnerable to cancer, and young adolescents with several partners are especially at risk (Birch, 1987).

However, towering above all of these is AIDS.

Figures for the US are alarming: 65,780 cases had been reported by June 1988, and of these cases half have already died. It is estimated that 1½ to 2 million are infected with HIV. Women and young people are increasingly affected. AIDS is the leading cause of death in New York among men aged 25–40 and women aged 25–34. Since the incubation period is gauged at about seven years, the clear message is that teenagers are very much at risk. The AIDS syndrome is no longer confined to New York, New Jersey and California, but is spreading across the country. Recent reports confirm the 1986 Public Health Services projection: now all 50 states have reported cases.

In Central African countries such as Zaire, Uganda and Zambia, 5–10 per cent of the population are estimated to be already infected with HIV. In Africa and the Caribbean men and women are affected in equal numbers. Females aged 15–19 have the highest rate of HIV positive cases. Depending on the region, 1–18 per cent of pregnant women and 27–88 per cent of female prostitutes are HIV positive.

Unless the spread of HIV is checked in some way, it is anticipated that during the 1990s the incidence of AIDS in Great Britain will rise greatly, although estimates differ. Worldwide, the Center for Disease Control estimates the cumulative total of cases will reach 270,000, of whom 179,000 will be dead.

> If these events occur, they will do so at a time when large numbers of people know how to prevent the spread of this most serious disease. We know, for example, that the virus responsible is transmitted in semen, vaginal fluid and blood. We know that it is not transmitted by coughs, sneezes, touch, social kissing, casual contact or by spending time in the same house, school or clinic as someone who has HIV infection. Thus, were every person to adopt reasonable and sensible precautions to ensure that they minimise the risk of coming into contact with, or transmitting the virus, the outlook could be far less bleak than the present scenario suggests. (Aggleton *et al.*, 1988)

The problem is that, just as with the discrepancy between knowledge and behaviour in relation to pregnancy risk, so it is with AIDS. Data indicate that, whereas the gay groups on both sides of the Atlantic have changed their sexual behaviour, heterosexual youth generally are not changing their behaviour at all. Many young men are not using condoms. Proof of this is found in the rise in the incidence of STDs and teenage pregnancy. McGuire (1983) illustrates some all too common attitudes: Lucy, a social worker with Planned Parenthood in a large US city, sees 110–120 girls (sometimes with boy friends) for counselling per month on average. She hears about sexual pressure on girls from boys:

> So I don't know what the teenage boys in general are feeling. I know here . . . the guys are interested in only one thing: the number of girls they take to bed. . . . Don't [the girls] mind that their boy friends are screwing around with everybody else in town? They know it. And they know their boy friends often want them to get pregnant so they can't go out with other guys.

Fred, MD, works in a public health centre in a large city in the US. He sees many boys at the centre's VD clinic:

> The male sexual role is basically part of the extremely macho, physical John Wayne type. In the subculture in the inner city among the blacks, it's the dude. The cool dude. The whole attitude towards sexuality is basically, and using a very bad pun, piecework, based on the number of performances. And the attitude, when they come in with VD is 'Wow, I'm really upset, I thought she was a nice girl'.

'Real men' 'screw around' indiscriminately, and if, by chance, they

> get involved with a situation where someone gets pregnant or . . . ends up giving you VD, then you've gotten burned. The nerve of this person to perpetrate this insult on you!

Syphilis is a serious disease; gonorrhea is a badge of honour:

> They can't wait to go down and show the guys the green drip in their underwear when they're in the gym. They laugh about it, it's a riot! You see kids twelve, thirteen, fourteen, and this is great, it shows they're a real man.

Adolescents are not well informed; or rather, even with information, they clearly find it difficult to translate this knowledge into responsible behaviour (Bowie and Ford, 1989). The problem is one of how sex education is handled, from both the giving and the receiving points of view. AIDS is today a necessary part of sex education and must, like all the other aspects of this literally vital subject, be sufficiently prolific, specific, group targeted and continuously programmed for young people to assimilate the information, understand its importance and to learn to put it willingly into practice. As with all responsibility and sex related education – education about HIV is needed before young people become sexually active so that they are helped to translate appropriate beliefs and attitudes into responsible action. This must undoubtedly take place before children reach the fourth form (or year 10) in Britain or the eighth or ninth grade in the US.

Karen Hein's report prepared for The National Invitational Conference in March 1988 shows findings which highlight specific developments in the transmission of HIV among adolescents, as well as the continuing sense of invulnerability to the virus among this group. Adolescents are more vulnerable to HIV than they imagine: 45 per cent of cases of AIDS in the 13–21 age group were infected with HIV through heterosexual contact; 10 per cent of mothers to babies with AIDS in New York City were under 21. In 1987, in a survey of 25,000 new-borns in New York State an alarmingly high rate of HIV antibodies was found. In New York City 1 in 61 infants was born with positive antibodies. In the Bronx, it was 1 baby in 43. By January 1988 there were 557 children in the US under 13 diagnosed as having AIDS: 61 per cent of them had died.

High rates of infection are indicated among childbearing women who become sexually active younger and younger in areas where intravenous drug abuse is a major associated risk behaviour. Minority group women living in areas of poverty are considered to be directly in the path of the AIDS epidemic. Yet advertisements warning of the causes and dangers and prevention of AIDS are geared to middle- and upper-class white adults rather than to the young and non-whites. White adolescents are more knowledgeable about the cause, transmission and prevention of AIDS than are black adolescents, and blacks are more knowledgeable than Hispanics. Also, since the interval between HIV infection and AIDS onset is likely to be seven or more years, a person who is HIV positive will not necessarily appear ill, will have no symptoms, and yet can pass on the virus – possibly unknowingly.

It is known that pregnancy can accelerate the course and severity of HIV infection due to alterations in the immune function in the mother's body. Biochemical complications in adolescent girls mean that the body is more susceptible to all sexually transmitted diseases, which include HIV (Hein, 1987). Young females are greatly at risk, and they are the bridging group to other groups, their future adolescent partners, and certainly their future children, for it is estimated that 60 per cent of white and 80 per cent of black urban females have had sexual intercourse by the age of 19, amongst whom the condom is not popular, and few are inclined to think about the future; there is also a high prevalence of intravenous drug abuse in urban areas.

In New York City, female partners of high risk males were far more commonly adolescents than adults, and represented almost half of all New York teenage AIDS cases. New York accounts for roughly one-third of all AIDS cases in the US and also accounts for 20 per cent of the reported cases in adolescents (Hein *et al.*, 1988).

A survey of high school students in New York City (Hein, 1988) revealed a decline in the use of drugs, alcohol and tobacco due to a changed perception of risk. But in areas of HIV prevalence, there was nearly 40 per cent high school drop out. This proportion therefore was not reached in schools in those areas of high risk. Since behaviour is influenced by drug use, and drug use is connected with school drop out in New York City, the risk of HIV infection there cannot be ignored. In the Bronx drugs are a major risk factor in the spread of HIV and therefore of AIDS. Two-thirds of AIDS cases there are associated with drug use, and half of the Bronx's 60,000 to 70,000 intravenous drug abusers are thought to have positive HIV antibodies. This group consists of young black and Hispanic adults between the ages of 20 and 40; they have multiple sexual partners and are major contributors to the risks of heterosexual transmission of HIV.

The levels of knowledge directly relate to the perceived risk. If young people cannot relate to the information, their perception of risk is unrealistic. In spite of the warnings, they cling to the belief that AIDS cannot be transmitted through heterosexual intercourse. They think that, so long as they are not injecting drugs or indulging in homosexual sex, they are untouchable.

In the US one of the main feared transmission routes of HIV to the young female population is indirectly through intravenous drug use. Thus a 16-year-old girl, for example, who is in a sexual relationship with an older boy who is a drug user, may not be aware of the connection between AIDS and IV drug use, or understand its severity. As with education for pregnancy prevention, all too often it is simply assumed by service providers that scientific and medical information is all that is needed. Only when the information is packaged differently to meet the needs of the particular target groups, and the programmes include exercises aimed at changing attitudes and behaviour (such as assertiveness training) can they have some effect for change. Some school-based communities in the US are beginning to reap rewards of programmes delivered in this way (Hayes, 1987). The number of teenage pregnancies in those communities has fallen significantly. Behavioural changes are possible, and this is hopeful.

We are not doing so well in Britain. Complacency as to the perceived relatively minimal danger of the AIDS epidemic in Britain is ultimately no defence. If Britain's trends follow America's, AIDS cases are sure to increase, and possibly in the way suggested above, through ignorance and lack of understanding. The British government's methods of educating the public have so far been of the fact-giving kind, tinged heavily with moral overtones. The two information campaigns in 1986 – which took the form of full-page newspaper and magazine advertisements, as well as those on television and a leaflet for every household – were aimed specifically at increasing public awareness of the sexually transmitted aspects of the disease, endeavouring to bring about behavioural change as a means of containing the epidemic. Evaluations of these campaigns found that, if anything, people were less sure of the facts than before and more confused and anxious about what they thought they knew. Confusion as to the principal causes of AIDS seems to have been increased by a nation-wide campaign to do exactly the opposite (Aggleton *et al.*, 1988).

Where government campaigns may have lacked a realistic approach, in Britain now, as awareness and sheer case numbers increase, many organisations are funding and operating surveys, clinics and Buddies/Helpers programmes to promote understanding, prevention and treatment of HIV, and support for those infected. But the risk of AIDS still appears remote to an adolescent. This is in part due to their NOW approach to life; they see things in concrete rather than in the abstract. If something cannot be seen, it is not there – like pregnancy at first. Decisions in youth tend to be based on the here and now, not the long term. Peer pressures – operating with the same approach to life – override the risks. Almost anything which is distasteful will be denied. This has a good deal to do with fear, which makes people very defensive. Teenagers will find it difficult to appreciate that AIDS can kill unless they have a great deal of very carefully handled education programmes.

Many adults are equally unwilling to face the facts of HIV and AIDS, and parents with this attitude are not helpful in developing a sense of responsibility in today's children. Reactions of anger and outrage or stony silence are no doubt expressions of unadmitted fear, but such responses are not uncommon in adults, operating the same denial system as the teenagers when something unpleasant threatens their lives.

This danger has never been so acute in Britain until the present time, except perhaps in the capital and some major cities, where inner city drug abuse is a serious problem. However, it may only be a matter of time before it spreads to other areas. Meanwhile educators in every field must take note of factors which currently prevent proper grasp and understanding of the significance of the causes and transmission of HIV, of AIDS itself, and of 'safe sex'.

The child's pre-school years and after

Several longitudinal studies are available now which chart the experience of the children of teenage mothers. Kiernan reports on a British sample born in 1946. Compared with women who became mothers in their early 20s, teenage mothers were more likely to come from younger, poorer, larger families. Both they and their husbands had low status jobs and low self-esteem (Kiernan, 1980). Further research has revealed a higher rate of marriage breakdown for this group following earlier parental marriage breakdown and a tendency to neuroticism (Kiernan, 1986).

A study of about 400 children born to teenagers in the 1960s in Baltimore, US, found over 17 years that children who have more than one care giver are more likely to thrive and to develop well. In this study Furstenberg *et al.* (1987) found that the amount of time the adolescent mother spent with her child was inversely related to the child's cognitive abilities. Children of mothers attending school or holding a job – and hence spending some time each day away from their children – scored higher than those whose mothers stayed at home with the children. The suggestion is that the child benefits from a more mature, less emotionally involved and more experienced care giver; the grandmother or a close female relative often performs this function well, as do professional child minders who make good relationships with their charges' mothers. Furthermore, those children whose mothers were out studying or working were better off economically and more supported emotionally than those of mothers who stayed at home. The mother's socio-economic status is strongly associated with the child's cognitive development. By age 5 children of teenage mothers did worse in tests of vocabulary and behaviour (Wadsworth *et al.*, 1984). The effects of poverty and deprivation on a teenage mother's child seem to be ameliorated if child rearing is shared with another adult.

A large study in Bristol has been following a national sample of children born in one week in April 1970 (Butler, 1988). Within the least fortunate 10 per cent, young mothers featured fifteen times as frequently in the extremely poor group; these families were more isolated, and preschool education was practically non-existent. Accidents were more common to children under 10 of young single mothers. Diet was also found to be a problem for children up to this age. As social class and income go down, for example, the proportion of sweets and other carbohydrates consumed by these children increases. On the other hand, protein intake – a vital ingredient in a child's diet – decreases.

By age 10, parents of 18 per cent of the children reported physical problems, 6 per cent of which had not been picked up at any preschool or school age medical. At age 16, still 16 per cent of the children had medical or educational problems, 5 per cent of which had not been previously picked up. Our inference here is that these figures attach themselves to the difficulties faced by adolescent mothers, since they are among the most deprived, the least resourced and the least prepared for the responsibilities of parenthood. Their children are more likely to suffer inadvertent and irreversible damage.

SECTION TWO:

Why Worry?

Chapter 7

Implications of Teenage Motherhood

In this chapter we look at some of the factors that seriously deter teenage parents from earning a viable income and from creating an independent family unit. With too much too soon in terms of responsibility, but too little in terms of vocational and life skills, young mothers, their partners and their children are not only poor – with the disadvantages and vulnerability that go with poverty – but in need of considerable welfare support and resources.

Teenage mothers as an underclass: their quality of life

In 1957 one British baby in twenty-one was illegitimate. In 1985 that ratio was one in five. Social changes during the 1960s, with an increase in economic prosperity and greater sexual freedom for the young, have almost certainly contributed to the current trend of both rejecting marriage to legitimise the birth, and keeping the baby, when once it might well have been offered for adoption. The status of motherhood for an adolescent causes a dependence that she will find very hard to shake off. If she is still at home, sooner or later she will want a place of her own with her infant, and she is bound to be housed by the state. If she is a mother under 16, in both Britain and the US she has no legal or financial status. As a minor, she is still dependent on her parents. Between 16 and 18 she is not fully included in the bureaucratic and legal scheme of things. Economically, during her teen years, she is a disaster. In both Britain and America teenage mothers represent a substantial proportion of the state dependent population.

Teenage mothers and their partners typically do not do well at school, and few get opportunities for further training. They are, as a direct result of these disadvantages, unable to find satisfying work. They are not deemed worthy of help towards improving their skills and the quality of their lives, for the first step in demonstrating a level of confidence in this section of potential workers, child care provision, is not available to them. Nursery places are limited and minding is costly, and these young parents are on the margins of poverty and inexperienced in asserting themselves against bureaucracy. Teenagers who become mothers help perpetuate the cycle of disadvantage and the reality of an underclass (Field, 1989).

Disadvantaged children are those most often from homes run by parent(s) who are on welfare, unemployed, disabled or sick. Parents' attitudes are crucial to a child's social and intellectual development. It is likely that parents in these circumstances are ill-equipped to show interest or encouragement in their children's attainment at school, and at age 11 such children show typically low scores on basic maths, reading and comprehension. These scores reflect social circumstances and not ability levels. If disadvantage continues up to puberty, it accumulates in adolescence and seriously impedes attainment thereafter (Wedge and Essen, 1982). Teenage parenthood is a possible outcome at this stage. Inequalities at birth and in school are likely to be reinforced later in the labour market (Field, 1989); if this occurs, their lower status on the income scale may become permanent.

In Britain it seems, in terms of education, training and employment opportunities, teenage mothers are not deemed worthy of equality of opportunity. The broad assumption is made by the government that school leavers who are either pregnant or mothers do not require work or training, since they have already chosen a full-time occupation. While their 16-year-old peers are obliged to take up a government sponsored training scheme as they leave school, school-leaving mothers experience a very unequal opportunity indeed, and are expected to draw income support straight away.

> The Government believes that on balance the best interests of lone parent and child, and society generally, are best served by this arrangement, rather than by the lone parent embarking on a course of full time training at such a crucial stage of the child's pre-school development. (Letter from the Employment Department to a British education authority)

The basis for this rationale may well be the fact that the government is not prepared to fund child minding provision for school leavers who have not demonstrated hitherto any commitment to study or work and who themselves could not afford child care. The use of doubtful moral arguments in the sentimental mode to persuade people of its integrity is nothing new. Young single mothers as a body have little strength to resist this kind of legislation. It may be that, as a result of pressure from interested agencies, the government is reconsidering this policy.

Britain is not the only country where this provision is insufficient. Hayes (1987) found that the US in general is sadly lacking in affordable child care provision to adolescent mothers, both those still in education and those who have left it. New Jersey is an example of quite inadequate child care provision. To every subsidised infant place in nursery and day centres, there were 17 babies to teenage mothers queuing up for it. These young mothers have next to no opportunity for employment, training or completing their education while no facilities exist to look after their children. Mothers in such circumstances are very poorly supported and often become severely depressed (Johnson and Ziskin, 1988).

While child care provision remains a problem, teenage mothers may well find the struggle to work or train too daunting to pursue. Not many unsupported young mothers possess sufficient self-esteem or a sufficiently positive idea of their future to be motivated towards a goal they are made to feel is not for them anyway. One way of maintaining the status they have already acquired is to have more babies, since they already feel trapped at home.

In Britain, however, at the age of 18, young people taking up Employment Training are currently provided with £50 per week towards child care provision for their offspring. By the time they reach the age of 18, the lives of 16-year-old mothers who did not benefit from this funding earlier have usually taken a course in which training is no longer perceived by them to have any place. Perhaps the changes related to training schemes in Britain that are currently being discussed will improve the anomalous situation and help reduce this discrimination.

It seems that everything is against teenage parents of both sexes improving their lot. If work or training is taken up, these young parents will be at the bottom of the income scale and are likely to be financially and socially crippled. Petty thieving and crime may be their solution. If they remain unemployed, welfare entitlement takes no account of their burden of disadvantages. There is evidence of greater discrimination among young blacks, who highlight the weaker points in the fate of the most disadvantaged, and who are most likely to be in the ranks of the underclass (Cross and Smith, 1987). Regarding youth training and job prospects, Field (1989) wrote:

> Because the poorest are directed to those schemes least likely to result in gaining a job, they are in fact being selected for unemployment and possibly membership of the underclass at the end of their courses. This outcome of the YTS courses completes the process of marginalisation to the fringes of society; from the poorest homes to the poorest school performances, to the greatest difficulty of obtaining work, to placement on those training schemes least likely to lead to full time paid employment. Once in the adult world of work, the underclass faces further discrimination when it comes to selection for the primary or secondary labour market.

While the government aims to reduce welfare spending, and does little about employment incentives to young people, including young parents, reliance on welfare will remain high, and the cycle of disadvantage will continue. As the gap between the rich and the poor widens, their disadvantage increases. There is a geographical factor too. McRobbie (1989) reviewed research studies, suggesting young mothers have created yet another North–South divide:

better work opportunities mean that those in London do much better than those in northern or Midland cities.

Many teenage mothers have to cope with more than mere poverty. The association with violence has already been documented (chapter 6) and this is often maintained into the next generation. Today's abused child is often a consequence of its parent's experience of abuse and is likely to be tomorrow's abusing parent. Deprivation and abuse can create a self-perpetuating cycle.

Relationship and parenting patterns are learnt from one's own parents and family. They are unlearnt with difficulty and only with longstanding help. Birch's (1987) South London sample contains many cases where teenage mothers had grown up with mentally ill or alcoholic relatives. Young parents who have experienced poor parenting models are likely to lack many essential qualities for good parenting themselves, such as, for example, an understanding of the needs of babies and infants, a tolerance for lack of sleep and a certain selflessness. Many young people find relationships difficult to sustain, and adolescents in our society are expected to be prone to mood fluctuation. Unfortunately this is not consistent with stability in relationships. And, as has been previously said, marriage at this point more often than not means divorce within a few years.

To add to these numerous deficiencies, when they are housed at the state's expense those who are isolated from their mothers often find themselves on bare, soulless, run-down estates, on the edge of town, where fear and isolation impede social life, and even shopping in the bleak malls and precincts is a miserable experience. With small children in push-chairs and very little money, they are unable to benefit from the choices available by shopping around.

What is the quality of life for these families? What have their children got to look forward to while their parents are struggling at every level of their existence? It seems that, in spite of the difficulties and responsibilities of parenthood, many teenagers feel that having a child is worthwhile. But since adolescent relationships are commonly unstable, few young mothers are able to offer their children a stable environment and emotional security, for their immaturity is combined with adverse social and economic conditions.

Birch (1987) discusses the link between deprivation in lower socio-economic groups in urban areas to the cycle of maternal nutritional deprivation. Low income families in run-down areas have large families and eat a poor diet. Nutritional deficits in the mother may originate at her own birth, not during her pregnancy or the birth of her child, and have serious implications for the long-term prospect for families in inner city areas. Much research is being done to monitor the effects of nutritional deficiencies, and enough is already known to give cause for concern for the physical, emotional and social health of the generations of children who as young adults beget children in deprived environments.

Janet, mentioned at the beginning of chapter 6, did not have enough good childhood experiences to take with her into motherhood at the age of 15. Typical of the lost adolescent looking for roots, rejected by each separated parent, she longed for love and affection. Disappointment goes with such a young woman and clouds her perception, affecting her behaviour and reflecting on her child. Her immaturity coupled with her sadness and her often unexpressed rage do nothing to enhance her life which is already adversely affected by poor economic conditions, low social status and poor education and training opportunities.

The adolescent mother's rage may well be directed at her own mother, only her mother is not often there to receive it:

> It was my mother's voice again yelling at me I was no good, I couldn't do nothing right, exactly her voice just as though she was there. It wasn't a baby I hit, it was my mum, I hit her right in the mouth with my fist, just like I always wanted to when I was a kid and couldn't. I don't expect you to believe me, but it's the truth. (Renvoize, 1978)

Things tend not to turn out as the young mother hoped. Not surprisingly the baby becomes the scapegoat, since the baby is the perceived cause of frustration. Neglect and abuse of the baby may well come into the picture at this stage. A 16-year-old mother, whose home experience was little other than smothering attention or shouting and swearing, behaves in similar ways with her child, teasing him and punishing him mercilessly over the months and years until he no longer flinches, but accepts it all blandly. He gets used to lying late into the morning in a cold, wet nappy until his mother chooses to get up. He learns to go hungry until his mother's money comes through. Instead of putting dangerous things out of his reach, once he has damaged himself she will shout at him, accusing him of being stupid, possibly accompanied by slaps or a beating.

It is enormously difficult to extricate yourself from dependent relationships when few resources are available to you. Depression and hopelessness are powerful preventers of action. Depression among mothers of young children is common, especially in inner city areas and among deprived groups, among which adolescent mothers feature strongly (Richman *et al.*, 1982).

Vulnerable and needy women tend to attract similar men (Norwood, 1986). They may have a baby to make everything right, but end up by making things worse than ever. Many teenagers hope that, by having a baby, they will hold their boy friend. Many also believe that, if the relationship is not going well, a baby will put the seal on its commitment. This is not to say the pregnancy is deliberate but, once it is there, keeping the baby seems like the answer to the relationship problem. And this is not to say that the child is necessarily wanted for its own sake, but rather as the means to an end. There is a popular myth that a baby can mend a marriage. Of course this is rarely the case. Seldom does a new child mend a marriage or a relationship. Two unhappy or under-achieving people and a baby only combine to compound the misery.

The hitherto unchallenged fathers

We have dwelt on the plight of the single adolescent mother, poorly educated, dependent on welfare benefits, in less than satisfactory housing, struggling with children she has perhaps not always chosen to bring into the world. And we have said some-thing about the young fathers – often absent, often irresponsible, usually not in any position to support their children. For those fathers who want to and are trying to support their family, the struggle is often so hard that they may give up. Some fathers who wish to be involved may not be invited to do so. Others, not fully realising the responsibilities involved, blow hot and cold in their support. Models for fatherhood may not be immediate, since their own father may well have played an unsupportive role in family life, and examples of good parenting may be few and far between.

Part of the problem lies in simply being male. Fred, the physician mentioned in the section on sexually transmitted diseases (chapter 6) saw a good number of boys at a VD clinic in a public health centre in a large US city. He put the blame on society's sex role stereotyping, which limits and discriminates against men as well as women:

> Men don't get involved with children. They are basically not family-oriented. The families that I see have the children, they have the mother, they have the grandmother, and a couple of aunts thrown in, and the men basically are off somewhere being tough. (McGuire, 1983)

His argument is that the male is excluded from the family. He has no support and is not asked to give any – except to provide enough money. His picture of the boy friend is one we have glimpsed already:

> The baby is the little girl's doll, it's her private thing. Her mother's helping her raise it. And the role of the boy friend? The boy friend comes round from time to time and makes trouble; this is the way he's viewed. There is very little within the structure of American life that really gives male parenting much support. This is especially true in the black subculture . . . Men go to their jobs; they're not really terribly involved in the family. (ibid.)

From his experience Fred describes the adolescent male as 'the cool dude', clocking up the sexual performances. He claims that the typical American father does not change a nappy, cannot cook and does not know where anything is – and is not expected to. Fred blames television for the unhelpful models of fathers that families see every day:

> Think about how many times you turn on the TV and you see a man preparing a meal, say, or a man taking care of a child in some sort of reasonable, responsible way. Look at all the sitcoms, the man's always the idiot. . . . They're tough and

decisive, and they're uninvolved in anything except 'You say that again and I'll knock your teeth out!' Always having fights in bars, that's basically the role for the male. (ibid.)

Fred's experience points up the tremendous ignorance and insecurity among young men and demonstrates the difficulties faced by service providers, among whom Fred has a particular role.

Adolescent fathers have pressing needs which are not being met, nor even considered in a useful and practical way. Fathers have been ignored. The needs of teen mothers and their children can be seen in many ways as being practical in nature and it is always easier to deal with practical issues than psychological ones. Documentation on teenage fathers in both Britain and the US is sparse because teenage fathers have been regarded by service providers, by their families and even by themselves as irrelevant in their partners' and their children's lives. Often too young to have acquired a decent education, useful skills or good wages, they are difficult to track down and to talk to. Shame, doubt or fear can lead to denial of the paternity. All of these factors could well contribute to poor communication between the two youthful partners, neither of whom is likely to be a skilled communicator. He may feel he is obliged to adopt a 'hit and run' image to save face among his friends. He is given little encouragement to handle any of his feelings, whether they are about supporting his partner and her child, or about running off. He may well want to do the former but not know how. He may not want to face his responsibilities, or be able to cope with his feelings of guilt about that. Young teenage mothers are encouraged to talk, and we are beginning to understand some of their circumstances. We address their feelings and we help them to understand those feelings. The adolescent confusion of young fathers is not addressed to nearly the same extent. This may be because in general boys are not helped through puberty, their feelings and their sexuality are seldom matters of serious discussion. Few parents know how to deal with their sons' developing sexuality.

Since premature parenthood has serious negative consequences on the young mothers' lives, it may not be surprising that the same is true for young fathers. But the young fathers are at a double disadvantage during the first stage of parenthood: help and support are not immediately available. Adolescent mothers are more easily helped for two reasons. Firstly the physical fact of the baby's arrival demands it. Secondly it is more socially acceptable that women should seek help than it is for men. Reaching young men can be hard in this matter of adolescent parenthood, since services related to reproduction and parenthood are traditionally the preserve of women. And where funding is limited the emphasis for service has to be placed on the immediate problem, the primary client whose pregnancy denotes status. The young woman finds it hard enough to attend her first antenatal clinic. The young man would rather not venture anywhere near, if he does not have to. The 'macho' image may seem even more vital to maintain in such time of stress, and in his anxiety he might be quite unapproachable.

However, there is a dilemma. While there is the undoubted responsibility for the child by the father, whatever his commitments to the relationship with the mother, it may not always be appropriate to encourage him to stay in his relationship with her. The younger the mother, the less likely she is to want to continue a relationship with her baby's father. Miller (1983), in her discussion of very young parents, synthesises the point:

> The professional dilemma remains as to how much to encourage the relationship between the teenage mother and her baby's father. Clearly, they both share responsibility towards the child. Promoting their staying together, however, may result in a too early (teenage) marriage, with probable subsequent economic difficulty and perhaps a family size larger than desirable.

Conflicting views of motherhood among both boys and girls reflects society's ambivalence: that motherhood is natural, is inevitable, brings status, maturity, independence, but also that motherhood puts you on the shelf and turns a girl from being sexy to domestic. These perceptions parallel the ambivalence about young fatherhood: the pride in 'scoring', the need to make a baby to prove virility, and yet the fear of responsibilities, the lack of emotional constancy. A vast number of adolescent boys drift towards fatherhood with a mixture of fantasy, apathy and indifference. It must also be said that many father more than one child to a series of girl friends in the hope of finding their own ideal family, and some even deliberately father children to different partners with no thought of settling down or supporting them.

It is not sufficient to accept the fact that teenage mothers regard this state of affairs as inevitable. Many do, however, and they deal with their new responsibilities and their losses as best they can. It is not sufficient to know that fathers often shirk their responsibilities and to know that involving them might not be what their partners want. To adopt the punitive attitude that they should take on the consequences of what they helped to create, regardless of their feelings, would also be insufficient.

One reason for fathers being left out of the picture is that, as boys, where babies are concerned, they always have been left out. Often excluded from sex education, discouraged from talking about feelings, given little opportunity to learn about and understand female reproduction and periods, many of them have not expected to be asked about their feelings and responsibilities. They probably have not ever discussed sex and relationships in a guided, sensitive or unembarrassed way. If this lack has meant anything to them it has probably felt like rejection, and rejected people behave in defensive and aggressive ways. Apart from this basic gap in their positive experience, during their partner's pregnancy they do not undergo any hormonal changes which affect their emotions or their daily functioning, neither do they experience their body changing shape and moving mysteriously about. Not only are they far removed from that, but they see their partner getting all the attention from something they themselves 'did'. As we saw at the beginning of chapter 4, even married older fathers find this aspect of expectant parenthood hard.

The confusion and the ambiguities affect not only the individual teenage parents, but also the children. The security that both its parents crave and would like to have created may elude the child too unless both mother and father are content in their affections and their relationship. Sadly, this happens all too infrequently between adolescent parents. The fourth section of chapter 8 discusses some support programmes which are now addressing the needs of young fathers.

Costs and implications of teenage motherhood

The costs of early pregnancy and motherhood are not counted merely in terms of money spent on services; there are also great emotional costs involved. The impact of an adolescent pregnancy is far-reaching, and its effects are felt within the family and across the generations. Financial costs fall both to the state and to the families concerned. Funding in Britain for all the services required for adolescents and their children comes mainly from the state. In the US most services for pregnant and parenting teenagers rely on multiple sources, a mixture of private organisations and state budgets. While funding on both sides of the Atlantic is felt to be insufficient and sources must be lobbied constantly for more, nevertheless vast sums of money are spent annually in supporting a generation of young and inexperienced parents and a generation of potentially deprived children.

The short- and long-term costs to the individuals concerned are less quantifiable. Measuring misery, depression, deprivation is not so easy, but there are many studies which indicate that families and children of early childbearers do suffer, and that the patterns of early sexual activity and parenthood repeat through the generations. The continuing need that these patterns generate perpetuates both the expectation of and actual material dependence. The loss or lack of self-sufficiency in this situation helps to create low morale and emotional vulnerability. Such losses are costly to the human psyche.

Families which are formed as a result of adolescent childbearing start out with grave disadvantages. This cannot be denied, whether or not as the years go by some of these disadvantages are successfully dealt with. There is a wealth of evidence from those who have worked with teenage mothers and supported them through months and years of adverse circumstances to suggest that having a child in early teens almost invariably reduces their life choices and those of their children. Most young mothers recognise the fact that, if only they had delayed childbearing, the future might have been brighter for them, their partners and their children.

Early childbearing in itself need not be a problem. However, the social structure of the 'developed' world makes it one since, as we have already discussed, teenage mothers have no real status, and facilities to allow them to lead a positive and fruitful life are not readily available. The home environment is one of the strongest influences on children's development, and children of the poor today tend to grow up without the benefit of forms of support which would help them to realise their full potential. Emotional, intellectual, social and financial support are all in their separate ways essential for a child's healthy growth.

The time when all these factors are at their most influential is during the last few months in the womb and the first few years of childhood. The Jesuit saying 'Give me a child until he is seven' expresses a very profound observation, yet we still remain very ignorant about what influences children at an early age and what part these experiences play in the child's psychological development. What we do know is that one of the crucial times for learning is during the spurts in brain growth. The big spurt starts with the sixth month of pregnancy and slows at around the age of two (Brierley, 1987). This information provides us with a clear basis of understanding why the early months and years are so important, and why informed adults are concerned about very young parents who seem to be starting off their lives with so few resources.

There are numerous risks to children in these circumstances. Along with lower educational attainment, like their parents, go behavioural problems, problems with self-control and a likelihood of themselves becoming adolescent parents. Although, as we have seen, they start off bright and in some cases advanced for their age, as children of adolescent parents grow their cognitive functioning shows relatively low compared with their more fortunate peers. Furstenberg (1976) found that boys tended to be more affected, and developed more behavioural disorders – they were more troublesome in adolescence. Young children of adolescent mothers who saw their fathers regularly scored somewhat higher on the scale of cognitive functioning and behaviour, but later, at ages 15–17, their school attainment was 'dismal'. This may be for many reasons, but the point to make is that the influences are multiple and they interact with each other.

Various researchers who have used different tests have come up with the same results: children born to mothers who dropped out of school before their first pregnancy had considerably poorer cognitive performances than children born to mothers who continued their schooling during pregnancy or who continued after their first child was born. Such children are likely to be behind in school and need remedial help. It is not known how exactly a mother's educational attainments affect the cognitive ability of her child, but maternal support to enable her child to stay in school, and to set and achieve its own educational goals – in other words, to make optimal use of the educational system – seems crucial (Hayes, 1987, p. 136).

The great majority of teenage mothers become dependants on state benefits. Millar (1989) argues that in Britain single mothers of any age feel more secure with regular welfare payments than if relying on maintenance and meagre earnings; until the laws change regarding the financial status of lone mothers, dependence on state benefits should not necessarily be seen as a bad thing, although teenagers themselves would usually prefer a job. Furstenberg (1976, pp. 160–2) and others have found that American teenage mothers accept welfare payments out of necessity, not choice.

Many, it must be said, have little choice: they are forced out of their parents' home by circumstances (space, conflict); many others do not question their need to be self-sufficient, and expect state welfare provision. If they are deemed 'homeless' in Britain, they are put up at hotels and guest houses providing bed and breakfast for mother and infant until suitable housing becomes available. This is a policy that is both unsatisfactory for the families involved and expensive for the taxpayer, but it is the one currently pursued for the homeless population of whatever age in Britain.

American welfare assistance is marginally the least generous compared with that of other developed countries (Jones *et al.*, 1985). In the US there is a clear correlation between the adolescent mother's choice to keep the baby and remain unmarried, and her eligibility for the welfare benefit Aid to Families with Dependent Children (Moore and Burt, 1982), young fathers being unable or unwilling to offer support (see chapter 3).

The cost of keeping a young mother under 16 and her baby falls on the family in Britain, since no benefits are available until the magic age of 16. In the US, if the family are on welfare, the young mother may receive financial help under 16. If not, her family must bear the costs, as in Britain. If the mother is attending a school or a special unit where creche facilities are available, then day care at least is provided for infants. If not, the expense of childminding elsewhere has to be met, and if this is not possible, there are considerable costs in terms of missed education to both mother and child.

Investing in children in terms of giving them the best start in every sphere of their life does not seem to be the priority of either the British or the US governments, at least as regards those in most need of support. Keeping young parents dependent on the state for their essential livelihood forces upon them a lack of choice and a way of life that can only reinforce their sense of lack of control over their own and their children's lives. Thus their options are severely reduced.

The costs to the nation of the consequences of early childbearing are very difficult to ascertain. American evidence (collected by Hayes, 1987, pp. 133–4) charts the extensive demands on the state resources that are created by young mothers. Such costs are at best estimates. For example, in the US in 1985, costs to be incurred over a period of 20 years (1985–2005) for teenage mothers giving birth to half a million babies in one single year were estimated to be $6.4 billion. If all these births had been delayed until the mothers' twentieth birthday, just over one-third of that amount could have been saved. In New Jersey alone, if all teenage births in 1984 had been delayed until the mothers were 20, it is estimated that some $50 million could have been saved (Johnson and Ziskin, 1988).

To help explain the above speculation, over half of the 1975 AFDC budget goes to households where the mother was a teenager at the time her first child was born: around 6.5 billion dollars, plus over 2 billion more when health costs are added. Ten years later, in 1985, total AFDC spending – including food stamps and Medicaid – had nearly doubled, to 16.6 billion dollars. Young mothers are not only more likely than older mothers to be receiving such aid, but the amount of their grants individually is larger, primarily because they have larger families.

Family planning services are required by law to be available to all AFDC recipients in the US. With an estimated 7 million poor and near-poor women annually needing organised family planning services, and the annual cost per head being in the region of $82, the total annual cost for this service would be in the region of $560 million. Although funding for these services has increased rapidly over the last two decades, present funding comes nowhere near meeting the need (Levitan, 1985), and about one-third of low income women received no subsidised family planning services in 1983. While setting aside large sums of money on efforts to reduce teenage pregnancy, and providing additional federal funds for individual states to use under maternal and child health headings, at the same time, by under-resourcing family planning services the Reagan administration failed to provide assistance to the poor in limiting their family size, thus undermining efforts to reduce state welfare expenditure and to promote independence.

The picture is no different in Britain where comparisons of this sort are equally valid, although of course the figures are lower. For example, Laing's study (1982) concluded that, for every £100 spent on family planning services in the public sector, health and social services can expect to benefit by £130 in savings from each avoided unplanned conception, and by £530 in the case of unplanned, premarital conception (Bury, 1984). Similar calculations are reported from the US (Rodman *et al.*, 1984). The benefits of preventive investment costs far outweigh the costs of support services.

For costs of a different nature, the monetary consequences of early, unintended childbearing are often dismissed by adolescents, as the expenses of contraception are perceived as socially and personally more significant. From her research Luker (1975) suggests four categories of costs perceived by women as arising out of the use of birth control. Firstly, the social/cultural implications discussed in chapter 2 and the *laisser-faire*/responsibility ambiguity of being sexually prepared. Secondly, the social and possibly financial costs of obtaining contraceptives. Thirdly, the costs to the relationship of maintaining contraceptive use when male attitudes still oppose their use. And fourthly the biological/medical costs to the body of some birth control pills and devices. In relation to these disadvantages, starting a family is not perceived as costing very much to adolescents at the time of making these choices.

Neonatal care for underweight babies is another example of potential savings from preventive investment. In New Jersey, the average cost of medical resources to keep a low weight baby alive in a neonatal care unit is $9000, while prenatal care throughout a pregnancy costs only $1200–$1500. The state must also bear the cost of these low weight babies born to young, welfare-dependent mothers should they develop handicaps of any kind and require long-term medical, social and educational provision outside the normal expectation (Johnson and Ziskin, 1988). It can be seen that continuing health care and hospital costs to the children of young parents are considerable. The cost of treatment for sexually transmitted diseases is also greater among this age group than among older parents. The cost to the state of education facilities outside the normal state provision is similarly significant. Special units, alternative schools, home tuition are all expensive extras, the costs of which fall to the state, and would be unnecessary if funds were first of all directed towards education in sexual responsibility among adolescents.

With family breakdowns and behavioural difficulties adding to the problems in a young family living on the edge of poverty on state benefits, social workers are part of the family system; they must also be paid for. As family supports they are a costly addition to any state budget. And since unplanned babies to young mothers are more likely to be abused and neglected, more likely to be conferenced on and taken into care, than those whose birth was delayed and planned, costs that are possibly not considered by the general public begin to assume large proportions. The charges of fostering and adoption and keeping children in the care of the local authority cannot just be measured in financial terms. The misery and anguish suffered by parents and children before, during and after the separation can be devastating and can have lasting damaging consequences to both parties.

Behavioural and psychiatric problems among young mothers and their children incur financial costs over a number of years as well as causing irreversible family breakdown. These problems could be prevented if political vision and funds were available to break the cycle of need. But already in the 1990s this view is shifting in Britain, as the teenage population dwindles, for the theory is that young school leavers will be sought after for employment, and having babies will not seem the only way of seeking status and independence. However, child care for those who do have children would be built into the employment arrangements. Or so let us hope and work towards. By contrast, in the US there is currently great concern about education programmes not keeping pace with the growth in technology and children leaving school with even less skills than hitherto. Employment prospects in these forecast circumstances would be bleak indeed for young parents. Their children would no doubt multiply as a result, for, as we have seen, there is a definite correlation between teenage unemployment and early parenthood.

Not all mothers who give birth in their teens fall by the wayside. Many return to their education after a few years, when their children are older, and if they have not been too browbeaten over the intervening years by unsatisfactory relationships, more children than they had planned and financial strain. Teenage mothers in Baltimore who returned to education after a gap of years actually did better than some who finished school with neither qualifications nor children (Furstenberg *et al.*, 1987). The situation of the young mothers had improved considerably by the time they reached their thirties. Many, for example, eventually continued their education: about one-third received some postsecondary education and 5 per cent completed college. Two-thirds were employed at the end of the research, and only about a quarter were receiving public assistance. Significantly, the majority who were doing well financially were currently married or cohabiting, yet their marriages had been largely unsuccessful. In other words, having a baby while still at school and missing the chance of obtaining a high school diploma seems to spur on some young mothers to skills training or academic heights later in life. This evidence is encouraging.

One of the pupils of the Bristol Unit, now aged 29, returned one afternoon and told her own story to the 15–16-year-old mothers there:

When I got pregnant I was just fifteen. My school asked me if I wanted to go back into the fifth form so that I could take my exams. But I'd heard of this special unit where there were girls in my position, and I thought I might as well go there and sit quietly for a year. I was really stupid. They didn't do exams then. I've paid for my laziness ever since. When Susie was two – I was still with her father – I had another child. After that my boy friend said we should do something about it cos he didn't want loads of children. I hadn't thought about it. It was him who saved me from myself. I began to realise there was more to life than babies. So I started looking for work or training. I've done every job you could think of. I've done all the training I've had the time for, but I still have no other qualification than a typing one. I've learnt to sell myself at interviews, and be clear about how my children will be cared for, even when they're ill. Now I'm a housing officer with a Housing Association and I've got my own house – I bought it off the Council. I've earned everything I've got and it's been a long hard slog getting it. I was lucky, my mother was a support. I didn't realise what a fool I'd been to reject my last year of schooling and doing some exams – until I was 17, and then it was too late. But you'll have to find it out for yourselves.

The overall picture remains of young families who need a great deal of support and encouragement on every level, and at some considerable cost. In chapter 8 we discuss some of the ways these are provided.

Chapter 8

Current Operational Policies

This chapter looks at a range of services, both preventive and supportive. The intention is to provide the general picture of good practice; obviously the full picture cannot be given here. There is a great deal being done in many areas, many authorities, many districts and by many devoted and committed people. Nevertheless the implication is always there that service supply falls short of need. Research evidence shows that sex education programmes can help to reduce sexual intercourse among young adolescents, to increase contraceptive use among those who are sexually active, and thus to reduce unwanted pregnancy.

It is important to stress that there are two separate aspects to the whole issue of teenage pregnancy. Firstly, to effect pregnancy prevention by encouraging responsibility in relationships and a recognition of choices and the importance of good decision-making for the future. And secondly, to offer effective and sufficient support to the young mother and her child, in order that they have the best start possible in the circumstances. The clear implication here is that if the first issue were realistically addressed, the second would not be the enormous problem that it is today.

'Sex Education' in schools

'Sex Education' (Personal and Social Education in Britain; Family Life Education – FLE – in the US) is the short-hand term for education for sexual responsibility, family relationships, consideration for self and others, and many other related topics. In Britain sex education in schools was an option until 1986, when the Education Act (no. 2) gave school governors the power to decide whether sex education should be taught in schools, and if so, what the content of such a programme should include. The governing body of a school, which includes a proportion of elected parent representatives, states the school's policy on sex education, and it is the head's duty to ensure that the staff put it into practice. School governors also now have the right to accept or reject parental requests to withdraw their children from sex education provision. Such provision should include, says the Act, a contribution to the teaching about HIV and AIDS.

In Her Majesty's Inspectorate report (1986) *Health Education 5–16* the section on sex education in the secondary school (11–16/18) stresses the importance of sexual relationships in our lives and justifies sex education as crucial for preparing children for their future responsibilities as adults and parents (para. 44).

The recent changes in sex education provision in Britain show a recognition of the importance of sensitivity in sex education as well as some move to establishing programmes which are directed to school children of all ages. Circular no. 11/87 states:

At the primary level particular care and sensitivity is needed in matching teaching to the maturity of the pupils involved, which may not always be adequately indicated by chronological age. At this level, teaching should aim to help pupils cope with the physical and emotional challenges of growing up and give them an elementary understanding of human reproduction. Pupils' questions should be answered sensitively and with due consideration for any particular religious or cultural factors bearing on the discussion of sexual issues. (DES Circular 11/87, para. 15)

For secondary schools the Circular continues:

In the secondary phase, sex education does not usually feature as a discrete subject on the time table but is commonly subsumed within a broader programme of personal and social education or health education. Whilst the physical aspects of sexual behaviour may well be encompassed within the teaching

of biology, opportunities for considering the broader emotional
and ethical dimensions of sexual attitudes and mores may arise
in other subject areas. (DES Circular 11/87, para. 16)

These observations suggest some understanding of the need for
sex education in schools. If this need were met, young people
would have a better chance to understand themselves and the
consequences of their sexuality than the previous generation had.
The HMI report (1986) was concerned to see that, whatever the
government's policies in this area, the significant benefits of sex
education from an early age should be stressed:

> Research has shown that if children are not provided with
> correct information about human reproduction when they are
> ready, they invent their own explanations. These can be even
> more amazing than the truth and in the long term may be
> confusing and anxiety-promoting and require much unlearning.
>   (Went, 1988)

Although it is *still not mandatory* in Britain to include sex
education on the curriculum, the Department of Education and
Science and Her Majesty's Inspectorate demonstrate (albeit from
different standpoints) a very clear commitment to sex and relationships education and wish to encourage schools to develop such
programmes. Responsibility for this rests solely on the governors,
and parents must be given the opportunity of approving the
programmes. Many schools, however, do not include sex education as such on their syllabus, but deal with sexual responsibility
issues as they come up within their more widely-scoped 'social'
education programmes. The latest thinking is that 'specialist'
speakers should not be invited and that teachers within the schools
should be expected to take on all aspects of such programmes.
Carol Lee's book *The Ostrich Position* (1983) describes captivat-
ingly the role of the sex educator in Britain, and the crying need
for such 'specialists'. Sadly, the Department of Education and
Science currently feels it is no longer appropriate to employ such
specialists. Ashton and Seymour (1988) describe an abortive
attempt to set up a comprehensive programme in Liverpool.
    The great majority (94 per cent) of British parents wish their
children to receive sex education at school (Allen, 1987). The

parents themselves admit to embarrassment when talking about sexual matters and feel ill-equipped to instruct their children satisfactorily (Lee, 1983). American parents feel the same; 98 per cent of parents report needing help in talking to their teenage children about sex and seven out of ten want teenagers to be taught about contraception in schools, although most parents believe that the responsibility for this should not be with the schools alone (Guttmacher, 1981). This proportion is similar to that found in Britain (Allen, 1987). However, while many parents think they *should* discuss sexual matters with their children and may be willing to do so, they are unable to provide their teenagers with accurate information on most of these issues. Studies have shown that less than 50 per cent of women knew the most likely time of the month when they could get pregnant; only a few per cent more knew how long a sperm could live inside a woman after intercourse; a mere 18 per cent knew that pregnancy can occur 48 hours after ovulation (Rodman *et al.*, 1984).

At the end of the 1970s sex education in the US was mandatory in only three states and the District of Columbia. Only seven other states encouraged it. Six of those states and DC encouraged schools to discuss birth control, and three positively discouraged such instruction. One state (Illinois) along with DC encouraged their schools to discuss abortion with their pupils, and three specifically discouraged it. Twelve states and DC required parental consent to their children's attendance during sex education classes. Many of the school districts that provided sex education gave parents the option of excusing their children from such courses. Policy was extremely varied and for the most part left to the local school districts. It was estimated that many children, about four-fifths of 12–18 year olds, were not receiving sex education.

Even mandatory sex education does not mean that all children are instructed. In Maryland, for example, which is one of the forerunners in sex education, and which has required sex education since 1973, still only one-quarter of students take the sex education courses on offer. So, although schools may put on courses which are mandatory, student attendance is not.

Where sex education does exist, it may be a separate course, a section of a course, a single lesson, a film (with or without discussion follow-on) or it may be overtly or covertly integrated into other course work. Whatever form it takes, it may be available to 35 per cent of public and private school students; 40 per cent to teenagers aged 13–19; 70 per cent to teenage women aged 15–19 (Rodman *et al.*, 1984). In New Jersey, where the numbers of teenage pregnancies are among the highest in the US, a survey of all school districts (NJNAP, 1986) found that FLE was taught in schools in all districts, at Elementary level (up to 14) and Secondary level (up to 18), covering all topics but not in all classes. Some parents were involved in developing the curriculum. Two-thirds of the schools taught contraception in at least one high school grade. This represented progress. A later survey, however, found that New Jersey still lacked 'substantive resources to implement the full scope of the family life education mandate' (Johnson and Ziskin, 1988).

Much sex education still consists of giving information on the menstrual cycle, venereal diseases and reproductive anatomy, rather than providing a full programme to embrace such topics as contraception, masturbation, decision-making, emotions and personal values. Kirby (1984) estimated that less than 10 per cent of all American students took comprehensive sex education courses.

Gradually the climate has been changing, as awareness of the need for relationships education has grown. More and more schools and organisations (Planned Parenthood, YWCA, etc.) are operating programmes to help young people take responsibility for their behaviour. However, until there is an overall federal policy the difficulty inevitably remains that all students do not get the benefit of airing and discussing *all topics* and that *contraception and responsibility for one's own fertility* – a most essential part of such a programme – is not always dealt with.

Regarding effectiveness, results of surveys differ, but the general picture in the US is that, among those students who took a full course on sexuality and responsibility in relationships, sexual intercourse took place to the same extent as among those who had not; however, if they had benefited from a course, they were more likely to have used contraception at first intercourse and were less likely to have experienced a premarital pregnancy. One high school programme in Minnesota, which combines family planning services with education, dramatically decreased teen pregnancies. Over a three year period this programme produced a fall in the pregnancy rate of 56 per cent among adolescents in one school and

23 per cent in another. It seems that this sort of programme is effective and could be used elsewhere (Rodman *et al.*, 1984).

There are two major difficulties with the delivery of sex education. Firstly, society's ambiguous attitudes to sex, denying its reality and its consequences for teenagers on the one hand, while on the other advertising its fantasy and mystery – the 'naughty but nice' syndrome. Lee (1983) speaks for sex educators generally. Other people blame them for getting children to talk about sex.

> While adults in general baulk at telling young people the facts, those of us who do are always going to run the gauntlet of public disapproval. It is so easy for moral indignation to be raised against us. Spurious statements attacking us are commonplace.

Secondly, while society on both sides of the Atlantic is beginning to wake up to the necessity of an overall mandatory sex education policy, the training of teachers in this area is sadly lacking. No specific training is given to teachers who are given the responsibility for such programmes, and many, though willing, like the parents feel inadequate for this. And now, since reliance on specialist speakers must dwindle, the onus is very much on individual teachers. At a time when the teaching profession feels hard-pressed and low in morale, sex education increases the burden of teachers' duties. The subject matter requires tremendous personal awareness as well as sensitivity, in both handling and delivery. Yet no formal training is offered to those who are expected to provide it. The result of this confusing and ill-thought-out expectation is that in practice teachers feel inadequate and are unable to carry out the required task, and the students are very poorly served indeed.

Sweden is the first country in the world to have established an official sex education curriculum for schools. It is compulsory and extended to all age levels. Contraception and human relationships are dealt with in depth. In the survey of 37 countries carried out in 1983 by the Alan Guttmacher Institute no other country came anywhere near Sweden in this provision. One reason put forward for this is the fact of carefully planned links between schools and contraceptive clinic services; these links were set up in 1975 following the liberalisation of the abortion law. Interestingly enough, both abortion and pregnancy rates for teenagers have dropped dramatically in Sweden since that time, although the same cannot be said for adults (Jones *et al.*, 1985, 1986; Goldman and Goldman, 1988).

While Canada, England and Wales and the US generally leave it up to the local policy-makers, the Netherlands takes a more pragmatic view and encourages the teaching of contraception by subsidising mobile educational teams under the guise of the private family planning association (sex educators, the very people British schools have lost). With the added bonus of some excellently directed materials on contraception and sex-related topics in the media, youth surveys show that knowledge of how to avoid pregnancy appears to be virtually universal (ibid). The policy in France is that sexuality is dealt with in schools for all adolescents, although in practice interpretation of this provision is left with the local decision-makers.

For the teachers, knowing what they should be doing is one thing. Actually doing it is quite another. Doing it effectively is another thing again. Children cannot benefit if their teachers are ill-equipped and ill-trained.

For adolescent students, if they are fortunate enough to have access to an effective course, having the knowledge is one thing, but we know that an enormous number of school students do not even have the benefit of that knowledge, since they were either not obliged to attend courses or they were not in school at the appointed time. For many of those who are able to benefit from sex education programmes, putting the knowledge effectively into practice is still difficult, it seems.

In Britain the problem of premarital, unintended teenage pregnancies is not going to go away. In the US the problem is proportionally much worse. Except for the rare innovative programmes, sex education is fulfilling neither the requirements of the political briefs nor the request of the parents, nor of the young people it purports to support.

The provision of birth control for young people

Growing numbers of teenagers use family planning clinics. Numbers in the US have risen from under 400,000 in 1971 to over a million and a half in 1983 (Vinovskis, 1988, p. 36). During the first half of the 1980s the number of family planning clinics increased in both Britain and the US, offering full and confidential advisory services to all, including adolescents. Even so, among NHS Family Planning Clinics in England and Wales, the relative number which were known to run young people's advisory services was small – about one in 22 (Bury, 1984). Unfortunately, due to financial constraints in Britain, this provision is suffering threats of cut-back instead of being increased yet further, and the service that is provided does not necessarily meet the needs of the adolescents it is specifically designed to help. By contrast, the growing move-ment to provide birth control clinics in American high schools is beginning to help meet some of the young people's needs in the districts where these clinics exist (see below). One of the great advantages of such school-based clinics is their accessibility to young males as well.

Unfortunately, the same tendency applies to family planning services as to so many others: while being easily accessible to the middle and upper income women, poor and young people find it that much harder to take advantage of what is theirs by right. The New Jersey Network on Adolescent Pregnancy (1986) estimated that:

> in 1984 . . . only about 25% of the state's women at or below 150% of the poverty level who needed family planning services had access to free or subsidised services. Similarly, only about 28% of the teens at risk of pregnancy has similar access.

In New York, where teenage pregnancy is an urgent problem, a number of organisations have been set up specifically to help young and poor people, and there is considerable emphasis on pregnancy prevention. Planned Parenthood (which started in 1916 with the first birth control clinic in the US) has clinics in the South Bronx (New York's highest teen birth rate), Manhattan and Brooklyn. The Community Family Planning Council has a net-work of reproductive health service provision which is free to all under 21: 40 per cent of their clients are teenagers. Both these organisations also offer multiple services of support, education, training and counselling to encourage a way of life other than early childbearing.

Teenagers are more likely to use contraception now than they were 10 to 20 years ago. The advent of the pill in the late 1960s brought a new freedom for men and women and a real shift in sexual responsibility from the man to the woman. However, with the anxiety about the possible side-effects of the pill prevalent during the late 1970s, and the newly learned freedom for men, together with the apparent reluctance of the adolescent to be seen to be planning her sex life, contraceptive use among teenagers remains erratic and confused. This in spite of the variety of methods available and the improved accessibility of services, as well as the very real threat of AIDS today.

McGee (1982) gives a clear synopsis of the difficulties faced by both client and service provider. Adolescents are inexperienced at arranging their own health care; the communication and negotiation required in intimate relationships are difficult for them; they worry about being seen going to a family planning clinic; and they are self-conscious about their bodies to the extent that they are equally as reluctant to touch themselves in the use of contraceptive devices as they are to be examined by a doctor. Studies consistently show that teenagers are ignorant about the risks of pregnancy and do not believe that pregnancy will happen to them. Given all this, the problems of obtaining and using contraceptives seem to many young people far greater than those of unwanted pregnancy. Over half of a sample of schoolgirls in Bath, England, knew that contraceptives were available free from family planning clinics, but more than one-third did not know where these clinics were (Hill, 1988).

The development from a dependent child to an independent adult is the hallmark of an adolescent, and in the process of this development, long-term rational anticipation of possible consequences is a skill that has to be learnt. The condom has a poor image today in spite of information and propaganda about AIDS. Therefore if the girl feels unable to ask for the pill or fails to take it regularly, contraception is rarely used. Very young pill-takers find the routine and the continuing motivation difficult, as affections fluctuate and change targets, and they move in and out of relationships. This is very much the general picture for teenagers, and the younger the partners, the greater the fluctuation and the greater the risk of pregnancy.

In 1974 the British DHSS recommended that all health authorities should be encouraged to set up special sessions for young people. This recommendation was updated in 1980. In the US, while family planning services were available mainly at private clinics until the 1960s, from 1967 such services were required by law (the Child Health Act) to be made available to all recipients of AFDC. In 1970 funds for these services were authorised, as well as for training and research in the field of birth control (Levitan, 1985). Teenagers, including minors, have excellent access (Rodman *et al.*, 1984) to family planning at these clinics and a majority do not require parental consent. In spite of the not uncommon public resistance to raising sexual awareness and encouraging responsibility among the young (see Lee's comment, beginning of chapter 8), much research has found that adolescent sexual behaviour has changed only in the direction of greater responsibility with the increased availability of family planning services. Christopher (1987), for example, found from the evidence available from studies of the clientele of such clinics that the positive consequences of these clinics have not been sufficiently stressed. Most of her clients (Haringey, London) were 17 or 18 and wanted advice on a safer method of birth control. Working-class girls were in a particular double bind, feeling trapped by their culture into non-use, and yet needing reassurance that use was OK. A middle-class girl is congratulated for her sense of responsibility. A working-class girl can be severely punished for hers (Bury, 1984; Skinner, 1986). The international study by Jones *et al.* (1985, 1986) found that those countries with the most effective programmes for sex education have the *lowest* rates of teenage pregnancy, abortion and childbearing.

Family planning services are free to all teenagers in Britain regardless of their status. Medical practitioners may require parents of young women under the age of 16 to be party to their advice. This depends on the discretion of the doctor concerned, and the question of confidentiality. In the US family planning services are available free to teenagers in families eligible for Medicaid (a federal-state programme of medical care for those on very low incomes), and otherwise to those who are fortunate enough to have access to clinics whose policy is to provide free reproductive advice to those who require it (including school-based clinics). Other clinics charge a modest fee. The same question regarding discretion and confidentiality applies to girls under 16. Those who do not qualify for Medicaid must consult a private doctor, thus incurring considerable expense. Pharmacists' supplies are also expensive. Private physicians are on the whole unwilling to provide services to Medicaid patients, thus making it quite difficult for young people in rural areas with no clinic in the immediate vicinity.

In Britain the condom must be paid for except when obtained from a family planning clinic. The pill is the most freely available form of contraception for women – it is the one most handled by GPs. By contrast, in the US there seems to be some ambivalence about pill use among both practitioners and potential young users. The fact that US medical practice requires that a pelvic examination be performed before the pill can be prescribed is, for many adolescents, a daunting influence against this method. We have already discussed the ambivalence of adolescents towards their own bodies. There is tremendous antagonism in a young person of either sex to another person examining them physically. It must be remembered that sexual activity, including intercourse, usually takes place in the dark, under covers, and the younger the participants the more likely this is. It should not be beyond human ingenuity to realise that, because of this legal/medical requirement, girls will be put off the simplest and most effective method of birth control.

The postcoital contraceptive pill – the 'morning after' pill – has been available in Britain for several years, and many young women have made effective use of this method. There is, however, considerable ignorance among the young about the function of this pill, and they are not aware that it is effective up to 72 hours after the unprotected intercourse. In Sweden, in spite of that country's success in terms of general compulsory sex education in schools and the low teenage pregnancy rate, the 'morning after' pill is not available, as it is considered not entirely moral. In the US the federal Food and Drug Administration has not approved postcoital use of pills. Jones *et al.* (1985) report that no plans exist as yet to market them, although they are available in some college health clinics and rape treatment centres.

As discussed in chapter 2, most of the clients presenting for contraception at clinics have been in a stable relationship (Skinner, 1986; Christopher, 1987; McGuire, 1983) for on average 6 months and are not virgins. Many of them have not been using any form of contraception. The rest have been using an unreliable method. A good many of them are already pregnant on first presenting at clinic.

Abortion, perceived and used as a means of birth control, is unfortunately not uncommon. In the US abortion facilities are more available in the cities. In England and Wales abortion is available free of charge under the NHS, although, due to bureaucratic delays, almost half of British women choose to pay for abortion in the private sector. In the US most women must pay for abortions themselves, and for a second trimester abortion the cost can be substantial (Jones *et al.*, 1985). The availability of abortion is – perhaps more than any other service – subject to fluctuation according to changing political forces. The 1973 Supreme Court decision to allow abortion to all who are deemed to require it was revoked in 1989, and the decision whether to offer it or not is once again with each state. Some will continue to provide abortion services and some will not. Economics and politics will continue to influence the outcome.

Compared with the situation in the US, medical services of all kinds are easily accessible in Britain, which should not make contraceptives difficult to obtain if they are really wanted. British teenagers grow up accustomed to attending clinics and the doctor's surgery for all sorts of things and therefore (in theory) need not feel self-conscious.

> This combination of ease of accessibility and familiarity with the health care system probably serves to remove many of the social, psychological and financial barriers to contraceptive services experienced by young people in the US. (Jones *et al.*, 1985)

In fact, this is exactly the environment that school-based clinics hope to create. For while Britain's teenagers still find it difficult to go and seek help and advice on birth control, young Americans find it even more so.

As part of a fresh initiative in the US, there is a now a growing network of school-community links in the form of school-based clinics. In an article on School-Based Adolescent Health Care Programs, Keenan (1986) outlines their ethos, their function, their staffing and their funding. The idea is to use the public secondary schools as principal health care settings for adolescents. In 1985 they numbered 60 nationwide. In New Jersey alone between 1986 and August 1988 the number went from 0 to 29. It is hoped that, as their effectiveness in adolescent pregnancy prevention is recognised, federal funding will be allocated to all districts. And since this sort of service, like many others in the US, relies so heavily on private funding, in 1985, where state money was not available, the Robert Wood Johnson Foundation linked with other foundations and corporations locally to set up 12 school-based adolescent health centres in six cities, with plans for 20 more to follow.

At present these programmes are run at centres within the school setting where teenagers of all ages go for all regular medical matters – periodic medical checks, immunisations, sports and employment physicals – which are staffed by adults who teach on the health promotion and sex education curricula in the schools, and also offer counselling and advisory services. All adolescent health problems are dealt with here – alcohol and drug abuse and the associated trauma, contraception, pregnancy, family problems – the idea being that these issues are present in the community and are so far not being effectively addressed. If the community's children get no help now, the community will be severely damaged later. This scheme, put into practice in a number of school centres in a number of states, looks as though it may be one of the best so far in combating adolescent pregnancy, and is a heart-warming sign of far-sightedness which other states and nations might do well to heed.

These centres are staffed by paediatric nurse practitioners, an innovation for American public schools – as it would be in Britain – for the contribution which nurses have been (and mostly still are) allowed to make in schools is severely limited. These projects look as though such nurses are beginning to flourish in the American school setting and thus contribute to the broad but detailed health care approach which the school-based centre offers.

These programmes function not just as part of the school health programme, but as integral parts of the mainstream health care system. Thus their funding does not come from education budgets, but from licensed medical facilities such as community hospitals and other outside sources. They are not influenced in any way by the schools in which they are located. The paediatric nurse has all the professional back-up she needs. This includes on-site physician and social services support, and the ordering of care as needed from clinical psychologists, health educators, substance abuse counsellors and nutritionists. The emphasis is on comprehensive health care for each individual. Since the main issues are seen as preventable problems such as drug abuse and pregnancy, the projects emphasise preventive on-site counselling, prompt referrals and follow-up.

A mere 20 per cent of the services offered at school-based clinics are for family planning but, nevertheless, the mere fact of providing such services can generate vehement opposition. The Catholic Church has made a strong stand against such activities in state schools: declaring that teaching the values of chastity and fidelity should take their place and, what is more, be sufficient; that federal and state laws should be amended to exclude contraceptive advice and services to young people; and that abortion only teaches and encourages violence. However, this is a minority voice, and the general trend in the US is now to realise that helpful, preventive action is essential. School-based adolescent pregnancy clinics serving males and females show very promising results (Kirby, 1984).

On a lighter note, Planned Parenthood of America have thought up and started one or two interesting schemes to prevent a second pregnancy. In Denver in 1985 the 'Dollar a Day' pilot project for teenage mothers got under way and proved quite successful; the figure of only 17 per cent repeat pregnancies within two years was less than half the national average. Now Planned Parenthood plans a scheme of offering $10 a week to teenage mothers-of-one not to get pregnant again. Says Cathleen Gentry, director of the San Mateo branch: 'We pay people not to grow crops and we pay people not to work. So why shouldn't we pay girls not to get pregnant to show that we value them? (*TES*, 26/8/89).

Very young teenagers have a particularly difficult time obtaining birth control information and services because, for one thing, they may have not reached the class or grade where sex education comes on the agenda, and for another professionals and adults in general have mixed views regarding the suitability of such services to minors, and the picture this creates is a cloudy one. In the US some states offer contraceptive advice to young people under 16, others do not. Most clinics will help any young person, but there is always the chance that an individual professional may feel uncomfortable without the child's parents' consent. This is the case in Britain too. All adolescents are at the mercy of the local service providers. And because legislation remains vague for the very young, and embarrassment is a real barrier to accessibility of services, once again: the younger the adolescent needing help, the less likely she or he is to get it. On the other hand, if the US school-based clinics really take off, the young students may find it all a great deal easier, as these clinics should be able to offer the necessary services to students early enough.

Very little has been said here about specific innovations in Britain to help adolescents prevent pregnancy. This is because there is relatively little recognition of the problem and therefore very little going on in this area. A discussion of what we feel should be happening is provided in chapter 9.

Educational provision for teenage mothers

Education is every child's right and a legal requirement. If, within the child's school years, she becomes pregnant and chooses to keep the baby, that education suddenly threatens to disintegrate, to become difficult to handle, and sometimes to be not worth the struggle. Or maybe it was all these things before, and motherhood seemed the easiest way out. However the individual student perceives it, the parents are obliged to see that their child continues her schooling, and the state must see that it is provided.

The school leaving age in both Britain and the US is 16 but, whereas in Britain students may leave at 16 with several qualifications (which are useful and valuable in the adult world), in the US students must remain in school until age 17/18 in order to graduate. Thus the emphasis on education has a different bias in each country.

In Britain some education authorities are at pains to provide alternative education of some sort to school age mothers aged 16 and under, but thereafter it is very much a question of local political will and enlightened professionals as to whether or not education is provided for young mothers wishing to go on to do further education studies or training of any kind. Very little thought has yet been given to the logistics of attending school, college, training centre or the workplace five days a week with a child who would need alternative care. In the US there is considerable awareness and enthusiasm among professionals both within and outside education, and among the students themselves, to carry on with school work, with absolute acceptance of the fact that the Diploma is a vital passport to the future (McGuire, 1983).

In the last decade or so quite an extensive number of initiatives have been taken both in Britain and in the US to provide alternative education for school students who are mothers, in order that they should not be too disadvantaged in terms of school-leaving qualifications in relation to their peers. The provision is not adequate to fulfil the need in either country, and it is extremely variable. Always, however, considerable emphasis is placed on parenting skills in all centres for pregnant and parenting teens. Some are in operation on a part-time basis only with peripatetic staff; others are like small schools and well resourced. Some have creche facilities, others do not. In each case, alongside the academic curriculum, however broad or limited that might be, preparation for parenthood and parenting skills is part of the programme. Where US student mothers continue to attend their school, parenting skills may feature less than for those who attend special centres. Some have social workers attached, some have health workers or nursery nurses, others have teachers only.

Provision in England and Wales for mothers aged 16 and under has increased with awareness of the need all over the country. In a recent survey (Dawson, 1987), which represents 60 per cent of the 105 local education authorities, a diverse picture emerges; diversity of provision – less than one-third provided a special centre with a creche, less than one-sixth provided a special centre without a creche, the rest (that is half) offered provision of the drop-in variety; diversity of space and resources – some centres operate in one room where everything goes on at once, others have the run of a suite of rooms. Group tuition was offered by 54 per cent of the local authorities. Home tuition was the most common provision, hours ranging from 3 to 15 per week. The type of provision clearly depends on the geography and the demography of the authority as well on political priorities. It is worth noting that 40 per cent of the authorities did not reply, our implication being that they probably offered sparse provision if any at all. Exam subjects were offered by all authorities, some more than others, but by no means all the school age mothers offered this rather specialised and individual teaching take advantage of it. Many do take a number of exams and do well, but some take only one or two and some take none at all.

> Simone attended one such centre from the age of fourteen when her child was born. She was entered for four GCSE subjects, but the date of her 16th birthday meant that she was allowed to leave at Easter. She could not be persuaded to stay on and take her exams, for which she was well – if not overly – prepared, and in fact dropped out of the system altogether at Christmas, having finally had one too many rows with her mother, made herself 'homeless' and been put into temporary bed and breakfast accommodation on her way to a local authority flat.

For young mothers over 16 in Britain the variety of choice that is available to their peers is sadly limited, due to lack of foresight and understanding on the part of the education authorities. Day care for their children is not automatically available, such facilities being underfunded to an extent that waiting lists for all state nurseries are long, and children considered to be at risk of parental violence are at the top. Although those who work with teenage mothers feel strongly that they and their children are at risk of a great deal of damage, the local authority cannot afford to hold this view, since resources are severely restricted. The few who manage to be found child care tend to start government training schemes and courses to learn skills ranging from business studies and typing and clerical work, to community care, to painting and decorating. A 16 year old leaving school with a baby rarely continues her education at a college of further education to take A levels, for example.

In England and Wales the majority of girls who become mothers have a poor chance of completing their schooling fully before the age of 16, and after that they have little chance to do so straight away. In Scotland, however, one project seems to fulfil a number of requirements in a most suitable setting: Wester Hailes Education Centre, Lothian, combines education to mothers under and over 16, child care on site, transport, an adult atmosphere (a pool and cafeteria) and a wide range of subject choice in a community school for students of all ages, that is 11–80 plus. All the young student mothers get free bus passes. It is a model for us all in Britain. One most important aspect of this project is the secure and free child care facility alongside the availability of education to age 18, and the encouragement to do further study. Young people are stimulated and enthused, surrounded as they are by a varied community whose common aim is creative and fulfilling education, and where this ethos is *the norm*.

The US provision is generally much nearer this model than is the rest of Britain, in that the school system there invites and expects students to stay on longer and is more realistic about care of their infants, although programme design depends on district policy and the school superintendent or head (Miller, 1983). There are inner city areas where the problems of teenage pregnancy and motherhood are particularly intense. For example a report of New York City Teen Parenting Programmes (Thomas, 1989) gives us an idea of the sort of educational provision available among an urban population where the highest rate of teenage pregnancy is recorded. In New York City it is the right of every child to receive high school education until the age of 20, although at any one time over 13,000 will be mothers.

The sheer numbers have forced awareness of the problem upon the city; there is a large number and considerable variety of alternative schools and child care available now for these young mothers, should they wish to continue with their schooling. In doing this they will have to struggle with caring for a child and obtaining a school-leaving certificate. In the case of alternative schools this certificate is usually the GED (General Education Diploma). If they have until they are 20 to do this there seems plenty of time, opportunity and support to achieve it. Federal funding provides the basis for these centres; commitment from the City, however, is the main financial resource, and charitable institutions provide the rest. YWCA (Young Women's Christian Association), LYFE (Living for the Young Family through Education), TAPCAPP (The Adolescent Pregnancy Care and Prevention Program), 'The Door', Covenant, to name but a few, offer a wide variety of free preventive and support services. They are invariably for young women aged 16–21/25, some are also for fathers, and these organisations include education up to the GED (Thomas, 1989).

Other cities, other states, have their own arrangements. While schools in Britain do not offer nursery facilities for staff or student babies, many American schools realise that this provision is the only answer to the problem. Many may think it shocking, but at least this practical solution means the young mothers have a chance to complete their education and step on to the labour market ladder with pride and a sense of self-worth. Those districts where school-based clinics have been set up in some cases offer child care for the student mothers. Such students have the opportunity to continue studying for their high school diploma. If there is not a high school with this provision located in a school age mother's area, she has a problem – unless an alternative school is available.

One example of a teen parent alternative school is cited by McGee (1982). The programme takes place in a family resource centre in Michigan which offers services and preschool facilities to the whole community, similar to that in Wester Hailes, in Scotland. One-third of school age mothers in the area attend (public transport is provided) and a small number of fathers, making – in 1982 – about 100 students a year. The education emphasis includes career development, job preparation, subsidised work experience and child care provision; in other words, everything to encourage a young parent's working towards academic qualifications, skills and a positive future.

Most education programmes for pregnant and parenting teenagers in Britain and the US serve only a proportion of the eligible population, because, although it is illegal to exclude pregnant and parenting teenagers from school, many fail to attend for all sorts of reasons. No creche at the school, hypocritical staff attitudes, transportation difficulties, lack of family support – some or all of these may cut through all the good will and practical support available.

Support programmes for pregnant and parenting teenagers

As can be seen from the previous chapters, teenage mothers still need the support of the education and public service agencies. There is today in the US a growing awareness of their need for health and welfare support. That level of awareness has not yet come to Britain.

All adolescents are eligible for social worker support if it is deemed necessary. Inevitably the availability of service does not meet the need, and many teenage parents and their families are difficult to help. Many have complex problems which call for a variety of helping skills. Many agency offices simply do not have enough personnel to cope with the demand.

Health visitors have statutory duties to visit regularly, but in practice this sort of support for the young mother and her new baby varies tremendously and inevitably depends on the sort of case load a worker has. Regular visiting in inner city areas is as difficult for health visitors as it is for social workers, and given that the teenage mothers move fairly frequently, service providers must rely to a certain extent on their adolescent clients coming to them. Only one of a sample of 50 teenage mothers in Camberwell, South London, saw the same health visitor over a two-year period (Griffiths *et al.*, 1986).

Health clinics have regular times, but many of these young people find it hard to motivate themselves to attend. Some young people alienate themselves from their helpers by being awkward. Some helpers are not adequately experienced to handle very young mothers. A 30+ year-old mother of a teenage mother may feel resentment at a young social worker or health visitor in their twenties entering her home and giving what sounds like advice on how to cope with her own family.

Marietta, a mother at the age of 15, living with her mother in an inner city area in Britain, had a social worker until some misunderstanding occurred. Marietta needed a great deal of support in a number of ways. It was felt she kept undesirable company and was easily influenced. She was picked up frequently by the police with her friends and attended court a number of times. Since the birth of her baby there was very little contact with the social worker. During Marietta's final months at the centre – which included a second pregnancy and a rather late termination, two court appearances, sitting an exam and efforts to arrange training for her and child minding for her baby – contact with the social worker was difficult to maintain. As a result Marietta had no support on leaving the centre. The social services agency had removed her name from their books.

All single teenage parents aged 16 and over are eligible for benefits which will keep them on the poverty level; in the US some of these take the form of Medicaid and food stamps.

Facing an 'adult' problem in an adolescent is not easy for society to do, and if recognition is slow in developing, political affirmation of the problem is slower, and funding slower still. In the US school-based clinics are one solution favoured by many to some of the associated problems in some locations and districts (see the second section of this chapter). And those fortunate enough to benefit from health care within the school setting may do so without the embarrassment that usually accompanies pregnancy. Funded by Health Care institutions, not Education, and targeted specifically at the young for the benefit of individuals, families and society in general, community services such as these sound like the ideal. Nevertheless, like every service, they have their limitations. They are closed during the holidays and outside the school day; they are not financially feasible within a school of less than 100 students; their existence remains highly controversial; inevitably service staff are under considerable pressure as many of the adolescents have multiple needs which cannot all be addressed. And at a time of general fiscal constraint in all areas of human service institu-tions, heavy reliance year after year on public and private monies adds to the work- and worry-load of personnel.

School-based clinics are able to offer help to all adolescents in the community and to refer them on if necessary. They may not, however, do anything for those who will not seek their services. Nor can any other agency, however well intentioned and however relevant the programme they offer, fulfil the needs of adolescents if those adolescents will not take and use what is offered. In New Jersey, for instance, there are hundreds of private agencies (aided by state funding) which deliver services to adolescents, but each has different criteria and constraints according to its funding. Young people who do not fit these criteria risk not receiving the services available. Once again, the familiar phrase: those who appear most at risk are the least likely to benefit.

Public support of teenage mothers varies in the US from state to state. Official sources provide most income support and public health facilities, and help to administer education and welfare support services, most of which are, however, directly supplied by local non-state agencies (Foster, 1986, ch. 4).

Although in theory prenatal care during pregnancy is available to all, such facilities are not always accessible to those who need them. In New Jersey, for example, there is a lack of subsidised or low cost prenatal care in certain parts of the state. UK residents perhaps need to be reminded that free services are not necessarily available to teenagers in the US. It depends on their parents' dependence on state aid in the form of AFDS (in which case they may be eligible for Medicaid) or on the type of services offered in their state of residence (NJNAP, 1986).

The Alan Guttmacher Institute (1981) reported that in 1978 in the US two-thirds of the 11,000 mothers under age 15 got no care in the first trimester of pregnancy, and one-fifth got none, or none until the last trimester. Half of the 203,000 mothers aged 15–17 got no care in the first trimester and one-eighth none, or none until the last trimester. For those aged 18–19 the comparable proportions were two-fifths and one-tenth. Not only does the likelihood of receiving care improve with age, but so does the quality of that care, as older mothers are more receptive and less anxious.

In the US Medicaid is the source of funding for 19 per cent of deliveries to teenagers, as against 5 per cent of births to women aged 20 or older. Private insurance pays 39 per cent of births to 15–19 year olds as compared with 79 per cent of births to women of 20 and over. About 1.6 million US teenagers have no health insurance – as might be expected. Teenagers are twice as likely to have to pay for their own deliveries out of their own or their parents' pocket than women aged 20 and over. Clearly, funding is more of a problem for expectant teenage mothers in the US than it is for those in Britain, where the National Health Service provides a free service for all.

Many special prenatal care programmes for pregnant teens exist in the US. However, evidence shows that in 1981 sustantially fewer than 20 per cent of pregnant teenagers were served by such programmes across the nation. The Alan Guttmacher Institute (1981) found that out of 125 cities surveyed (with populations of 100,000 or more), 107 reported some kind of special programme for pregnant teens. Most were small; only 31 provided for 1000 or more a year. Things have moved on in the States since then, but although provision has improved, several problems are identified as preventing effective prenatal care provision to teens: funding; isolation of personnel and overstretched work load; attracting and reattracting clients; identifying and drawing in the neediest ones; treating them as adults when they do turn up; time shortage preventing dealing with the clients in a holistic way – only treating the immediate issue; lack of time and funding for follow-up (McGee, 1982). This is a familiar story. Those in most need at all stages of pregnancy – the young adolescents – are less likely to benefit from the services that are on offer, and their children are more likely to suffer lastingly as a result.

McGee (1982) cites three examples of programmes which use social services agencies as a base. Firstly, a mental health agency uses volunteer paraprofessionals who themselves were teenage mothers. They make weekly visits to teenage mothers offering guidance and information about child development. Secondly, a YWCA, using public and private resources, offers a wide Pregnant Teen/Teen Mothers Programme: emotional, social, vocational, academic, parenting education and support, with a particular focus on drop outs. The Director of the project voices the ethos of all services providers to teen parents: 'We believe that when these young parents feel fulfilled themselves they can be better parents.' Lastly, yet another programme for teenage mothers, operating in a voluntary capacity, offers education which is less academic, counselling, employment guidance, 'Men's Night' events. Referrals are made through school and welfare links; there is child care, a health clinic, WIC (women with infants and children) food pro- gramme and help with transport.

There is an initiative under way in Britain to support mothers and their young children, and a great many of the mothers are teenagers, or were at the birth of their first child. The work of The Child Development Programme in Bristol (Barker, 1989) focuses on the preschool child's development and the untapped capacity of the mother to foster this. Barker believes that certain groups of parents are not given sufficient opportunity or credit in helping their children to develop healthily:

> The programme arose out of the conviction of a number of concerned people that the problems faced by parents in the more disadvantaged areas of the UK and the high demands made by modern parenting, contribute greatly to childhood morbidity as well as to later ill health, poor educational performance and social malaise. In other words, such state expenditure on ill health, on providing social welfare services and attempting to minimise the damage caused by educational failure, can be traced not only to socio-economic conditions but

also to an inadequate foundation in the early years. The quality of parenting is considered to be the most important contributor to these early problems, although the key role of societal and structural factors is also recognised.

Barker's programme is a parent support programme in which health visitors aim to empower parents and help them to develop their parenting skills in all areas of early development. Health visitors in this programme go into homes on a regular basis, covering a wider range of preventive and developmental work than that usually undertaken by health visitors. Barker argues that the welfare system as it exists today in Britain offers on the one hand 'professionals who know best' and take the responsibility away from parents, on the other a sadly inefficient and deficient service. Parents are often made to feel inadequate and powerless. The health visitors' programme focuses particularly on language stimulation, cognitive and social development, nutrition and over-all health. By their building up the confidence and sense of achievement in the mother, the child begins to thrive.

Barker's work demonstrates what can be achieved and thereby shows up the poor conditions existing in many homes, both in the children's developmental retardation and in the parents' lack of motivation through ignorance and low self-esteem. The health visitors' input helps the parents to feel that they are in control and are confidently responsible for their children. The results of the first phase (completed in 1984) point to a considerable degree of achievement: an increase in parental responsibility in the areas of general health, nutrition, language, cognitive and social changes in the children, and a decrease in child abuse due to the programme's ability to help parents to a fuller understanding of their potential. Teenage parents are among those visited on this programme, for it is in the disadvantaged areas chosen for the programme that the majority of teenage mothers are to found.

Twenty-one Health Authorities throughout Britain were actively involved in 1989 and others are joining the programme. This venture has proved its worth. More like it need to be put into operation. For programmes like this one do exactly what is needed; they help children to develop in a healthy way and enable their mothers to be part of this healthy development.

The Barton Hill Young Mothers Group in Bristol was formed

out of a recognition of the isolation of teenage mothers, the poverty trap they were in and the need for mutual support. With local authority funding in 1986, these young mothers produced a slide/tape presentation, *Too Much Too Soon*, which they show to groups at secondary schools in an endeavour to point out the realities of early, unplanned motherhood, and to encourage pregnancy prevention. Highlighting the difficulties of very young motherhood, these young mothers encourage the adolescent audience to think carefully and behave more responsibly towards themselves and each other as well as towards a possible pregnancy when embarking on a sexual relationship:

'I didn't think it would be like this, you know. I could have been a physiotherapist by now. That's what I wanted to be before I got caught with her. . . .'

'You just don't realise – well, I didn't, and look what happened to me . . . two kids before I realised that I simply didn't want to be here. And it's too late now. . . .'

This group of mothers (aged 17–25) is an excellent example of peer education. They are in the unique position of having the opportunity of expressing clearly the discrepancy between thought and action among adolescents and putting this across in an acceptable way to those most vulnerable, boys and girls equally. The young mothers also support and encourage each other in planning a future which will help them back into education or training and out of state dependence and poverty. A video update, made by the young mothers and based on their own experiences, will be available early in 1991.

Programmes for young fathers are somewhat slower in developing in Britain than those for mothers. But in the US there are some very interesting initiatives in programmes which aim to help young fathers. Teen Fathers Collaboration (Sander, 1986) offers a range of services to adolescent fathers, both married and unmarried, in a number of areas. These include counselling (individuals, groups and couples), job-related and educational services, parenting skills classes, prenatal and health care classes, family planning, and labour and birthing classes. Sited in hospitals, schools and social services agencies, 395 young fathers and prospective fathers from a variety of ethnic backgrounds have been involved. It was found that, just as girls are trying to live women's lives too soon, so are the boys trying to be parents too soon – but with considerably less support. They too feel isolated, confused, ignorant; worst of all they feel useless. From the operation of these programmes, several points are clear. Firstly, if the father desires to have no connection with the mother and his child, he will neither want nor be enticed to take part in any programme to support his new status. If the mother wants nothing to do with him, the same applies. Secondly, if the father can be tracked down or encouraged through the programme by the mother to join in the various activities of the fathers' programme, then he will slowly begin to enjoy his role. Thirdly, the mother/father/child group benefits enormously from his inclusion. The mother blossoms, the father gains understanding and confidence, the child has the chance of a really good start in life. Given the opportunity to care for their children, as well as receiving continuing support, fathers can present a very different picture from the scared runaways so frequently seen.

TAPP in Louisville, Kentucky, offers separate programmes for teen mothers and fathers. In New York City, where the need is great, there are many programmes for young parents. TAPCAPP (mentioned in the previous chapter) provides a haven of individual counselling, health care, community education (nutrition, budgeting, Maths and English), and parenting skills. The project operates in an area where 45 per cent of the population are teenagers – half of whom are unemployed; the pregnancy rate is the highest in the city, the school drop out rate is 50 per cent, the adolescent crime rate is the third highest in the city, infant mortality is the highest in the city and the incidence of paediatric AIDS is also the highest in the city. This project had groups for fathers and grandmothers, but they were unfortunately discontinued (Thomas, 1989).

Other initiatives involving young fathers in the US are currently operational. New York City boasts several centres for adolescents where fathers are helped and supported in understanding and acting out their parental role (Thomas, 1989). In an area where life style is erratic, where drug abuse is commonplace, where sexual exploitation is rampant, where up to 50 per cent of young men truant from school and fail to get a satisfactory education, and where employment prospects are extremely low for such people: constancy in a parenting relationship must seem the last improbability for a teenager. Federal funding and New York City funds support these centres; one of these is specifically for black youth, to discourage too early parenthood as it is perceived as threatening the black community. The National Urban League's programme, Manhood and Fatherhood: Adolescent Male Responsibility in African American Families, has as one of its slogans: 'Not all brothers should be fathers'. On the assumption that single parenthood and poverty help create social disadvantage in generation after generation, the NUL targets young black men and advocates and encourages responsibility in parenting as well as in preventing parenting. One of their posters reads:

> *Be careful. Be responsible.* Being a father is a lot more than just making a baby. And if you really want to know how a real man handles sex and deals with being a father, call or stop by your Urban League office. *Don't make a baby if you can't be a father.*

In Britain, where, admittedly, the problem of adolescent parenthood is not so dense, the very fact of the numbers of teen parents remaining relatively small means that services specifically designed to cater for them simply do not exist. In Britain support services of the kind under discussion here are nearly all state-funded, whereas the American system favours funding from a variety of public, private and semi-private sources. Individual clinics in Britain, GPs, Family Planning Clinics, Community centres, etc., welcome young people and in some cases offer support groups, but there are very few locations which give up time and services to teen mothers alone.

Of the few that do, the one in Haringey, London, is chiefly for contraceptive advice (Christopher, 1987). King's College Hospital, London, has been running an antenatal clinic for teenagers since 1980. Other clinics offer young mothers support services with varying degrees of appeal. Many of the young mothers in real need would not make the effort to use these services. They can only be encouraged to do so, and service providers usually have little time to 'sell' their provision outside the centre. An adolescent parent needs an adult head on her shoulders to seek out all the advice and information and accept the practical help available as she makes the transition from pregnancy to parenting services. Despite the quality of services on offer, many clinic personnel are justifiably frustrated by their inability to help all those who need it in the way they need it.

One programme designed to help children also provides a long-term supportive role for the parents. In the recognition that children from poor homes need preschool programmes to compensate for the deficiencies of their background, the US government initiated a major educational programme called Head Start in 1984. Focusing on 4 and 5 year olds (school starts at age 6 in the US), it is the largest public funded child care and development programme in the US. In spite of its obvious benefits, and the significant contribution it has undoubtedly made to many children and their families, in 1984 Head Start only managed to reach one-fourth of the eligible children. Other compensatory programmes also exist to help children catch up in all aspects of their development (Levitan, 1985). This programme is already costly, and there is insufficient funding for all eligible children to be catered for in this way. Until there is, the healthy development of deprived children and their families will continue to be impaired, and the unseen costs continue into adulthood.

Scandinavia appears to have both the political will to find solutions and the resources to make them happen. In Copenhagen, for example, a city of one million people, there are 600 day care centres. Parents pay up to 35 per cent of the cost, and state funding makes up the remainder, or pays the entire cost for poor parents (*New York Times*, Aug. 1988). British and American policy-makers might learn from the Scandinavian experience that it pays to invest in children.

State housing policies for teenagers and their children

Many teenagers continue to live at home with their parent(s), their siblings and their babies – for it is not uncommon for more than one daughter to produce a baby at roughly the same time, despite overcrowded conditions.

> A mother, still in her thirties, had her three daughters living with her, aged 19, 17 and 13. Also living in the house were the husband of the eldest and the child of the 17 year old; the 13 year old was pregnant but living in a children's home for a while as everything had got too much for their mother.

When independent accommodation is available in Britain it is likely to be substandard housing on inner city or peripheral estates. In the former the traditional urban way of life has degenerated over decades through poverty and neglect; whereas in the latter the soulless, featureless environment is often without centre and denuded of adequate facilities – even of trees. People become vulnerable and easily influenced when placed in these circumstances. Too dejected to be able to do anything about them, they are no longer able to control their lives in a positive way.

Janet, however, aged 15, was aware of what was possibly in store unless she managed to get herself and her son out of the rut:

> Look at this! Houses and shops boarded up, litter and filth everywhere, miserable people in the streets, nothing to do! I don't want my son growing up in this sorta place. It's not nice.

The same rule applies to housing as with everything else to do with the poor: the less income they have at their disposal the more they have to pay out. Eligibility for public housing in the US is restricted to households with annual incomes below 50 per cent of the median income in the local public housing area. The average public housing household has an income of 30 per cent of the area median. This is another way of saying that, whichever way you look at it, the worse off get the worst deal, and teenage parents who are lucky enough to move into state-subsidised housing are contributing to the perpetuation of poverty and disillusionment among the families that dwell there.

In Britain public sector housing boomed in the postwar period and during the early 1950s, initially under a Labour government with a strong commitment to better housing for the poor. High-rise blocks of flats followed in the 1960s. As part of the Great Society's anti-poverty legislation, a similar building boom occurred in the US in the mid 1960s under Lyndon Johnson: affordable housing was considered as essential as other services for the poor. Throughout the 1970s and the early 1980s public housing in Britain and the US worked in tandem with other state-funded services, and subsidised rents were of considerable help to a young impoverished family. In recent years, however, there have been major changes in how housing is provided.

Local authority new building has been severely restricted by rate capping, and much of the existing stock has been sold to sitting tenants. Today in Britain the poor availability of public housing seems to make no difference to young people's behaviour – a fact that surprises the government – for this knowledge is tempered by other knowledge: bed and breakfast accommodation while you wait, at the local authority's expense. Many young parents expect to be housed and find local authority bed and breakfast provision the only option. Some Housing Associations and cooperative schemes provide only a limited substitute for a council flat or house, and their waiting lists are also long.

There are few homes and halfway houses for young mothers to go to when they leave home, where collective living might ease the burden of isolation. A few places exist where pregnant teenagers and adolescent mothers and babies may spend some time while they establish their new identity, but they must soon move on again. In New York City 'Covenant House', for example, takes in mothers and babies and tries to move them back home or on to mother and baby homes where it is at all possible (Thomas, 1989). Other US states offer small hostels for a lucky few, including New Jersey where one teen mother residence opened recently. These are for the most part privately funded, and some are mostly for girls with emotional/behavioural problems also, such as the Chitterton Care Center (Bedger, 1980). A tiny percentage of adolescent mothers have the good fortune to stay briefly in this sort of caring environment. Other homeless mothers may be successfully fostered with their child: a scheme recently set up in New Jersey trains foster parents in working with teen parents. But this provision is rare. In Britain hostels for young mothers and their children are few and far between, and plans to develop this sort of provision meet with bureaucratic procrastination almost everywhere. The problem in Britain is that the state will not provide, and private bodies who might put up some funds do not yet see this area as a priority. In this respect Britain is far behind the US. Foster care for a teenage mother and her child is less and less available. One reason for this is lack of social services funding, another is the fact that adolescent mothers are a different prospect today from a decade ago.

So where do single teenage mothers go to live with their child? The majority, it will be recalled, remain single for several years. If they marry they are likely to be single once again fairly soon. Many are forced to remain in their parents' home until there is a

chance to move, or else they live with their relatives or the father's
family – if they are on good terms with them. In any event, the
choice is small between the waiting list of the local housing
authority, and temporary accommodation, usually provided in a
cramped hotel room with minimal cooking facilities. In London it
is often miles away from the teenager's home area.

Once established in her local authority flat, Clara found that
independence wasn't as easy as she had hoped. Her boy friend
came to see her and spent the night. He somehow managed to
spend the next night, and the next.

Clara was not at all happy about this. She had a good
relationship with him, but was not ready to settle down with him
– she was still only 16, had managed to get on a training scheme
and be found a sponsored child minder, and she wanted to get
on by herself for a while. It was difficult to turn her boy friend
out. If she did not, however, she risked losing her housing
benefit, without which she simply could not survive. If she did,
she felt that she would also be risking her relationship. It was a
real dilemma for her.

Girls in this position are very vulnerable. Their boy friends are not
always as understanding or generous as they might be. Many
young mothers in Clara's position have given in, and ended up
losing everything they had begun to work for, for even the boy
friends leave in the end as the relationships dwindle for lack of
outside interests and stimulation, and because of their youth and
few hopes.

Clara's boy friend was fined for 'actual bodily harm', banned
from the city but did not go to prison, as this was his first
offence. He returned to the city and asked Clara to marry him.
She was stronger than most in her position and refused. She was
subsequently questioned because he had previously brought a
prostitute to work in her home. She was terrified about the
statement she made for the court: she had not managed to
change her front door lock as she could not afford it.

This is not the picture Clara and others like her had in mind when
they applied for public sector housing.

It is possible that a girl might become pregnant in order to 'qualify' for a place in the housing queue. This is thought to be a serious possibility by some people on both sides of the Atlantic. When a British 17-year-old mother, living with her own mother and not getting on at all well with her, applied for a local authority flat she was told she would have a long wait – unless she got pregnant again, for that would ensure a quick move. So she did. On the other hand, a 16-year-old mother of two, living with and in fear of an alcoholic mother, was told by her local housing authority that she 'hadn't got enough points' to quality for a place of her own.

In Britain there is now concern in government circles: young single women are supposedly becoming pregnant deliberately in order to jump the housing queue and gain welfare benefits. It may be that they see themselves as mothers rather than as part of the labour force. Certainly the benefits they can claim may seem more attractive than the meagre training grant they would get at age 16. But Child Benefit has been frozen since 1987; grants for the poor are no longer as freely available as they were and loans have taken their place; there are restrictions on single mothers' employed activity; a lack of child care; poor quality public housing in unattractive and poorly serviced areas; these are not attractions. Punitive measures of these kinds show no care or thought for present or future generations. Once a mother, the young woman needs all the support she can get. If she has not managed to prevent pregnancy, and she has been allowed to choose to keep her baby – then, along with education and good health services, decent housing has to be her right as well as that of her child.

Training and employment prospects for parenting teenagers

The parenting of children in teenage years is a barrier to good employment prospects and thus to the ability to support a child. Market forces have made the employment prospects of young parents even worse in recent years, with unemployment rates higher among the unskilled and untrained. Many funders and organisers of training schemes do not appreciate the vital link between training and child care. Many others, including the British government, make the assumption that, with a child, work is out of the question.

Some schemes have been introduced to help them. In England there are no secondary schools offering child care to student mothers. However, young mothers aged 18 who take up the government scheme, Employment Training, are eligible for a child-minding grant of £50 per week. Unfortunately this is still not considered appropriate for young mothers leaving school at age 16 and wanting to train. Colleges of further education offer all kinds of academic and vocational courses, but very few provide a nursery for students' babies and infants. In Scotland the Wester Hailes Education Centre (see page 192) offers the best example Britain can offer of equal opportunities for all, in terms of educational opportunity and alternative care for students' children.

In the US teenage pregnancy is a relatively much larger problem and one that is addressed with more realism than in Britain. National qualifications are obtained at age 18, and not 16 as in Britain. More and more schools are providing nurseries for the infants of students in order to encourage them to continue their schooling. Once out of school the state nursery waiting list is as long as in Britain, and many mothers are prevented from working. There are, however, various training programmes federally funded for young people aged 16 and over, and projects here and there in the US have child care facilities on the premises (Levitan, 1985). But there are by no means enough.

No young people in Britain or in the US may draw benefits until aged 18, unless they are mothers; remaining in education may help advance their prospects further. The British government sponsored Employment Training programme provides further incentive with the extra £50 per week for alternative child care. But by this time the teenager who was already a mother at 16 is unlikely to be sufficiently motivated. Of course this is not true of all mothers, but if, in the intervening two years, she has produced more children, any training, work or study courses that are available become harder and harder to take up.

It is important that services and facilities are available, but availability is useless unless they are also accessible. In fact, few employment opportunities are accessible to a young mother, especially if she is single and feels trapped at home with one or more children. The range of self-help, and of educational and vocational programmes for both the employable youth and the employable poor may be wide, whether centrally or locally funded. But many potential workers lack adequate knowledge of the labour market; they may lack the confidence to go and ask about programmes, the skills to apply for courses, the patience, self-control and sufficient optimism to remain in the post they choose. This is a difficulty for young trainees of both sexes. Young people aged 16 need good models of working practice in their work or training place. This is not always forthcoming. Clara (see previous section) had not been on her Youth Training Scheme for more than a few weeks when one of the staff was suddenly not there any more. She heard that he, along with other staff members, had been fired at the end of the previous week with no warning, no official notice. Whatever the exact circumstances, Clara, young and new to work, ambitious, confused in her personal life, was determined to make a go of things. She was proud to be doing something with her life, beginning to feel she was secure at least in her career progress at last, and then she was faced with this example of working life: apparently no job is safe, no one is secure. Disillusionment set in once more.

The younger the parents the less likely they are to have good earning prospects. For example, in the US young men today with the weakest literacy and numeracy skills are eight times more likely to have illegitimate children than those with better skills, nine times more likely to drop out of school before graduation and five times more likely to turn to public assistance for basic income support (Children's Defence Fund, 1987). The problem of youth drop out, unemployment and early parenthood in the US is largely among the black and Hispanic population in inner cities. The reasons for this can be seen in various factors.

Firstly, the expansion of income support measured against the minimum wage makes it relatively attractive not to work. Secondly, as jobs have moved to suburbia and public transport has been curtailed, many central urban black residents no longer find work easily. And thirdly, those able to afford to move away from the inner city slums do so, leaving those areas relatively even more deprived. These trends apply to British inner cities also.

The quality and the quantity of government programmes offering training and work for young men and women in the US declined during the Reagan administration. There had been a shift away from serving employers (the labour market frequently failed

to match jobs with workers) towards efforts to help the disadvantaged (the inefficiencies of the labour market are still most notice-
able when serving the poor) (Children's Defence Fund, 1987).

In Britain, as the plethora of schemes and programmes continues to change confusingly, there is a general feeling that what is
offered is not always very relevant or even realistic in terms of the
labour market. Many 16 year olds embarking on a Youth Training
Scheme do not find it a rewarding experience, for they are not
stretched and challenged enough and tend to feel they are being
used as 'cheap labour'. Those who complete the two years may
find themselves as jobless and ill-equipped for available employment as before.

However, nothing that is available is of any use whatsoever to a
16-year-old mother leaving school (however many GCSEs she
may have) without alternative means of child care. Similarly
nothing is available which gives hope to a young father with few
qualifications and little confidence. Governments on each side of
the Atlantic must address themselves with greater realism to this
issue. The opportunity of gainful employment for a living, self-
and family-supporting wage is essential for each adult, whether
parent or not, in our present societies. Children of unfulfilled
parents are likely to suffer deficits similar to their parents in all
aspects of their lives. In this sad and short-sighted way the same
problems are perpetuated in successive generations.

Chapter 9

What Further Needs to be Done?

This final chapter sets out some recommendations for action and for future policy. It has to be accepted that many young people are sexually active in their early teens and that such activity can lead to unplanned pregnancy. Since adolescents who find themselves in this predicament have the right to choose the outcome of the pregnancy, it must not come as a surprise if many of them reject termination and adoption and choose motherhood. Society allows adolescents this choice and this decision. Society then has an obligation to carry through the implications of this. Young women who have been allowed to make the decision to become mothers are surely entitled to support in so doing. What otherwise is the point of allowing an adolescent to keep her baby? Or of allowing her to become pregnant? Or of allowing or tolerating her sexual activity in the first place?

Two things need to be done. Firstly, support for these newly created young and mostly female-headed families. We must certainly improve the support system in all its aspects so that the children have some prospect for a healthy, happy and worthwhile life. If we want healthy, happy children, we must first help the mothers in whose charge they are.

Secondly, there is prevention of the problem before it becomes one, and this in the long run would prove a far less costly business. Initially it is a question of acceptance of children's sexuality on the part of society. We must recognise education for sexual responsibility as an integral part of our social system. Institutions such as the family, the media and schools should ideally work together to help parents and children to understand that sexuality is one of many important attributes of human beings, and that it needs careful and sensitive nurturing, not wrapping up in myth and mystery. As for our sexual function: it is only one of many aspects of human relationships, and it is the responsible nature of human relationships that sex education should focus on. The recommendations outlined below deal with each area of need for young mothers and their children, and lastly with education and training for early pregnancy prevention.

Health care and moral support

Adolescent mothers and their children are disadvantaged in many, if not most aspects of their lives, and need reliable and consistent support for a considerable time. As young women become parents – sometimes even before they leave school – and their children begin life with loving but inexperienced and ingenuous mothers, sensitive help and guidance are required from the start. As an overall policy, since there clearly is a need, very young mothers and their children could be recognised as a category that merits a special slot on the clinic or hospital weekly timetable, whether it be for antenatal or infant check-ups. Many places already have such a system, and these are run by enlightened and committed staff. But many do not, and if each clinic, health authority or district were made aware of the special need, and were empowered to offer special services to these families, mothers would feel more valued and children would have a better chance in life. It is so easy today, when funding is limited and resources and personnel are lacking, to take the short-term view and get through the day's list of clients and be thankful not to have had to work too much overtime. But it is the long-term view we must have in mind, for without action for the long term, the children of these teenagers are likely to fare no better than their parents, and the problem really will not go away, even for the next generation. There is widespread fear among pregnant teenagers that antenatal staff will show a punitive stance to their pregnancy, and these fears need to be dispelled.

Health visitors can play a significant role in the young parent's life, as we saw in chapter 8. The work of Barker's team would be a useful model for authorities to adopt everywhere for disadvantaged and inexperienced young mothers, encouraging mothers to take control and pride in their children's development, and children to develop healthily.

Social workers also play an important role in the lives of many teenage mothers; in many instances they are the key link for a young mother between her needs and the various agencies that she depends on. These may be any one or all of the following: housing, welfare benefits, education and health. A social worker or counsellor is sometimes the only person a lone mother has to share her problems with. Very often it is the counsellor's role that is the only effective aspect of the job the social worker feels able to perform. In a world where crisis work increasingly takes over, this role may be diminishing. It would be ironic if so much social work effect went into fulfilling the statutory duties surrounding child abuse that vulnerable mothers were not given the help they need to prevent child abuse occurring. Girls who become mothers in their mid-teen years and who have little or no support from their own families need to rely on someone who knows the various other support systems, and who can lead them directly to the appropriate one. It would be helpful if social service agencies recognised this category of young mothers as requiring special attention.

The need to understand and recognise the responsibility of young fathers is crucial. More research must be done in this area, and more projects like Teen Fathers' Collaboration (Sander, 1986) in the US funded by the Ford Foundation (see chapter 8) could be set up in locations already used by service agencies. The confusion and rejection that young fathers feel when faced with their partners' pregnancy and motherhood are not taken sufficiently into account. Once motherhood is well under way and his child is born, the father needs to be involved – if that is what is generally wanted – for the benefit of all three people principally concerned. As we have shown, from a very early age boys are not encouraged to discuss relationships and parenthood, and they are in general even less experienced than girls in all matters to do with feelings, sex, relationships and the responsibilities of parenthood. Help for fathers in the very early stages of parenthood may be one of the clues to happier and healthier families, and thus to more balanced children than the classic disadvantaged child of the lone teenage mother.

Somewhere to live

Teenage mothers are encouraged to remain at home with their families for as long as possible. But if relationships break down or there simply is not room, the teenage mother and her child will sooner or later require their own home. In many cases – and these are usually the most needy – this requirement is sooner rather than later, and often of a crisis nature. The local authority is obliged to house the homeless mother and child, and when hotel accommodation in the form of bed and breakfast is all that is available, mother and child have a very poor start indeed to 'independence'.

There are two issues here. Firstly, young single mothers need shelter, and for many reasons it may be impossible to remain in their parents' home. Secondly, young mothers need support and guidance as they embark on parenthood, having themselves barely left childhood. Halfway housing in hostels with individual family units equipped with basic necessities, as well as comfortable communal areas, may well be an answer for some. Funding for these would have to be found from various sources. In the present climate in Britain it seems the state would not see fit to provide. In the US a start is being made in this area, with funding from both public and private sectors, but we have a long, long way to go before the need is met in any considerable measure.

Adolescents are possibly one of the most difficult groups of people to help, especially those who have become parents earlier than originally intended; personnel serving this group have to be particularly sensitive to their needs and whims, and particularly strong in reliability and consistency. It is such people as these who would be required as wardens of halfway houses, so that there is always a good parent model on the premises for help and support.

As a matter of policy single parents under 18 should not be housed in conventional public sector housing. The majority who are in such need as to require instant rehousing with their child are the very ones who are least able to cope with their newfound independence. As we have discussed in previous chapters, young mothers in this situation often find themselves prey to exploitations which they are too inexperienced to resist. They and their children are placed in moral danger when housed in this way. Their isolation exposes them to many social evils which they are too young – and too desperate in their need for housing – to have contemplated.

Young parents need help with handling money, sorting out their various benefits and understanding the relationship between benefits and income and, in some cases, maintenance. The warden of a halfway house could be the social worker described in the previous chapter. There is in any case a clear need for the different agencies to link up in some way and work in tandem to help these young parents get on their feet and provide the best for their children.

Clearer legal and financial status

The legal status of teenage mothers needs to be clarified, especially of those who become parents below the age of consent (age 16 in Britain and most states in the US). If the law relating to unlawful sexual intercourse is felt to be good, then it must be seen to operate. If not, it should be scrapped. Perhaps the age of consent should be lowered, in line with evident sexual activity which makes the law a bit of an ass.

Birth control advice should be a teenager's right, however young she/he is; and both advice and contraceptives, including condoms, should be free. Adolescents should know where they stand regarding confidentiality, and whether parents need to be told of their activities.

The right to choose the outcome of the pregnancy exists in theory, and yet the right to abortion is not clear-cut, and the right to give a child for adoption is not much talked of. A pregnant adolescent may well choose to keep the child. She may have first thought about abortion, but for various reasons may not have achieved it. When a mistake has been made through the fault of a hypocritical society, it seems doubly unjust that moral outrage should prevent its being rectified. Abortion within a reasonable period of gestation should be every teenager's right if she so chooses, but this right must be followed up with intensive counselling on both loss and birth control. If legal access to abortion for teenagers is cut off there will be more illegitimate and unintended births, and this will incur far greater costs to the state in terms of welfare support than the abortion procedure and the counselling involved.

Maintenance by the father needs to be looked at with objective sympathy. The father's responsibilities cannot continue to be ignored, and yet making legal requirements that he help maintain his child seems an insuperable task – and in many cases an unrealistic one. At present any maintenance paid by fathers and disclosed by mothers is deducted from benefits. This method does nothing to encourage either honesty or responsibility. A disregard of a proportion of maintenance would, we feel, be an encouragement to young single mothers to seek financial support from their child's father.

Teenage mothers find systems of state support very complicated and many need help in filling out forms and following correct procedure. These systems should certainly be simplified. Whatever their benefit or income, young mothers are almost invariably on the poverty line, and without means of child care or reasonable income they and their children are likely to remain there. Some financial incentive is necessary for young mothers to pull themselves out of poverty. One way of doing this would be to increase the earnings disregard – that is the amount of money a single mother can earn without having her benefits reduced. In Britain currently single parents are allowed to earn up to £15 a week without affecting their income support; this could be doubled with negligible cost to the state. Offering grants and loans to adolescent mothers is no answer to their financial problems, for their economic prospects are such that they will never be able to repay them.

Education

Education for mothers of age 16 and under must be seen to continue. There can be no question that, whatever a child's circumstances, schooling must be made available in an appropriate form. Both in Britain and the US the law makes it clear that this should be the case. And yet, when it comes to school age motherhood, many education authorities in both countries fall well short of the mark. School age pregnancy and motherhood are facts of life, and it is dim-witted to suppose or pretend otherwise.

Those responsible for providing education to these very young mothers – however small their number in any given authority – must offer an appropriate service. In the light of all the evidence about disadvantaged children to very young mothers and especially to parents with very few skills and no qualifications, it is both short-sighted and unethical not to offer them the chances to complete their education that are equal to those offered to their childless peers.

The Miles report (1979) recommended that school age mothers in England and Wales should return to their school to complete their education. Society has not thus far come to terms with the reality of school age mothers; education authorities think fit to provide alternative education either in small units (which have many advantages) or on an individual home teaching basis (generally considered unsatisfactory but better than nothing). In the US many districts have schools which keep their young mothers on, and provide a nursery for their children; other districts provide alternative schools for mothers with facilities for their children. Each of these solutions provides for both school age mother and her child, representing an acceptance of the situation by local districts. Our model would be Wester Hailes (chapter 8) in Scotland, where free education for young mothers is the norm and free child care provision is on site, until the mother reaches 18; she has a chance to take A levels and may be encouraged to continue with further education.

Teenage mothers who wish to continue their education after age 16 should find no impediment in doing so. Anyone of any age should have access to education, but especially young people, and especially those who have in the past not responded to schooling that has been offered. Young teenage women, who find themselves mothers earlier than they had hoped or expected, may express the wish to catch up on education previously missed, or to continue their education beyond 16. Teenage mothers in Britain should have the opportunity to study for more GCSEs or other qualifications, while teenage mothers in the US should be able to qualify for their diploma in the normal way. Since much evidence shows that the mother's education has a considerable and positive impact on her child's development, policy-makers – and then service providers – must be made aware of the importance of education for this group and be given the resources to provide it.

Training and employment prospects

It is unquestionable to us that, just as young women with a child should have the right to continue their studies if they wish, so should they have the opportunity to train or to work. Young women without a child, and all young men (regardless of parent status), have this opportunity. Education, training and employment represent passports to independence, self-sufficiency, satisfaction with life and a sense of achievement and fulfilment which enhance the human condition and the quality of life. If a parent has sufficient education, the chances are that training and then employment may follow. Without a completed education training is essential in order to obtain meaningful employment. For women of uncertain confidence and little sense of achievement, employment with neither education nor training is invariably poorly paid and dead-end type work.

Women who leave school at 16 with a child in Britain should have the same opportunity to train or work as their childless counterparts, and the same deal as 18-year-old mothers on Employment Training schemes: that is funding for regular daily child minding. It is iniquitous to condemn all mothers of 16, who may no longer attend school for lack of child minding, to live on income support as of necessity. In the US, where continued attendance at school is encouraged as a matter of policy, and where attendance at special centres is possible due to recognition of the exceptional need (as in New York, see chapter 8), training and employment prospects for those who are *poorly* motivated are barely accessible. And for young mothers with children in inner city areas where in any case jobs are hard to find, expectations are few, and there is little choice beyond welfare benefits and more children.

Our recommendations in this matter of further study, training or work stem from the notion of equality. Young women leaving school as mothers at any age need a great deal of support. Those who have little family support and few resources are those who most need encouragement and most need worthwhile occupations outside the immediate home setting. Our recommendations extend therefore to an encouragement of public thinking along the lines of greater value placed on women. Firstly, that child rearing is valuable and important work and should be valued in a way recognised by society – that is, by payment. Secondly, that if a mother wants to work and feel part of the social system in this way, if she wants to increase her knowledge and broaden her horizons, then her children need not be considered a hindrance to that; in fact the children invariably benefit.

We would wish therefore that more consideration be given to the contribution that all school leavers can make to the world of work and to the nation's economy, quite apart from the fact that satisfaction in a variety of activities means more interesting and lively people. The ripple effect of this reaches out to the whole family, and children flourish if their parents are happy.

One final but essential reason for this recommendation is the tendency of young mothers at home on welfare benefits to have no clear idea of their long-term future, or of their worth, and to go on having more children. Their poverty makes no difference in this connection: if they cannot get status any other way, having another baby will give it to them in the short term.

Child care

None of the recommendations in the previous two chapters makes any sense unless those young mothers who need help have someone to care for their children who is reliable, consistent, trustworthy and cost-free to the mother. Even if mothers do not have an immediate aim, if their child has a regular child minder they are free to investigate possibilities and seek advice. They have the chance for the first time in their lives to look outward, to extend their horizons, rather than perpetuating a possibly stultifying role by looking inward and staying at home.

One of the most difficult decisions a young mother has to make when she wants to take up work of some kind is which move to make first – look for child care or for a job. If she is resourceful and has family and education to back her up, and even someone to mind her child while she makes her choices, there is no problem. But there are many mothers without these assets, for whom no choice but motherhood on benefits is often the continuation of the downward spiral.

State-run day nurseries (funded by local authorities) are no longer as available as they once were to a majority of needy children. In most authorities today only those children considered to be 'at risk' are eligible for a place at such a nursery, and children of teenage mothers do not automatically have priority – although in a very few areas they do. With all the recent focus on the importance of preschool provision, we would recommend that funds be made available for more day care facilities free of charge for small children of mothers who want to work.

Since research has shown how beneficial the care of a child by someone other than the mother for even a few hours each day can be, some means should be found of providing this sort of service. As with other preventive measures, a relatively small amount of money spent in the child's early years represents savings many times that amount in the years that follow.

Preschool education is much discussed these days, but little seems to be changing in spite of evidence of its enormous benefits to both child and mother. The Head Start programme in the US, set up to provide early education for deprived children, has been found ultimately to save seven times the amount originally spent (Levitan, 1985). This sort of sum appears not infrequently in American research, but it is a measure of concern as well as of evidence that a little preventive work NOW can save a great deal LATER. Financial savings in this case also represent comparative improvements in the quality of life.

Governments must be convinced by the evidence from both research and the service providers that funding for child care at every stage is essential for the health and well-being of our nation's parents and children. It could even be said that the health of the economy also depends on this sort of provision.

Sex education

While support for teenage motherhood is essential – and costly – if we wish to create healthier, happier and more economically viable families, it must not be forgotten that much teenage pregnancy and parenthood could be avoided if appropriate prevention measures were taken, at relatively little cost. The provision of sex education remains, in both Britain and the US, on a patchy scale, as we saw at the beginning of chapter 8.

In order for young people to be responsible in their behaviour and in their relationships, several factors have to come together. Firstly, children need from birth to be well nourished in every sense, to be cherished, wanted and loved for themselves and not for what they represent. Many young parents need encouragement to do this. If parents can be helped to overcome difficulties and inhibitions in nourishing and cherishing their children, those children will fare better in this respect. Secondly, children must have facts and information from an early and appropriate age regarding their sexual functioning and the consequences of sexual activity. This must be reliably and sensitively given from a sound and confident source. Embarrassment needs to be overcome in the early years, and parents can help here by being good examples of affectionate and responsible people.

Sex education in schools needs to follow this model. It must start young, at primary or elementary level, and at least by the age of 9. Dealing with menstruation and touching on contraception with groups of 14 and 15 year olds is foolishly locking the door after many a horse has bolted, and yet this is not uncommon practice. As one girl in the Bristol Unit put it: 'Why didn't we have all this two years ago? It's too late. We would've been a lot better off if we'd been able to talk about these things then.' Responsibility for oneself and one's relationships, for one's future and for one's creations, as well as for the environment and one's place in it, is something that must be instilled into every child. It should start at home and should be part of the school's curriculum, featuring regularly over a period of many years as children develop and mature.

The fact that children mature at different rates should not deter any teacher or school programme. Children will absorb what is relevant for them at the time and put the rest aside: better to give out information early and risk repetition than to give it too late. This is one reason for a continuing programme of regular times for learning and discussion. Such programmes should in our view never discriminate between the sexes: both boys and girls should be fully informed about male and female sexuality and thus would benefit enormously in sharing thoughts and feelings about relationships.

Treated in this way, adolescents should no longer feel deliberately ignored and deceived. They need no longer feel they must not ask questions. They need no longer assume that everyone's 'doing it', so they ought to join in. Treated thus like intelligent and sensible beings, our children might just begin to behave like intelligent and sensible people. It must not be forgotten that expectations of our young have a good deal to do with what we ultimately find they turn out to be. Many adults, especially those at the helm of curriculum decisions, seem to forget that adolescents have the potential for making good decisions, and also for controlling their own lives. Boys must be included in all these programmes, and special attention needs to be given to their part and their responsibility in procreation, for up till now the consequences of teenage pregnancy have fallen very heavily on the girl (and her family).

The power of social attitudes is in our hands. We are part of that power. We can begin to shift the emphasis if we try, and all the evidence suggests that we should try. We are asking for a reappraisal of current policies on sex education; we are asking governments, local authorities and parent governor groups not to hide their heads in the sand, but to face the facts that information and discussion about sexual matters are vital for our children's well-being and healthy development in all aspects of their lives.

The school is certainly the place for sex education to take place in a routine and organised way. This is not to say that parents do not have a large part to play as well. Adolescents often find communication with parents difficult; but if adolescents have more chance to work through their own ignorance and embarrassment, this may help the parents and ease communication between the generations. At the same time other institutions, especially the media, must shoulder some of the responsibility for our children's present ignorance, and could do more to encourage a new approach to gender roles and sexual relationships. Contraceptives should be accepted as part of normal advertising programmes, especially those aimed at teenagers. This in itself, after the initial shock waves and streams of indignant (and embarrassed) letters, will help to create a more matter-of-fact attitude to conception and contraception that will foster responsibility in young people. All the evidence shows that more open display and discussion of sex in a straightforward and informative way does not encourage sexual activity where it was not known before; rather, it increases sexual responsibility in the use of safe protection against pregnancy and sexually transmitted diseases.

Despite all the progress in contraceptive provision, much still needs to be done for older teenagers. Skinner (1986, p. 154) describes (in a footnote!) how a teenage mother was counselled when in hospital after her second abortion.

> The young hospital doctor making his ward rounds stopped to talk to her about the pill, which she was to be given on her discharge. He told her simply how the pill worked, then explained to her how it should be taken . . . . His voice was low and his language simple. The girl contributed to their discussion, not the least intimidated or defensive because of her ignorance. He spent 10 or 15 minutes with her, and when he left the delighted girl said: 'Never in all the times I've been pregnant has anyone talked to me like that'.

The benefit to human happiness of that short interview seems comparable with a heart transplant operation, and it was a great deal easier to achieve. At least we should ensure that everyone gets *that much* out of the NHS.

Some problems arise from out-of-date terminology. Clinics providing contraceptive advice need to be named in a suitable way; 35 per cent of the sample of 133 fifth and sixth formers in Hill's (1988) survey felt that the term 'family planning' was inappropriate. Teenagers interviewed by both Sharpe (1987) and Birch (1987) did not attend clinic, as they thought that family planning clinics were places where people planned their families.

Training personnel who work with teenagers

People who work with adolescents need particular training in order to deal effectively with postpubertal change and confusion. Those who are in the position to advise and guide young people in decisions about their sexual lives need special training to help them make these decisions. It is not simply a question of handing out the pill or warning about the 'safe' period. It probably would not be an exaggeration to say that all adolescents are confused and embarrassed by sex at some stage during their teenage years, some are bewildered throughout that period, and many are alarmed and frightened. Where else will they find some sensible answers, some comfort and some understanding but from adults, both from the example they set and the way they relate to adolescents?

If those adults are themselves confused and embarrassed they are of little use to the young people they are trying to help. If teachers are expected to give classes and run courses in PSE/FLE they must be equipped to do so, both in knowing the subject matter and in having the confidence to handle it. Where such programmes exist, many teachers who are not trained in this area are expected to take them on. We strongly recommend that teachers who feel they are not appropriate or simply do not want to do so, should not be required to provide sex education in schools. We suggest also that those who are willing to take on this task should benefit from training courses for the purpose of educating effectively. At a crucial stage in their lives, sex and relationships and responsibility must be treated clearly and sensitively with adolescents. Teachers cannot do this unless they themselves feel clear and sensitive about the subject matter. Training and regular refresher courses would enable them to come to terms with their own feelings and sexuality. Many adults would admit to the need for help in this. It would certainly help our children if adults were less inhibited in helping them to discuss their doubts and anxieties. We cannot expect parents to make a start, but we could help this generation of adolescents become more helpful parents to their children.

Adults outside the school system who provide young people with services related to sex, reproduction and parenthood should also receive training, and for the same basic reasons. A great number already, like many teachers, provide a good and personal service to young people. It is also important that, where fathers are offered help and support, those providing such services should be male. Young men are in general too inhibited to discuss their sexual life or even the consequences of it with women clinicians.

This is often a make or break time for teenagers. The opportunity to talk freely, with enough time, and to return for more, is also important. If this opportunity is available – and known to be available – to young men and women, we might prevent many an unwanted pregnancy, and many of the unhappy consequences of unintended pregnancy described in these pages. We suggest training which would help staff, male and female appropriately, to empathise more with adolescents, and to help them listen better so that young people may gain self-confidence in a responsible way and feel empowered to take control of their behaviour. Again, for these adults, this would take the form of coming to terms with their own sexuality and resolving issues by raising awareness and discussion.

Adults may feel affronted at these suggestions. But perhaps there is less harm in admitting that some things are too difficult to face and help is needed with them, than in pretending that all is well. Children see through facades of pretence. Nothing is gained in the long term when adults who are unsure of their own ground try to help children to be sure of theirs. It does not work.

If these policies were carried out, the savings to the nation's budget would be phenomenal, but would not be immediate. We would have to wait a generation before we could see any improvement. Training for personnel working with adolescents would represent the beginning of greater knowledge and understanding of the complex nature of human sexuality and relationships. Meanwhile the other recommendations would also need to be addressed in order to support as they deserve the young parents today who became parents before they had intended, and to help their children develop healthy, happy lives.

Changing the popular view of teenage mothers

Teenage mothers get a bad press. This is hardly surprising: all the people who write about teenage sexual activity, and all the 'experts' on the subject, are considerably older than teenagers themselves. It is impossible for teenagers to control the discourse about themselves, and very difficult sometimes for them just to get a hearing. Gradually, throughout the media, this situation is changing: Sharpe's book (1987), based on British teenage mothers' own accounts of their lives, and McGuire's similar (1983) presentation of US mothers are notable milestones. We too have attempted to let teenagers' words illustrate many of the points that our book makes.

Our own views will by now be clear. We seldom feel teenage pregnancy is A GOOD THING. All of us reach the point of maturity at which we contemplate becoming a parent at different chronological points in our lives. However, in our view few teenagers appear ready for parenthood; and that is true of virtually all 16 year olds and younger.

Teenage motherhood is not, however, inevitably a disaster. Its success, in terms of the healthy development of both mother and child, depends above all on the right kind of help being available at the right time. One of our tasks in writing this book is to encourage everyone who is concerned with pregnant adolescents (including their relatives) to work to this end. When attending clinics or other kinds of services in connection with their condition, for example, teenagers should not be scapegoated.

Our other task is to seek prevention, in preference to cure. Calling for sexual restraint by teenagers might be useful, and receives added impetus with the threat of AIDS; but to assume that it will be entirely successful is simply naive. Teenagers need – and indeed deserve – access to appropriate contraception, just as older people do. And the creation of sexually healthy attitudes, needless to say, needs to be tackled from a child's earliest years.

References

Aggleton, P., Homans, H. and Warwick, I. (1988), 'Young people, sexuality, education and AIDS', *Youth and Policy*, 23.

Alan Guttmacher Institute (1976), *Eleven Million Teenagers* (New York).

Alan Guttmacher Institute (1981), *Teenage Pregnancy: One problem that hasn't gone away* (New York).

Allen, I. (1987), *Education in Sex and Personal Relationships* (London: Policy Studies Institute).

Ashton, J. and Seymour, H. (1988), *The New Public Health* (Milton Keynes: Open University Press).

Barker, W. (1989), Summary: The Child Development Programme. University of Bristol.

Bedger, J. E. (1980), *Teenage Pregnancy: Research Related to Clients and Services* (Springfield, Ill: Thomas).

Bettelheim, B. (1976), *The Uses of Enchantment: the meaning and importance of fairy tales* (London: Thames and Hudson).

Birch, D. M. L. (1987), *Are You My Sister Mummy?* (London: Youth Support).

Blondel, B. *et al.* (1987), 'Pregnancy outcome and social conditions of women under 20: Evolution in France from 1972 to 1981', *I. J. Epidemiology*, 16, 3, 425–30.

Bolton, F. G. (1980), *The Pregnant Adolescent: Problems of Premature Parenthood* (Beverly Hills, Ca.: Sage).

Bowie, C. and Ford, N. (1989), 'Sexual behaviour of young people and the risk of HIV infection', *J. Epidemiology and Com. Health*, 43, 61–5.

Brierley, J. (1987), *Give me a Child Until he is Seven. Brain Studies and early Childhood Education* (London: Falmer).

British Pregnancy Advisory Service (1978), *School Girl Pregnancies: an introductory report* (Henley in Arden).

Broverman, P. K. and Strasburger, V. C. (1989), 'Why adolescent gynaecology? Paediatricians and pelvic examinations', *Paediatric Clinic of North America*, 36, 3, 471–87.

Bury, J. (1984), *Teenage Pregnancy in Britain* (London: The Birth Control Trust).

Butler, N. R., Ineichen, B., Taylor, B. and Wadsworth, J. (1981), *Teenage Mothering*. Report to DHSS, University of Bristol.

Butler, N. R. (1988), Talk, 'Youthscan – A survey of British Youth', reported in *J. of Adol. Hlth & Welfare* (Winter 1988).

Campbell, A. A. (1968), 'The role of family planning in the reduction of poverty', *J. Marriage and the Family*, 30, 236–45.

Campbell, B. (1984), *Wigan Pier Revisited: Poverty and Politics in the 80s* (London: Virago).

Cartwright, A. (1976), *How many children?* (London: Routledge & Kegan Paul).

Children's Defence Fund (1987), *Declining Earnings of Young Men: their relation to poverty, teen pregnancy and family formation* (Washington, DC: Adolescent Pregnancy Prevention Clearing House).

Christopher, E. (1987), *Sexuality and Birth Control In Community Work*, 2nd edn (London: Tavistock).

Clearie, A. F., Hollingsworth, L. A., Jameson, M. Q. and Vincent, M. L. (1985), International trends in teenage pregnancy: an overview of 16 countries, *Biology and Society*, 2, 1, 23–30.

Corby, B. (1987), *Working with Child Abuse* (Milton Keynes: Open University Press).

Coyne, A. M. (n.d.), *Schoolgirl Mothers* (London: Health Education Council).

Cross, M. and Smith, D. I. (eds) (1987), *Black Youth Futures* (National Youth Bureau).

Dawson, N. (1987), Survey of educational provision for pregnant school-girls and schoolgirl mothers in England and Wales. Unpublished M.Ed. thesis, University of Bristol.

Dowling, C. (1981), *The Cinderella Complex: Women's Hidden Fear of Independence* (New Jersey: Summit).

Dunnell, K. (1979), *Family Formation 1976* (London: HMSO).

Elster, A. B. and Penzarine, S. (1979), 'Adolescent pregnancy: where is the unwed father?' *Paediatrics*, 63, 5, 824.

Family Policy Studies Centre (1986), *One Parent Families* (London).

Farrell, C. (1978), *My Mother Said: the way young people learned about sex and birth control* (London: Routledge & Kegan Paul).

Field, F. (1989), *Losing Out: the Emergence of Britain's Underclass* (Oxford: Blackwell).

Foster, S. (1986), *Preventing Teenage Pregnancy: a public policy guide* (Washington, DC: Council of State Policy and Planning Agencies).

Fox, G. L. and Inazu, J. K. (1980), 'Patterns and outcomes of mother-daughter communication about sexuality', *J. Social Issues*, 36, 1, 7–29.

Francke, L. B. (1978), *The Ambivalence of Abortion* (New York: Random House).

Francome, C. (1986), *Abortion Practice in Britain and the United States* (London: Allen & Unwin.)

Furstenberg, F. F. (1976), *Unplanned Parenthood: the social consequences of teenage childbearing* (New York: Free Press).

Furstenberg, F. F. (1980), 'Burdens and benefits: the impact of early childbearing on the family', *J. Social Issues*, 36, 1, 64–87.

Furstenberg, F. F., Brooks-Gunn, J., Morgan, S. P. (1987), *Adolescent Mothers In Later Life* (Cambridge: Cambridge U.P.)

Gilligan, C. (1982), *In a Different Voice* (Cambridge, Mass.: Harvard U.P.).

Golding, J. and Butler, N. R. (1986), 'The end of the beginning', in N. R. Butler and J. Golding (eds), *From Birth to Five: a study of the health and behaviour of Britain's Five Year Olds* (Oxford: Pergamon).

Goldman, R. and Goldman, J. (1988), *Show Me Yours: what children think about sex* (Harmondsworth: Penguin).

Grazi, R. V. *et al.* (1982), 'Offspring of teenage mothers: congenital malformations, low birth weight and other findings', *J. Reproductive Medicine*, 27, 89–96.

Griffiths, S. M. *et al.* (1986), 'Providing services for teenage mothers: experiences from Camberwell', *Public Health*, 100, 1, 33–41.

Hayes, C. D. (ed.) (1987), *Risking the Future: Adolescent Sexuality*. Vol. 1, *Pregnancy and Childbearing* (Washington, DC: National Academy Press).

Heaton, T. B., Lichter, D. T. and Amoateng, A. (1989), 'The timing of family formation: rural-urban differentials in first intercourse, childbirth and marriage', *Rural Sociology*, 54, 1–16.

Hein, K. (1987), 'AIDS in adolescence: a rationale for concern', *New York State J. of Medicine*, 87, 5, 290–5.

Hein, K. (1988), AIDS in adolescence: exploring the challenge. Report to the National Invitational Conference 27–8 March, New York.

Hein, K., Vermund, S., Drucker, E. and Reuben, N. (1988), Adolescent AIDS cases: epidemiological differences related to geography and age, Soc. for Adv. Med. annual research meeting, March.

Henshaw, S. K. and Van Vort, J. (1989), 'Teenage abortion, birth and pregnancy statistics: an update', *Family Planning Prospectives*, 21, 2, 85–8.

Hill, M. (1988), 'Do family planning facilities meet the needs of sexually active teenagers?' *B. J. Family Planning*, 13, 4, 148–51.

Hudson, F. (1985), The education of schoolgirl mothers: a case study. Unpublished M.Ed. thesis, University of Bristol.

Ineichen, B. (1977), 'Youthful marriage: the vortex of disadvantage' in R. Chester and J. Peel (eds), *Equalities and Inequalities in Family Life* (London: Academic Press), pp. 53–69.

Ineichen, B. (1979), 'The social geography of marriage', in G. Wilson and M. Cook (eds), *Love and Attraction* (Oxford: Pergamon).

Ineichen, B. (1984/5), 'Teenage motherhood in Bristol: the contrasting experience of Afro-Caribbean and white girls', *New Community*, 12, 1, 52–8.

Ineichen, B. (1986), 'Contraceptive use and attitudes to motherhood among teenage mothers', *J. Biosocial Science*, 18, 4, 387–94.

Jackson, S. (1982), *Childhood and Sexuality* (Oxford: Blackwell).

Johnson, R. L. and Ziskin, L. Z. (1988), *Alternatives: Report of the New Jersey Task Force on Adolescent Pregnancy* (New Jersey Dept. of Health).

Jones, E. F. *et al.* (1985), 'Teenage pregnancy in developed countries: determinants and policy implications', *Family Planning Perspectives*, 17, 2.

Jones, E. F. *et al.* (1986), *Teenage Pregnancy in Industrialised Countries* (New Haven, Conn.: Yale U.P.).

Jowett, A. (1988), *The Independent*, 28 April.

Keenan, T. (1986), 'School-based adolescent health care services', *Paediatric Nursing*, 12, 5, 365–9.

Kiernan, K. E. (1980), 'Teenage motherhood: associated factors and consequences: the experience of a British birth cohort', *J. Biosocial Science*, 12, 4, 393–405.

Kiernan, K. E. (1986), 'Teenage marriage and marital breakdown: a longitudinal study', *Population Studies*, 40, 35–54.

Kinard, E. M. and Klerman, L. V. (1980), 'Teenage parenting and child abuse: are they related?' *A. J. Orthopsychiatry*, 50, 3, 481–8.

Kirby, D. (1984), *Sexuality Education: an evaluation of the effects* (Santa Cruz: Network Pubs).

Laing, W. A. (1982), *Family Planning: the benefits and costs* (London: Policy Studies Institute).

Lee, C. (1983), *Ostrich Position* (London: Writers and Readers).

Lees, S. (1986), *Losing Out: Sexuality and Adolescent Girls* (London: Hutchinson).

Levitan, S. (1985), *Programs in Aid of the Poor*, 5th edn (Baltimore, Md.: Johns Hopkins U.P.).

Luker, K. (1975), *Taking Chances: Abortion and the Decision not to Contracept* (Berkeley: U. California Press).

Marshall, W. A. (1981), 'Changing patterns of physical development and health in children', in R. Chester *et al.* (eds), *Changing Patterns of Child Bearing and Child Rearing* (London: Academic Press).

McCarthy, J. and Menken, J. (1979), 'Marriage, remarriage, marital disruption and age at first birth', *Fam. Planning Perspectives*, 11, 1, 21–30.

McGee, E. (1982), *Too Little, Too Late* (New York: Ford Foundation).

McGuire, P. (1983), *It Won't Happen to Me: Teenagers Talk About Pregnancy* (New York: Dell).

McRobbie, A. (1978), Working class girls and the culture of femininity', in *Women Take Issue*, Women's Study Group, CCCS, University of Birmingham (London: Hutchinson), pp. 96–108.

McRobbie, A. (1989), 'Motherhood, a teenage job', *Guardian*, 5 September.

Metson, D. (1988), 'Lessons from an audit of unplanned pregnancies', *British Medical J.*, 297, 904–6.

Miles, M. *et al.* (1979), *Pregnant at School* (London: National Council for One-Parent Families).

Millar, J. (1989), Lone Mothers: Dependence and Independence: policy claim for single parents, Annual Conference, National Council for One-Parent Families, 14 April.

Miller, S. H. (1983), *Children as Parents* (London and New York: Child Welfare League of America).

Moore K. A. and Burt, M. R. (1982), *Private Crisis, Public Cost: Policy Perspectives on Teenage Childbearing* (Washington, DC: Urban Institute Press).

Murstein, B. I. (1986), *Paths to Marriage* (Beverly Hills, Ca.: Sage).

New Jersey Network on Adolescent Pregnancy (1986), *No Easy Answers* (Rutgers University).

Norwood, R. (1986), *Women Who Love Too Much* (London: Arrow).

Oakley, A. (1979a), 'The Baby Blues', *New Society*, 5 April.

Oakley, A. (1979b), *Becoming a Mother* (Oxford: Martin Robertson).

Osborn, A. F., Butler, N. R. and Morris, A. C. (1984), *The Social Life of Britain's Five-year-olds* (London: Routledge & Kegan Paul).

Osofsky, J. D., Osofsky, H. J. and Diamond, M. O. (1988), 'The transition to parenthood: special tasks and risk factors for adolescent parents', in G.Y. Michaels and W. A. Goldberg (eds), *The Transition to Parenthood: Current Theory and Research* (Cambridge U.P.), pp. 209–32.

Petchetsky, R. P. (1984), *Abortion and Woman's Choice: The state, sexuality and reproductive freedom* (New York: Longman).

Prendergast, S. and Prout, A. (1980), 'What will I do . . . Teenage girls and the construction of motherhood', *Sociological Review*, 28, 3, 517–35.

Pringle, M. K. (1980), 'Aims and future directions', in G. Pugh (ed.), *Preparation For Parenthood* (London: National Children's Bureau), pp. 54–61.

Pugh, G. (1980), 'Some current initiatives', in G. Pugh (ed.), *Preparation For Parenthood* (London: National Children's Bureau), pp. 9–42.

Renvoize, J. (1978), *Web of Violence* (Harmondsworth: Penguin).

Richman, N., Stevenson, J. and Graham, P. J. (1982), *Pre-School to School: a Behavioural Study* (London: Academic).

Rodman, H., Lewis, S. H. and Griffith, B. (1984), *The Sexual Rights of Adolescents* (Columbia U.P.).

Rubin, L. B. (1976), *Worlds of Pain* (New York: Basic Books).

Russell, J. (1981), 'Medical and social hazards of teenage pregnancy', in D. F. Roberts and R. Chester (eds), *Changing Patterns of Conception and Fertility* (London: Academic), pp. 183–92.

Russell, J. (1982), *Early Teenage Pregnancy* (Edinburgh: Churchill Livingstone).

Ryan, G. M. and Sweeney, P. J. (1980), 'Attitudes of adolescents towards pregnancy and conception', *A. J. Obs. Gynae*, 137, 3, 358–66.

Sander, J. (1986), *Working with Teenage Fathers* (New York: Teen Fathers Collaboration, Bank Street College of Education).

Sarsby, J. (1983), *Romantic Love and Society* (Harmondsworth: Penguin).

Schofield, M. (1968), *The Sexual Behaviour of Young People*, revised ed (Harmondsworth, Penguin).

Shah, F. and Zelnik, M. (1981), 'Parent and peer influence on sexual behaviour, contraceptive use and pregnancy experience of young women', *J. Marriage and Family*, 43, 2, 339–48.

Sharpe, S. (1976), *Just Like a Girl: How Girls Learn To Be Women* (Harmondsworth: Penguin).

Sharpe, S. (1987), *Falling for Love* (London: Virago).

Simms, M. and Smith, C. (1986), *Teenage Mothers and their Partners* (London: HMSO).

Skinner, C. (1986), *Elusive Mr Right: the Social and Personal Context of Contraception* (London: Carolina).

Sonenstein, F. L. (1986), 'Risking paternity: sex and contraception among adolescent males', in A. B. Elster and M. E. Lamb (eds), *Adolescent Fatherhood* (New Jersey: Erlbaum), pp. 31–54.

Strasburger, V. C. (1989), 'Adolescent sexuality and the media', *Paediatric Clinics of North America* (Adolescent Sexuality), 36, 3, 747–73.

Taylor, B., Wadsworth, J. and Butler, N. R. (1983), 'Teenage mothering: admission to hospital and accidents during the first two years', *Archives of Disease in Childhood*, 58, 6–11.

Thomas, S. (1989), *Study Visit to New York City: Teen Parenting Programs* (Bristol: YWCA).

Thornes, B. and Collard, J. (1979), *Who Divorces?* (London: Routledge & Kegan Paul).

Times Educational Supplement (*TES*), 26 August 1989.

Times Educational Supplement, 13 October 1989.

Vinovskis, M. A. (1988), *An 'Epidemic' of Teenage Pregnancy? Some historical and policy considerations* (New York: Oxford U.P.).

Wadsworth, J., Taylor, B., Osborn, A. and Butler, N. (1984), 'Teenage mothering: child development at five years', *J. Child Psychol. Psychiat.*, 23, 2, 305–13.

Wedge, P. and Essen, J. (1982), *Children in Adversity* (London: Pan).

Went, D. (1988), *Sex Education in the Curriculum* (London: Family Planning Association).

Werner, B. (1988), 'Fertility trends in the UK and 13 other developed countries, 1966–86', *Population Trends*, 51, 18–29.

Wielandt, H. and Boldsen, J. (1989), 'Age at first intercourse', *J. Biosocial Science*, 21, 169–77.

Williams, S. *et al.* (1987), 'Poverty and teenage pregnancy', *British Medical J.*, 294, 20–1.

Willis, P. (1977), *Learning to Labour* (Farnborough: Gower).

Wilson, D. (1978), 'Sexual codes and conduct: a study of teenage girls' in C. and B. Smart (eds), *Women, Sexuality and Social Control* (London: Routledge & Kegan Paul), pp. 65–73.

Wilson F. (1980), 'Antecedents of adolescent pregnancy', *J. Biosocial Science*, 12, 141–52.

Wolkind, S. N. and Kruk, S. (1985), 'Teenage pregnancy and motherhood', *J. Roy. Soc. Med.*, 78, 112–16.

Wynn, M. and Wynn, A. (1979), *The Prevention of Handicap and the Health of Women* (London: Routledge & Kegan Paul).

Yates, A. (1978), *Sex Without Shame* (London: Temple Smith).

Zelnik M., Kantner, J. F. and Ford, K. (1981), *Sex and Pregnancy in Adolescence* (Beverly Hills, Ca.: Sage).

Index

233